REVOLUTION
AND
RENEWAL

REVOLUTION
AND
RENEWAL

How Churches
Are Saving Our Cities

by Tony Campolo

With Stories by Bruce Main

Westminster John Knox Press
Louisville, Kentucky

Bible quotations are from the King James Version.

Excerpts from Robert Linthicum, *Empowering the Poor,* copyright 1991 Robert C. Linthicum. Published by MARC, a division of World Vision. Reprinted by permission of the publisher.

Excerpts from Eugene Rivers, "Ten Point Plan to Mobilize the Churches," *Sojourners* (February/March 1994). Excerpted with permission from *Sojourners.* (800) 714–7474. www.sojourners.com. Reprinted by permission of the publisher.

Excerpts from William H. Willimon, *The Intrusive Word: Preaching to the Unbaptized,* © 1994 Wm. B. Eerdmans Publishing Company, Grand Rapids, Michigan. Reprinted by permission of the publisher; all rights reserved.

Book design by Sharon Adams
Cover design by PAZ Design Group
Cover photograph: © 1999 Photodisc, Inc.

First edition
Published by Westminster John Knox Press
Louisville, Kentucky

This book is printed on acid-free paper that meets the American National Standards Institute Z39.48 standard. ∞

PRINTED IN THE UNITED STATES OF AMERICA

00 01 02 03 04 05 06 07 08 09—10 9 8 7 6 5 4 3 2 1

Library of Congress Cataloging-in-Publication Data
Campolo, Anthony.
    Revolution and renewal : how churches are saving our cities / by Tony Campolo ; stories by Bruce Main.
       p. cm.
    Includes bibliographical references.
    ISBN 0-664-22198-X (alk. paper)
    1. City churches.   2. City churches—New Jersey—Camden.   3. Camden (N.J.)—Church history—20th century.   I. Main, Bruce.   II. Title.

BV637 .C26 2000
253′.09173′2—dc21   99-049161

To Nina Campolo Goodheart,
my joyful granddaughter
who knows how to sing and dance
to the music of the city.

Contents

Preface

This is a book I've always wanted to write. I love the city, and writing about it and thinking about how it can be made more like the heavenly city is almost a preoccupation.

As I stroll down the streets of my own city, Philadelphia, I always feel a strange kind of excitement. I have the sense of being an alien in a strange and distant land. I am in the city but not of it. In spite of the many times that I have wandered up and down its streets, I still feel like a tourist. The tall buildings with their walls of glass lift my spirits much as soaring gothic cathedrals do for many who see them in such places as Chartres or Rheims. For me, the noises of the city have an entertaining quality about them, and the louder they are, the more I love them. Those sounds all speak to me of people on the go, heading for important meetings or making important deliveries.

The people of the city seem more interesting to me than those I meet in suburban shopping centers. From the crazy man who makes himself a self-appointed cop and directs traffic to the bag lady pushing the stolen supermarket cart filled with all her earthly belongings, I find urbanites anything but stereotypical. Businesswomen in the city seem somehow to combine a chic elegance with their high-powered efficiency. Businessmen seem to carry themselves with an air of extra importance. Their loosened ties and briefcases leave me with the sense that every one of them is a lawyer (and in Philadelphia that just might be the case) who just handled a case that was a matter of life and death.

Most of all, I like the ethnics. I myself am an ethnic, and I am not sure I would enjoy those mini-cities in the Midwest where everyone is an Anglo-Saxon and each seems to "belong." For me, that array of Italians, Slavs, and Jews who have aptly been called "The Urban Villagers" are of thrilling interest. They carry with them other ways of life from different

times and different places. These are the people who know who they are
and care not a twit as to whether they have dressed for the occasion. They
walk and talk like they are from some mountain village with a strange-
sounding name, and they act as though they own the streets they walk on.

There are street vendors who wink as they try to sell you imitation
Rolex watches or Givenchy ties for a few bucks a throw. And there are
the hucksters and hustlers who know how to con you out of all your loose
change, even when you know that they really do not need bus fare to go
to the bedsides of dying mothers. And I appreciate the African-American and Hispanic folks, once absent from the upscale shopping streets
but now a vital market in the downtown economy.

I love my city because it's the right size. Philadelphia is manageable.
Unlike New York, you can get to know it. In some ways it's a mini-Paris.
Philadelphia's Benjamin Franklin Parkway has the form and dimensions
of the Champs Élysées, and its Logan Circle is a postcard replica of Place
de la Concorde, sans the obelisk. It's not New York, but Philadelphia does
have theater and a good ballet troupe. Its orchestra may be the best in the
world. But the jewel of my city is the art museum. It sits on a hill apart
from the skyscrapers, and this yellow limestone masterpiece of Greek
architecture illuminated by spotlights each evening is, for my money, the
most beautiful building in the world.

Sadly, all is not well around this vibrant downtown circus maximus.
North, South, and West, you find ghettos and worse. Some parts of North
Philadelphia look very much like those European cities that were
bombed out during World War II. And, not far to the south of the business district, it is easy to find that strange section of town peopled by
pimps and druggies and worse.

East of center city Philadelphia, just across the Delaware River is
Camden, New Jersey. It is not part of Philadelphia, anymore than East
St. Louis is part of St. Louis or East Chicago is part of Chicago. Like these
other cities that grew up beside gigantic cities, Camden is both an extension of Philadelphia and a city with a character all its own. For the most
part, it lives off Philadelphia for its entertainment, and the Philly teams
are the focus of Camden sports enthusiasts. Yet, Camden has had its own
economic life, and with that life, its own destiny.

In this book we will look at both Philadelphia and Camden, but more
will be said about Camden. This is because over the past several years
some of my coworkers have developed ministries there. In the process,

we have gotten to know the city, to understand something about its people, and, most important, to impact Camden with programs that have softened some of the sufferings endured by its people.

From a sociological point of view, Camden is fascinating because it demonstrates how, in a short span of time, a city can change from being alive with hope to being a reservoir of despair. Camden is not difficult to study. Its history is easy to trace, the forces controlling its change simple to decipher, and its demographic transformation readily discernible. So, fasten your seat belts for a trip through a city that has died but is about to be resurrected from the dead.

In many ways this book is a blueprint or instruction manual as to how such a resurrection can be made to happen. It is a book filled with stories of the people of Camden, aimed at convincing the reader that Camden is worth saving. The first chapter is nothing but stories because I want you to get some glimpses of the children and teenagers who struggle there. This is also a book about the faith-based programs that are already giving the city some new signs of life. It is filled with proposals that could provide additional impetus to the coming resurrection. Most important, it is a book about faith. If faith is the substance of things hoped for and the evidence of things not yet seen, then this book is surely about faith. It is about the faith of some brave men and women who refuse to walk away from a disaster and who have committed themselves to seeing a city "born again."

This book would have never happened had it not been for some very "significant others." They include three special people who work hard in my office—Alison Caldwell, Valerie Hoffman, and Diana Robertson. However, special credit must be given to Sue Dahlstrom, who typed and critiqued what was written, and to my wife, Peggy, who has to be the best and most patient proofreader/editor in the world. To all of them I say, "Thanks!"

Chapter 1

Stories That Tell the Story

Zechariah, the Hebrew prophet, had a vision for the city. It was a city that was yet to be—a vision that generated faith in the face of the ugly realities of the Jerusalem of his day. Zechariah did not despair as he looked upon the devastation of blighted Mt. Zion, nor did he throw up his hands in surrender at the sight of grinding poverty. He did not lose hope in the face of the crime that pervaded Jerusalem's neighborhoods, nor did he deem incurable the social pathologies that destroyed the peace of that city. Instead, Zechariah looked beyond the sorry condition of the Jerusalem of his day and dreamed of a time when God would make its streets safe for children and for the elderly to once again venture out of their homes without fear.

We find the vision of this city that was yet to be in scripture:

> Thus saith the LORD of hosts; There shall yet old men and old women dwell in the streets of Jerusalem, and every man with his staff in his hand for very age. And the streets of the city shall be full of boys and girls playing in the streets thereof. Thus saith the LORD of hosts; If it be marvelous in the eyes of the remnant of this people in these days, should it also be marvellous in mine eyes? saith the LORD of hosts. Thus saith the LORD of hosts; Behold, I will save my people from the east country, and from the west country; And I will bring them, and they shall dwell in the midst of Jerusalem: and they shall be my people, and I will be their God, in truth and in righteousness.
>
> . . . .
>
> But now I *will* not *be* unto the residue of this people as in the former days, saith the LORD of hosts. For the seed *shall be* prosperous;

1

the vine shall give her fruit, and the ground shall given her increase, and the heavens shall give their dew; and I will cause the remnant of this people to possess all these *things.*

. . . .

So again have I thought in these days to do well unto Jerusalem and to the house of Judah: fear ye not. These *are* the things that ye shall do; Speak ye every man the truth to his neighbour; execute the judgment of truth and peace in your gates: And let none of you imagine evil in your hearts against his neighbour; and love no false oath; for all these *are things* that I hate, saith the LORD.

. . . .

Thus saith the LORD of hosts; In those days *it shall come to pass,* that ten men shall take hold out of all languages of the nations, even shall take hold of the skirt of him that is a Jew, saying, We will go with you: for we have heard *that* God *is* with you. (Zech. 8:4–8, 11–12, 15–17, 23)

Is that not what we all long to see happen to our own city? Is not Zechariah's vision a vision we can all embrace?

The way to transform the city that *is* into the city that ought to be is not easy to prescribe. The simplistic answers to the urban crisis that are flung about in cavalier fashion by journalistic pundits on C-SPAN do not readily work. The chaos and evils that wreak havoc on urban dwellers are not really addressed by the ideological rhetoric that comes from politicians on either the left or the right. Granted, there are those in each of the parties who have some good insights and suggestions to make, but in the platform of neither party do we find the sure formula to transform the city into what God wants for it to be.

The political left, generally expressing itself within the Democratic Party, tends to believe that ameliorating the problems of the city will be brought about by intervening in the socioeconomic order of the city and restructuring its institutions to facilitate justice and prosperity for all of its people. Political liberals believe that structural evil is what creates the pain and troubles of individuals, and that life will be good in the city only when the various institutions of the social order are transformed into paragons of virtue. The city, they claim, can only be changed from the top down. A good social system, they say, is what creates good people— and what they say is somewhat true.

Those on the political right, who usually identify with the Republican Party, believe that the city can be changed only from the bottom up. The city, they say, is nothing more than an expression of the character of the individuals who make it up. Consequently, the conservatives' approach to social change requires that we deal with those whose sinful behavior is destructive to themselves, as well as to others around them. Conservatives believe that ultimately *individuals* determine the quality of life in the city, and that urban policies should be designed primarily to convert individuals into good people. Good people, they believe, are what make a city good—and they, too, are partly right.

In this book we will affirm both the left and the right—both the liberals and the conservatives—both the Democrats and the Republicans. In this book we will contend that changing the city into the kind of place that actualizes Zechariah's vision requires *both* a "top-down" and a "bottom-up" approach.

If the church is going to be the "lead institution" in bringing something of the city of God to urban America, we believe that it must, on the one hand, address institutional evils and simultaneously challenge its people to bring the lost souls of the city into transforming relationships with Christ. We believe that the church must combat evil on the macro level by working to eliminate racism in the business sector, bring true justice to the courts and to the juvenile-protection agencies, end corruption in the housing authorities, improve the educational system, clean up the environment, create good recreational programs, eliminate the drug traffic, outlaw gambling, improve family services, and organize neighborhood people to address all the problems inherent in the urban social system. In this book we will try to provide some directives and guidelines for making the church effective in doing such social action. But even as we challenge the church to embrace the call to work for social change, we will, at the same time, remind the church of its God-given calling to bring individuals into the new life that comes from Christian conversion.

The kingdom of God in the city begins with persons who surrender to the lordship of Christ or it does not begin at all. While we believe that social institutions and urban culture condition what *happens* to individuals, we also believe that individuals make their personal influences felt on the societal level. But when we consider both sides of this interactive process, we must conclude that the conversion of individuals into radical followers of Jesus is what will get redemptive social change started. Therefore, we believe that whatever else the urban church may get into, it must always hold its ministry to individuals as primary and, like its Lord, "seek and save those who are lost." That is why, before getting into the roles that the church must play in bringing justice and creative socioeconomic change to institutional systems, we must first declare what the church can and should be doing to change individuals and to impact their lives with God's transforming love.

Over the years, I have been involved in urban ministries on both the societal and the personal levels. I have done my best to earn my credentials as an advocate for social action, identifying with those ancient prophets who demanded justice and help for the poor and oppressed. But over the years I have also recruited and organized an army of young people who have set up ministries that have reached out to distressed individuals in the city—especially to children and teenagers. These young volunteers, who come to us mostly from colleges and universities, have formed the backbone of a variety of programs for city people that are incorporated under the direction of The Evangelical Association for the Promotion of Education (now renamed EAPE/Kingdomworks).

During the last two decades, the young people who have come to work with EAPE/Kingdomworks have touched the lives of tens of thousands of children and teenagers who live in some of the worst ghettos of America. They have organized after-school tutoring and recreational programs. They have put together alternative schools, which have rescued the kids who were falling between the cracks of the public school system. They have developed youth programs in churches that had never before tried to reach the young people in their neighborhoods. They have placed teams of young adults in neighborhoods to go door to door with ministries of prayer and evangelism. And they have run summer day camp programs for thousands of children in urban neighborhoods across the country.

Of all the young people who have come to join our ranks of dedicated youth workers, none has proven more faithful and effective than a young Canadian named Bruce Main. Bruce now heads up our affiliate ministry, Urban Promise, in Camden. The work that Bruce has done has rightfully earned him the recognition of *Christianity Today* as one of the 40 most outstanding young Christian leaders in America.

For a decade and a half, Bruce has labored long and hard in a city which *Time* magazine labeled "the worst city in America." In local churches in a half dozen neighborhoods of that city, he has established a variety of programs that have turned "throwaway children" into college students of promise and led untold numbers of "lost" kids into lives of hope and promise. When it comes to change on the micro level, Bruce Main is a blazing example of what can be done. While calling for social change and supporting those who struggle against "the principalities and powers" that perpetuate structural evil within the institutions of the city of Camden, Bruce has not given up his first love, which is a personal ministry to the at-risk youngsters who roam the streets of the city.

I can think of no better illustration of how the church can bring the love of Christ to individuals than to give you a glimpse into some of what Bruce does in his daily rounds of service. Allow me to share with you some of Bruce's own stories. Read them and be inspired by what the church can do when it takes seriously its calling to rescue the perishing and care for the dying who live in the city.[1]

Baptism by Fire

Our mission organization had been using the almost vacant Baptist church for a year and a half. In that time carpets had been stained, door handles had been broken, and graffiti had appeared on the bathroom walls. Utility bills had skyrocketed, toilet paper was being used at an astronomical rate, and the Sunday morning service was being interrupted by the restless commotion of over a hundred city kids. Our mission organization was covering the costs, yet it still appeared that this mission project was becoming a little too expensive. After all, what was the payoff? What was the church gaining from the project? There were no new members. The weekly collections were not increasing. And there were no visible signs that the children were changing.

The deacons finally called me into the pastor's office one Sunday after church. It had been the usual banner morning. Some child had clogged the toilets, and one of our five-year-olds had thrown a tantrum during the responsive reading. I approached the office with some trepidation for I knew that the news was not going to be good. Stepping into the office, I was greeted by the stares of five elderly men. The deacons. They made up one half of the attending congregation.

"Have a seat, Bruce," gruffed one of the aging men. I sank into the collapsible, cold metal chair that had been placed there especially for me. The pastor, who was sitting behind the desk, took the initiative.

"Well, Bruce," he began slowly, "you know your youth program has been in the church for about a year and a half." I braced myself for what was to come. "People in the congregation are beginning to wonder whether it's making any difference. The people need to see some change."

I could see the deacons nodding in unison with the pastor. Obviously they had had a meeting previously and the pastor was simply seizing the opportunity to collect some political points to substantiate his leadership.

"What we really need, Bruce . . . what we *really* need are baptisms." I almost fell off the chair. After all the discontent, after the relentless criticism, all I needed to do was get some kids baptized? *It couldn't be that easy.* I don't want to take the sacrament of baptism lightly, but it was difficult to believe that a baptismal service would make the deacons happy. Had I misread them? I have never been one to play the political game or sacrifice the spiritual integrity of a person to prove a point. We had, however, had a number of children commit to following Christ, so there was a strong possibility that some of them might want to be baptized.

"I think it could be arranged," I replied, repressing a smile. "Give me a week and I'll see if there are some interested candidates."

"How many do you think there might be?" asked one of the deacons who had yet to make a comment. I did a quick tally in my head.

"Probably fifteen to twenty," I said with a tinge of satisfaction and pride, for the church had not seen a baptism in the past ten years and now the deacons would have to contend with the fact that they did not even have enough robes to clothe all the children who would desire baptism.

Just then the old deacon curtly commented, "You know that they'll have to be interviewed by our committee. Yes, every one of those children will have to be approved by the deacons." I began to sense what was going on. Baptisms were not the real issue. The issue was power and control. With the presence of the outreach program, the leaders had lost control of *their* church. Their hope was to back me into a corner. But to their surprise I responded to their game. They thought I could not deliver with the baptisms; I caught them off guard. But even now, their power had, once again, to be asserted. No child was to be baptized without *their* stamp of approval.

The night arrived when the children were to be interviewed for baptism. The kids were nervous and scared. They feared these white, old men who seldom smiled or made them feel welcome. Seated in the back room of the church, the fifteen baptismal candidates huddled around in a circle and waited to be called.

"Kenyatta Mickey," yelled a voice from down the hall. Kenyatta hesitated. The ten-year-old little boy didn't want to move from his seat. He just sat there and shook his head at me and mouthed the words "not me."

"Come on, Kenyatta," I whispered, not wanting the deacons to hear of the problems we were having. I reached, grabbed his hand, pulled him to his feet, and walked him down the hall. We entered the office. There were the five old deacons, sitting in the same five seats, staring at us with the same blank faces. There were no cordial greetings. There was no "Welcome, young man, it's so good to have you interested in surrendering yourself to Jesus." Just the blank stares and the penetrating eyes. I could see little Kenyatta begin to perspire. What an introduction into the Kingdom! The poor kid. He was terrified, he was nervous, and he was definitely not experiencing the warmth of Christian fellowship.

"When did you become a Christian?" started one of the old men.

"This summer at the church camp." By this time my heart was leaping for joy. My pride was screaming silently that there were kids changing because of this program.

"How has becoming a Christian changed you?" asked another deacon, still without expression or warmth.

"Well, I used to be bad. I got'n all kinds of trouble, and fights, and I said a lot of bad words. Now I don't do all that stuff," replied Kenyatta while satisfaction wrinkled across his brow. After a few more questions and a sermon from the oldest deacon about the importance of tithing, they released Kenyatta from his interrogation. Kenyatta flew out of the door and skipped down the hall with his arms raised, screaming, "I did it! I did it!" When Kenyatta got back to the group, he burst forth with his story. The others were relieved that he returned alive and yet envious that he had finished.

One by one the children went through their **interviews.** One by one they returned by running down the hallway bubbling over with joy that they had completed the encounters with the deacons. What an introduction to the Christian life: horror, fear, and intimidation.

The day came when the children were to be baptized. Ten minutes before the service, when I was already dressed in my robe and hip waders, the pastor called me into his study. He informed me that the deacons had decided to vote the Outreach Program out of the church. I stood in his office in total disbelief. Fifteen children waiting in robes to be baptized, fifteen children who had given their lives to Jesus, fifteen children and teens who had been approved by the deacons, and yet they secretly decided to vote us out of the church.

As I baptized the children I felt both joy and sadness. Joy because these beautiful children were making a statement to their families and friends; sadness because the deacons were going to ax the very thing that Jesus commissioned us to do—reach those who are lost and preach the good news to those who need Good News. The church had lost its vision and had become a place where power could be misused, where peace and quiet and reverence were treasured and children were not counted as real humans. Ironically, as I scanned the congregation between immersions, I saw not one deacon.

The program was to leave. But before the deacons could bid us farewell, the decision needed to be brought before the congregation and voted upon. Realizing that the deacons had a sort of intimidating presence, with the ability to sway the congregation, we decided to visit the congregation individually and get their feelings about what was happening in the church. Were the deacons actually reflecting the sentiment of the whole body? Was the leadership really listening to the concerns and interests of the congregation?

We were greeted with some surprising responses. Overwhelmingly, the responses of the parishioners were positive. Although many were elderly, couldn't get out to church too often, and "didn't understand the ways of the youth," they did believe that the church needed to become more community oriented and that the children were the future. We encouraged all to get out to vote.

The day of the congregational meeting arrived. The twenty or so members gathered after church. In addition to the members, we had encouraged some of the parents to come out and share what the programs had done for their children. About fifty children were outside the church, waiting and praying for the outcome of the vote. They were concerned that they wouldn't have a place to go after school and in the evenings. They were concerned that their clubs and activities would be canceled.

One of the deacons got up to speak. A hush fell over the group as he began to speak. "The deacons of the church feel that it is time for the Outreach Program of the church to be terminated. We come here today in full confidence that you will vote in agreement." One of the older men in the church, Mr. Brown, stood up. I had never heard him speak publicly before. He was a quiet man, so to see him rise to speak was a surprise. "You know, in the Bible Jesus speaks about the disciples who shooed the children away. If I'm not mistaken, Jesus got a little mad. In fact," he continued, gaining a little momentum, "Jesus said that we have to become like little children to get into heaven, didn't he?" A few of the deacons were getting a little restless. Old Joey Brown wasn't about to sit down, and he was obviously having an impact on the crowd. "If we turn away these children, I think Jesus will be real mad."

Old Joey sat down. He had said more in those two minutes than I had heard him say in two years. But his words had gone forth with power. However inarticulate he was, the words had made an impact. Before anything more could be added, the deacon seized the floor.

"We need to vote! All those in favor of keeping the program, raise your hands." Fifteen of the twenty hands shot up. Only the hands of the deacons did not come off their laps. The program would remain! We still had a home. The children would have their facility. But the best was yet to come. Although the outcome was obvious, the administrating deacon now asked, "Those who oppose the program, raise your hands." Fully conscious of the stares of the congregation, only two raised their hands. The other two walked out of the church and have never returned. The last deacon just sat, a little bewildered, unable to comprehend what had happened.

When we walked outside, the children came running up to us. "Did we win? Did we win?" they screamed. When they heard the news, they erupted with a yell of approval. Two of the boys I had baptized just weeks earlier said they had been on their knees praying the whole time. Now they were beaming because their prayers had been answered. God had heard them. They would not lose their church—a place that, for many, had become their home.

⌐ ⌐ ⌐ ⌐ ⌐

Prejudice Alive

"We better get outta here quick! Who knows what they'll do with a bus full of niggas in this neighborhood," yelled fourteen-year-old Gooter. The old church bus, packed with teenagers, instantly erupted into a roar of laughter.

Little did Gooter realize that his joke would hold a prophetic message. Already I had sensed the urgency to get the bus started and out of the neighborhood. I was panicking. There I was, in one of the affluent white suburbs of South Jersey, in a bus filled with black city kids.

Before I knew what was happening, three police cars had encircled the bus. An officer, who looked like General Patton, approached the bus and yelled, in a demeaning tone, "We've already had ten complaints from the neighborhood! You've got 15 minutes to get the bus and all these kids out of here, otherwise I'm taking the whole bunch down to the station." Probing the officer for an explanation for his panic crossed my mind, but I could see that he wasn't in the mood for dialoguing about the injustice I was sensing, so I bit my tongue.

But the teens did not bite *their* tongues. "This wouldn't happen if we were white," exploded one young man from the back of the bus. The comment somehow carried over all the yelling and discontent that was surfacing quickly and pierced my heart. The young man was right. The hostility and rudeness of the police would not have existed if the bus had been full of middle-class white kids. If these kids had had influential fathers and mothers in the community, they would not have been treated in similar fashion. And somehow they knew this truth. And it made our children angry.

To this day I am still amazed that the officer did not offer me a "jump," or provide some options as to what we could do to get the bus rolling. After all, are not the police a public service, paid by the public to serve the public? And yet we were not served, we were not helped, we were just reprimanded and ordered to get out of the neighborhood or be arrested—for the crime of breaking down on a public road.

For those of us who did not grow up in poor urban areas, who did not walk the streets of high-risk communities, and who were not born with a skin color that has been victimized for decades, it is hard to understand the stigma that these children carry with them. They are harassed in shopping malls, they are stopped unnecessarily by police, and they are denied the privilege of cashing checks or receiving an education that is comparable to that of their suburban counterpart who lives five minutes away.

And people say that the plight of the urban poor is in their own hands. "Why don't they just go out and get a job?" says the conservative critic. But if the jobs are in the suburbs, and if the dignity of our urban youth is stripped from them when they go to the suburbs, then how can they get jobs?

As Christians we must begin to break down the barriers, stereotypes, and fears that exist between the people of the suburbs and the people of the inner city. Some of America's finest youth are poor. Some of America's finest youth do not have the opportunity to hide behind the garb and pallid veneer of middle-class protection. The fear of the unknown has always been a problem for humans. Never has it been so apparent in the fears of urban youth. Not all are drug dealers, not all are on welfare, not all are lazy, and not all have no vision or hopes for the future. Recently *Time* came out with a story about our city. Our young women were portrayed as people whose only ambitions in life are to become "hairdressers" and yet end up as whores. Our young men were portrayed as young gangsters who tote $400 grenades and cradle Uzi machine guns under their jackets. And yet as I talk with our youth, I hear dreams of becoming doctors and lawyers. I see young men and women striving to become significant people in society.

The reaction to the article by the youth in our city was interesting.

Many wrote to *Time* and challenged its view of city kids. Others started groups that will strive to get urban youth more accurately portrayed in the media. Our organization sponsored a gospel choir tour to California, which gave our youth the opportunity to speak in front of large crowds and share boldly that they were from Camden—the same city that *Time* plastered "Who Could Live Here?" above its name. "Who could live there?" heralded our lead tenor to an audience of over 2,000 college students. "We live there!" He then motioned to the sixteen other youth behind him, dressed sharply in bright blue and red choir robes. The audience exploded with applause.

The media does its job in highlighting the urban problem by painting bleak pictures and holding up the negative. But the media portrayal is not all accurate and the images that it has created must be re-created. Christians must take an active role in this re-creation. The media will continue to uphold the negative and enforce the stereotype, and those who read the papers and watch television will continue to base their judgments on what they experience first- or secondhand, and not from their encounters with real people and real hearts. Let's be courageous. Let's take risks to get to know the unknown—because in the unknown, in the quest to discover, we will find beauty and life that will ultimately enhance our own.

◻ ◻ ◻ ◻ ◻

Mysterious Samaritan

One morning after church, as the congregation was slowly shuffling toward the exit, an elderly woman named Mrs. Bennett grabbed the arm of one of the intern staff. Mrs. Bennett was a widow, somewhat hard of hearing, lived in the neighborhood, and had been coming to the church for years.

"Stand right here beside me," she whispered in a tone of desperation.

"Why?" echoed the staff worker, who was now a little perplexed as to why Mrs. Bennett wanted her to stand in this particular spot.

"You see that woman over there?" Mrs. Bennett gestured with a tilt of her head. The intern turned slowly and noticed an elderly black woman coming up the center aisle of the sanctuary.

"Sure, I see the woman," replied the intern, who by now was a little confused as to why such a big deal was being made out of the departure of one of the church members.

By this time Mrs. Bennett had grabbed the intern's arm and pulled her close to her rickety body, all the time making sure that the intern stood between her and the black woman. Finally the woman passed and the elderly Mrs. Bennett released her grasp of the intern's arm. A look of relief came across her face, much like the look of someone after they have withstood a very tense trial. She thanked the intern with a deep sense of gratitude and then whispered, "She always wants to give me a hug."

Mrs. Bennett, who had grown up in the South, was not going to be hugged by a black woman.

About two weeks later Mrs. Bennett was out for her weekly milk run to the Three Brothers Store on the corner of Fortieth and Westfield Avenue. Her normal route consisted of four city blocks. She would leave her house on Thirty-seventh Street, shuffle half a block to Westfield, make a left turn, and then walk about three blocks to the corner store. This particular day Mrs. Bennett, after picking up her milk, began to feel a little faint and decided to sit on the curb outside the store for a few minutes to catch her breath. While resting, a little black girl walked by and saw the old woman in distress. Feeling led to help, the little girl called to the old woman, asking if she could use some assistance in carrying the milk to her home. Unable to hear the question, Mrs. Bennett just sat and stared at the little girl, all the while nodding her head up and down in rhythmic fashion.

Taking the nod as her cue, the little girl hoisted the aging lady to her feet, picked up the milk, and began the laborious four-block trek to the lady's house. Upon arrival, the little girl shouldered Mrs. Bennett up her stairs, handed her the milk, gave her a big hug, and then blurted out, "God bless you."

The event went unnoticed until the following week at church. After service Mrs. Bennett cornered one of the interns and relayed the story. As one who previously had been unable to understand why we would want to work with these children, she concluded the conversation by claiming that we "must be doing something good."

After hearing the story, my curiosity got the best of me. I wanted to find out the identity of this little Samaritan. I began to drop little hints throughout the children's programs. Finally I posted a little reward for anyone who could tell me the name of the anonymous helper. At first I sought out all the well-mannered little girls. "Was it you, Francis? How about you Taquea, Susana, or Joy?" But I drew blanks. Finally one day I got a lead. Someone had seen Tiombe help an old woman down Westfield Avenue. At first I couldn't believe it. Tiombe was far from the angelic child. In fact, a week earlier I had suspended her from the program for fighting.

Odd as it may seem, the day before Tiombe was suspended from the program her class had studied the story of the Good Samaritan. Tiombe had heard the Word spoken and had then implemented it. The Word had become flesh; the Word had come to life through the actions of a child. And because the Word had not lain dormant in the subconscious of someone's mind, it sent a life-changing message to an old churchwoman who had probably heard sermons on the story for years. Ironically, scholars will continue to debate the sources of the story, and pastors will continue to exegete "the text" with precision, but it will be the simplistic obedience—the literal obedience like that of a child—that will speak the loudest and change the hardest of hearts.

How Good Is Good?

"The Good Samaritan took a risk! If we are to follow the way of Christ," I said in a final crescendo, "we too must be willing to love without considering the cost."

I closed my sermon with a prayer and dismissed the congregation. There was the usual milling around in the vestibule. On their way to the door, a few commented on what had been said. The final cluster of people began moving toward the side exit. We chatted about the coming week and how bitterly cold it had been. It was December and the cold chill of the eastern seaboard had settled for the winter. Outside, the frigid winds ripped through the row homes and hurled the debris of the street into the darkened alleys.

As we were ending the conversation, there was a knocking on the door. I opened the door and in rushed a man, his arms tightly wrapped around himself. "Geez, it's freezing out there!" he exclaimed. I studied the man for a moment. His hair was greasy, his beard unclipped, his teeth tobacco yellow, his fingers dirty and cracked—he'd not had a shower in days. Before I could introduce myself, he started his story.

"Could you help us? Me and my wife got no place ta go. All we got is our car. We'll freeze ta death if we stay out tonight."

"Well . . ." I stuttered, not knowing quite how to handle the situation since I wasn't familiar with any shelters that would be open at that time of night. It *was* cold. And I just, after all, had finished my best Good Samaritan sermon. "Exactly what is it that you need?" I continued to probe, stalling.

"There's a motel a few blocks away that we could get a room at. It'll cost only about $30 for the night, I guess. Could you help us out with a *loan?*" By this time I could see those who earlier had been escorting me to the door watching me with intense interest. Just moments ago I was telling them the Good Samaritan was a standard for all Christians to live by. Now my words were coming back at me and cutting to the core.

But I didn't have $30; that was just as real as my sermon. And I didn't think my wife would be too happy if I came home with a couple of strangers. I shot up a silent prayer and grabbed for another idea. *They could stay at the church.* This was, after all, The House of the Lord. Why shouldn't it be used in situations such as this? "What about just staying here for the night?" I suggested. "We can put you and your wife on a couple of couches, and we'll give you something to eat in the morning." I was pleased with myself, my quick thinking, and God's answer to my prayer.

"Now, Bruce," muttered Deacon Smith, who had remained behind and was watching this drama with growing concern. He was obviously annoyed. "You know the church policy." To be honest, I didn't know the church policy. I was only the "resident missionary," still too young and naive to know that church doors couldn't be thrown open to meet unplanned-for needs. "A situation like this would have to be voted on and approval would need to be granted by the committee," he concluded.

I winced. It took a moment to process what had been said. Not only was I hearing correctly, but the deacon had the bad form to point all this out in front of this freezing homeless man. I was embarrassed, and I quickly tried to come up with something to say in defense of the church and of Jesus. We would all go home to our warm beds that night, yet here were a man and a woman who needed a place to sleep and warm their bodies. My indignation rose. The church would be empty; it *could* keep them warm and shield them from the bitter wind for one night. But the need could not be met. Votes needed to be taken and insurance policies reviewed. No room for risk.

While we had been talking, a gentle, white-haired woman slipped an envelope into my hand and whispered, "This should cover them for the night."

I motioned the homeless man aside and passed him the $30. I apologized about the situation and suggested he come back the next day. There were some chores around the church. I could pay him a few dollars that could help him with further financial needs. He thanked me and left. I wasn't optimistic. I'd often heard empty promises from those we'd helped.

To my surprise, the next morning the couple showed up. Rested and clean, they looked like new people. I showed them the kitchen. They made a pot of coffee and fried some eggs. With a little food in their stomachs they were eager to do some work around the church. I was ecstatic! This was one of the few times we seemed to be helping a couple who really needed it. They were receptive to discussions about faith, and they even wanted to get involved with some of the outreach programs at the church.

Over the next few weeks, the couple came to the church to wax floors, do office work, and help with our after-school programs. In both of them I saw a renewed sense of happiness. Soon they would be able to find employment, I prayed. And with enough money saved, they could possibly get a small apartment.

Christmas. The other missionaries went home, leaving their living quarters empty. This seemed to be the perfect opportunity. The couple could stay in the staff house for two weeks, work at the church, and save enough money to make a down payment on an apartment and get their lives started again. Christmas would not have to be spent on the street. It would be spent in a warm place, with comfortable beds and cheerful decorations. Our homeless friends had gotten a break that few in their situation get. I was pleased, too, that we had been able to be Samaritans.

New Year's was a dreary day. The phone rang. I recognized the voice as my homeless friend. Something was wrong.

"I had an accident and I'm in the hospital," he began. He paused.

"What . . . what happened?"

"I borrowed one of the staff cars and went to Philadelphia. Somebody ran into me as I was coming off the bridge. The car has some front-end damage. Don't worry, I'll be able to fix it." He assured me that he would look after any damages. He claimed that he had been in the auto body business before he was laid off. Within a few days, he claimed, the car would be fixed. I had little interest in the Rose Bowl or any other football game for the rest of the day.

A few days passed, but there was no progress made on the car. In the meantime, the police called, inquiring why this man was riding in a car registered to another person. He said there had been evidence of alcohol in the vehicle and on the breath of the driver.

The car never got fixed. It had to be sold for parts. The homeless couple disappeared. They were spotted wandering the streets, but they never got involved in the church again. The whole escapade had turned out to be a costly endeavor with no "payoff."

Did we do the right thing? There was nothing to show for what we had done. There was no boost in church membership; there were no souls saved; there was no friendly couple who now had a home. We were out about $5,000. We'd been burnt.

But, Samaritan, at what point does one stop giving? Should we protect ourselves from being taken advantage of? Must there be a "payoff"? What is a good way to give, and what is poor stewardship?

Tell us, Samaritan: How much did the encounter cost you? We know there was a needy man left at the inn with the promise that you would return and pay whatever was needed to cover the remaining expenses. How much were the expenses? Were you ever thanked?

The fact is that the Samaritan saw a need, a desperate need. He did not calculate the cost as the other passing people did. He just let the compassion of his heart guide him. It was that kind of spontaneous compassion that Jesus affirmed.

The homeless couple is now gone. Right now they may rest in a warm bed, or they may continue to fight the cruelties of life on the street. I don't know. I do know one thing, however, and that is, for a brief moment of their lives, they experienced a little taste of God's Kingdom on earth. It may not have been much of a taste, but it was *a taste*. And who knows? It could be that their brief brush with God's people will one day call them back to the Author who can provide warmth, security, and an eternal home.

❏   ❏   ❏   ❏   ❏

The Holiness of a Broken Door

I once met a Catholic priest who had a fascination with doors. He believed that the front door was the most important part of a church. The door, he claimed, should be something that beckons people to come in. It should be something intriguing, something that "whispers the mystery that lies beyond it."

The door of our church used to be white, shiny, and metallic, smooth and new looking; it could have graced the cover of a church supply catalog. The door was seldom used. As a matter of fact, the door reflected the church that existed inside the door—unused. With only a couple of hours of use of its hinges each Sunday, the door had little chance to tarnish its beauty. It just sat there, not living up to its calling as a church door—that is something that is used to allow people to enter a place where the mysterious Divine dwells.

But last week we had to replace the door. Since our rambunctious youth program arrived at the church three years ago the door had changed. The shiny, white metallic finish had been dulled by the continual touching and thumping of dirty hands. There were gouges, dents, and holes in the door created by kids who were late for events and needed to be heard. The bright brass trim around the mailbox had been ripped off. The inner core of the door could now be seen and had begun to spill its contents onto the surrounding sidewalk. Perhaps the brass had been stripped to be sold or taken off in an effort to rob the church. Whatever the case, the fancy trim was gone. All that was left was an ugly, roughly cut metal hole, through which the mail person could shove the mail each day.

Days before the door was replaced, it would hardly open. The only hinge connecting the door to the frame was the top one. And even that hinge had been reset a number of times. The other hinges had long ago been ripped out of their homes and tossed in the scrap pile. As the door was opened, shut, slammed, and propped over the last three years by children, teens, and staff, the door collapsed. Finally the screws gave way, and the wooden door posts disintegrated.

So the door was replaced. The cost: eight hundred and fifty dollars to put in a new frame and metal door. Unfortunately the trustees in our church didn't share in the same door theology as my priest friend—that a door should create a sense of mystery and intrigue. We got a new, white, shiny metallic door.

Although I grimace over this expense in our budget this year, I do have to chuckle over the fact that we wore out a door. Children broke the door! Not intentionally, but because they wanted to get into the church. Something was happening inside these walls that was calling them off the street to come into this place where God lives. The door had begun to serve its purpose. Despite its lack of ascetic intrigue, the door had begun to live out its calling as the threshold leading to one place where God dwells.

What was taking place on the inside had become intriguing and a mystery to the little ones who desperately wanted to get in.

The more I have thought about our door, the more I have wondered how many churches in America can boast over the fact that they have had to replace a door because of the dents and holes made by young people trying to get in.

But if the church really lives up to its calling, should it not be replacing its doors more regularly? Wouldn't it be exciting if churches across America all of a sudden had to start ordering custom-made doors to replace all the doors that were being broken. Just think how wonderful it would be if churches had to start hiring special "door ministers" just to keep doorknobs from falling off and hinges from snapping. Right next to Minister of Music and Christian Education Director in next year's budget would be "Door Minister."

Yet if the church really does become that "beacon of light on a hill," those who surround her should be lured and drawn in through the doors. If the church becomes a vibrant and integral part of a community and if spirituality does begin to intertwine itself with everyday life, doors should wear out. The church should be a place of traffic.

What changed in our case? Why did the church begin to change from a mausoleum to a beehive of activity? Why did children from the community start coming to a church that had lost its voice in the community? One of the reasons is that we started going into the community and extended an invitation to its people to come. But the invitation was not just to come and fill our pews for an hour Sunday morning. Children were invited to come and express themselves through dance, play like creative children, study things that are fun and interesting, sing crazy songs, eat ice-cream sundaes, go on trips to out-of-the-way places, and produce their own silk screened tee-shirts. In short, we tried to make what was behind the doors of the church intriguing. We tried to evoke the curiosity of our children. We created programs that would speak to the needs and desires of children and teens. Since 50 percent of our city's population is under the age of eighteen, we decided to make children our focus. After-school programs, evening Bible clubs, computer class, and dance class are just a few of the events we designed to make the church an appealing place to come. And they have come. And, Lord willing, the children will continue to come. And, quite probably, a few more doors may be broken before it's all said and done.

❑   ❑   ❑   ❑   ❑

Behold a Child

Sounds of music fill the air. Fifty children are on their feet, singing, clapping, and dancing. The room is exploding with excitement and spontaneity. Nothing has been taught, rehearsed, or practiced. These are children—God's children—who are responding spontaneously to music. The song changes, the beat shifts, yet the children still stand and lift their voices to the Lord.

There is a particular song that really gets the children excited. It's not a rap song, nor is it rock and roll. The song is Jewish in origin, and it has a very strong Middle-Eastern beat. But each time the song is played, the children begin to dance. They twirl, they spin, they lock arms with one another. There is laughter and it is a joyful time.

But this motion all takes place in the basement of the church. When the children go upstairs to the sanctuary, they somehow believe that this type of worship is not appropriate during service. They lose their spontaneity and their freedom.

One day the "Jewish" song was played in church. Although the beat was a little slower, the children still recognized it. Upon hearing the song, a little nine-year-old girl named Kusa burst up from the pew and started to dance. Before she realized that no one was following her lead, little Kusa grabbed one of the staff by the arm and hoisted her to her feet. She linked arms with the woman and then began to twirl her around. Absorbed in her own world, Kusa was having the time of her life. She was praising God the way she wanted to—the way she knew how to.

After a few moments, Kusa snapped out of her trance only to see the other people in the sanctuary staring at her. By this time, the other children—who normally would have been dancing downstairs—were laughing at their friend. Kusa caught on and began to slow down. Finally she stopped her dance altogether and took a seat back on the pew. The staff worker, by this time, had also found her way back to the pew, not knowing what to think and feeling terribly awkward.

Never again did Kusa dance in church. Never again did she feel the freedom to respond to praises and songs in the way that felt most natural to her. Those around her had crushed her spirit. They had sent a message that she was wrong and foolish for doing what she did.

It is interesting that we are called to be like children by Jesus. In fact, if we desire to enter into the Kingdom of heaven, we must become like little children. And yet what does it mean to become like a child? Part of what it means is to shed the expectations and veneer of "propriety" created by other adults. It is others who often crush the childlike spirit in each of us that desires to be nurtured and released. Jesus holds a child on his knee and basically tells the adults who surround him that they are to become like this little one.

Children are our greatest teachers. If children "behold the face of God," then we must draw near to them and tap into the mystical connection they have with the Divine. If a child can reflect the heart of God, then we must allow ourselves to be taught by the little ones of this earth. In their spontaneity, their freedom, and their imagination, they can teach us what it means to be a child of the living God.

▭ ▭ ▭ ▭ ▭

Power of "The Story"

Two children left the room with tears running down their cheeks. Another student sat hunched over, her head buried in her lap, sobbing uncontrollably. The remaining students sat with their eyes riveted to the television.

Fifteen minutes earlier, it looked as if our teen Bible study would be just another dud. The kids were acting tough and cool. They wouldn't sing the songs and everyone wanted to be the clown when games were played. The young men present had just finished running the streets and still held their macho guard securely in place.

The ladies were talking trash and exchanging verbal blows with the young men who dared challenge them. The atmosphere was far from spiritual. The climate was far more conducive to a neighborhood brawl than to a Bible study.

This was our Easter Club. More than ever I wanted to communicate the message of the Cross to these kids. As part of the program, there was to be a clip from the movie *Jesus of Nazareth*. I had seen the crucifixion scene earlier and had been very moved. I prayed that some of our teens would be just as moved.

As I started the film, the kids were still making their little quips; the words of Jesus could barely be heard over the laughter and jokes.

Then something strange happened. As Jesus was being flogged by the Roman guards, a silence came over the room. Jesus was nailed to the cross; the teens remained speechless. The jokes stopped, the verbal jesting finished. All eyes were on the television. And then, to my amazement and surprise, tears began to flow. I could not believe what I was seeing. Both boys and girls began to drop their guard and experience grief.

After Jesus uttered the words "It is finished," I walked to the front of the room and turned down the volume. I asked the kids to bow their heads and reflect on what they had seen. I explained the rest of the story—that Jesus had died, then victoriously, triumphantly came back to life. With their heads bowed, I prayed for the group, then dismissed them all to go.

To my surprise, nobody moved. Silence. Forty kids sitting silent as if they wanted more. I couldn't figure out what was going on. From the back of the room came a voice that shattered the silence. "Yo, Bruce, ain'tja gonna show the rest of the flick?" The others chimed in with agreement. So there we sat, huddled around the TV for the next forty minutes, watching the end of the movie.

A few years ago I did the same club. In a suburban community in Southern California, I showed the same film to a group about the same size. The reaction of the affluent students was totally different. There were no tears. There was not the same fascination with the character Jesus, nor the same identification with his pain.

Inner-city kids see slasher movies all the time. People are killed in their own communities frequently and they talk about it casually, candidly. Death and suffering is part of their life. So why all the tears when Jesus is put on the cross? Wasn't this just another movie? Wasn't this just another person who lost his life? No. The cruel death of God in the flesh struck a responsive chord. For a moment the children saw a man who felt the hurt and some of the victimization they have experienced. That man was God. For children who live in a broken city, seeing anguish and pain on the face of God touches something deep within their souls.

Christ's story continues to be a story for those who hurt. It is this story, and this story alone, that is always the story for the poor and oppressed—not only because the Bible "tells us so," but because the children who sat in a room that night, watching their Savior being crucified 2,000 years ago, tell us so.

Out of the Mouths of Babes

Prayers had just finished. The tops of thirty little heads vanished and their faces stared at me once more. A hand flew up in the second row. It was little Yolonda.

"Can I say something?" she whispered.

Nodding in approval, I motioned her to rise. Off the pew she rose and came toward the front of the group. With her head bowed, she stood silently as if she was trying to figure out what to say. The rustling of winter jackets told me that the children were becoming restless.

"You know how my father has been missing," she quietly began, breaking the building noise of restlessness. Tears began to well in her eyes. It was going to be difficult for her to continue. "They dragged him out of Cooper River yesterday afternoon. He's dead."

Little Yolonda then bowed her head and began to shake uncontrollably. The seal had been broken, the pressure released. Yolonda had finally been able to share the immense burden she had shouldered for the past day. A few of us came forward and put our arms around her. The other children began to pray for her. The prayers ended and I led the trembling little body to the side of the sanctuary and sat with her. She continued to cry and cry.

Her moans and wails echoed through the spacious sanctuary, creating an atmosphere much different from the regular Monday night mood. As the children's choir began to sing, their voices were challenged by the repeated sobs of the little girl who had just lost her father. And yet, as the sobs and the wails met the voices of the children, the collision began to create a remarkable sound. The pain being expressed seemed to be driving the children to sing from their souls. They were producing a sound that I had never heard. The words of the spiritual began to live and echoed through the sanctuary with unusual intensity.

> In times of trouble, He will hide me,
> In times of trouble, He will hide me,
> Whom shall I fear?
> Whom shall I fear?

The words, with all their power, embraced me and the weeping child. We were enveloped in the sounds of the other children. The pain of little Yolonda had touched the open wounds of the other children, and they entered into solidarity with their sister.

The tragedy of Yolonda's life is that she had not had anyone to listen to her story. The news of her father's death had come secondhand. And even with the news, there was still confusion as to whether he had been killed or whether he had ended his own life. Little Yolonda had not had anyone to listen and help her make sense out of the whole episode.

But for a moment the church and her choir served as it should. The church became a place of safety, a place where she could be vulnerable and share her deepest hurts. When this happened, the Spirit came and touched her little friends, who responded by singing with power and conviction. The children became her priest. And through their prayers, compassion, and inspired song, they became the agents through which God chose to bring comfort.

I don't believe that any other person or group could have ministered as well as our little, off-note, often raucous choir did that night. I don't believe that the world's best child psychologist could have aided her mourning process any better than her listening friends. Nor do I believe that even the finest of choirs could have brought more solace to her soul. God chose to use the humble that night. Out of the mouths of babes came the healing message of the loving Christ.

▭ ▭ ▭ ▭ ▭

A Moment with Angels

Cities are places of extreme contrasts. A city block is packed with life, excitement, and opportunity. Children play; talk is loud; music and sound is everywhere. It's a beehive, buzzing with life. For those with eyes for redemption, the sight can be exciting. Where else can there be such a place for the spirit of Jesus to mix and mingle, touch and heal?

But the opportunities are tarnished by the pervasive hopelessness. Youthfulness is shrouded by the early death. Beautifully aged architecture is bathed in dirt and trash. One only has to see a child skip rope with high-speed dexterity in the shadow of a crumbled man, cradling his bottle of Firebird, to understand that nowhere are the contrasts more apparent than in the city.

Choir practice had ended. For some reason the children had been able to focus their attention for one hour and twenty minutes. Signs of good discipline were beginning to show, and the children—all thirty-five of them—were beginning to make the connection between good sound and hard work.

In the midst of this sometimes loud and raucous group is a little girl named Ieysha. Because of a slight speech impediment, she is reluctant to look you in the eyes, and she seldom speaks. And the children are quick to tease her for her disability, most likely because of her apparent beauty. With a complexion that is light and golden, she is the envy of those young ladies with darker skin. For some reason, in our community, the youth uphold the fair complexion and the dark is scorned. Her eyes, big and brown, are stunning when they catch your gaze.

But when she sings she tends to forget what others have said about her. She lifts her eyes from the floor and an angelic quality exudes from her face. This particular night, she had joined in unison with the other children and been swept away in the song. Who knows where the song had taken her? Maybe she had departed from the world, which up to this point had been so cruel, to another place where she was free from her disability and free from those other girls who always teased her behind her back.

I managed to get all the children into the van. It was a tight fit, and the ride was not without the occasional outburst. I had already dropped off about half the children and was making a right turn off Twenty-first toward McGuire Apartments. Ieysha would be next to get off the van. I slowly moved down the darkened street toward her apartment. The cement wall to my left had been claimed by one or two of the local gangs and was covered with different color spray paints; an abandoned car sat to my right.

I noticed two people on the sidewalk in front of Ieysha's house. The lighting was poor, so I couldn't make out who the people were. As the van's tires nestled against the curb, I could hear the profanity and screaming above the idle of the van. Suddenly one of the two leapt off the retaining wall in front of the house and ran in front of the van. The headlight clarified the image for me. It was a man. He was bending down and picking up a bottle off the street.

By this time Ieysha had began to scream and yell profanities at the man outside the van. She hurled herself over the bodies of the other choir members, opened the side door of the van, and raced out into the night. Her cousin flew out of the van behind her and grabbed her by the jacket. As her cousin held her, little Ieysha continued to scream at the man.

"Get away from my mommy!!! Get away from my mommy, you bastard!!!" she yelled and sobbed uncontrollably.

By this time the man had found a bottle. He picked it up, cocked his arm, and hurled it at the head of Ieysha's mother. Ieysha's mother had seen it coming and ducked, and the bottle sailed by her head and smashed into the wall behind her. Seeing that the bottle missed, the man got in his car and began driving off down the road. With hammer in hand, Ieysha's mother rushed toward the car and launched the hammer at it. The hammer missed and the car sped off.

I sat in the van without moving. The whole episode had happened within a minute. The children in the van were silent. They could see that I was troubled. Finally, one asked me what was the matter. I was too numb to respond, too saddened to do anything. Ieysha and her mother were now inside, her cousin back in the van, and the children wanted to continue their van ride home as if nothing had happened.

That night I dropped off the last child and began to weep. I wept for Ieysha, for I now understood her rage and her lack of confidence. I shuddered to think what had taken place in front of her eyes. I cringed to think of what a man who could throw a beer bottle at a woman's head from less than ten feet away could do to a little child. As I shut off the lights in the sanctuary that night, I couldn't help but reflect that only an hour before a little girl had sung the praises of angels, and only moments later had been snapped back into reality by having the vilest of curses pulled from the depths of her being.

The contrast between the sacred and the vile, the angelic and the demonic, was so vividly clear in that little eleven-year-old child. Embodied in this little child is the contradiction of the city. A place of hope and a place of despair. A place where angels can live, and a place where their wings can be broken and crippled.

❏ ❏ ❏ ❏ ❏

Gifts of Reconciliation

There was a rush for the van. Besides the usual pushing, shoving, and name calling, I noticed one of the older boys trying to pick a fight with one of the younger girls. It was Tyrone. I didn't like Tyrone; he was a thief. Two weeks prior he and his friend had broken into the church and stolen all my prizes for the children. When confronted about the break-in, he lied.

I knew it. Witnesses told me. Yet still he lied. No hesitation in his voice, no lowering of his eyes, no remorse. My resentment toward him was building.

Now Tyrone was back, causing more problems, more headaches, and more stress for me and the staff. My anger, which had been stewing over the past week, quickly surfaced. With all that excess adrenaline, I began to shake. I had to act. Before I knew it, I had Tyrone's jacket in my grasp and I was throwing him out of the van.

"What the —————— do you think you're doin', man?" he lashed out!

"Get out of here, you're not going to disrupt my kids!" I shouted back in his face. I was out of control.

"You ain't gonna touch me like that and get away with it!" he screamed. "Come on man, hit me. Hit me. Hit me, pussy!" He continued to egg me on in a fanatical manner. By this time I *wanted* to fight. With anger intense and my adrenaline out of control, my fists were all but breaking the air between us.

Watching, with eager fascination, were my after-school program children—the same children whom we had been teaching repeatedly about nonviolence. All I knew was, if I struck him, five months of teaching would be gone and fighting would have license in our programs. So, with all the self-control I could conjure, my face ashen with rage, I turned, got in the van and drove off . . . defeated.

For three weeks it sat on the window sill in my living room. Wrapped in white paper and tied with a bright red bow, the box of peanut-butter-filled chocolates waited to be delivered. Christmas had passed; it was mid-January. My peace offering for Tyrone had moved no closer to his hands since the day I had wrapped the gift.

Each day the box taunted me. It became a painful reminder of the forgiveness that needed to take place. My intentions had been good, but when it actually came to putting words into action I just couldn't swallow my pride and deliver his gift and apologize for the way I had treated him weeks earlier. In addition to my gnawing conscience, my wife decided to get in on the action. I can still hear her words: "Honey, when are you going to get that box off my window shelf? It's collecting dust." Each day I assured her that it would be gone.

Finally one day I saw Tyrone in the street outside my house. This was my chance. I grabbed the box, tucked it under my arm, and headed for the door.

"Yo, Tyrone," I yelled. "Can you come here for a minute?"

Tyrone gave me a startled look and slowly moved away from his friends. As he got a little closer, I took the parcel from under my arm and passed it to him.

"Um . . . here's your Christmas present." I was not doing well. But Tyrone was caught off guard. He looked utterly flabbergasted, confused, and perplexed. He was speechless.

As I left him standing there, I glanced back to see him cautiously opening the box, holding it at arms length. It looked as if he was working with a bomb squad defusing an explosive. I smiled as Tyrone, surrounded by his curious friends, opened the box that he was sure contained a bomb, a snake, or some other object of revenge.

The next day, an hour before our program began, Tyrone appeared at the church parking lot. He wanted to say something to me, but he wasn't sure how to say it. Maybe he wanted to say he was sorry. Maybe thank you. But he just stood there. Finally, I motioned him into the van, which weeks before had been the scene that had divided our relationship. He escorted me on my errands. While riding we chatted about things that interested ninth-grade boys. There was no comment about either our dust-up or the chocolates. Later that week Tyrone showed up for church—the first time he had been there in six months.

A broken relationship had been restored. The anger and frustration that had festered between us was dissolved, simply by a little gift of chocolate peanut butter balls.

Tyrone has disappeared. I have no clue as to his whereabouts. I don't know whether he is still stealing and fighting or living the life that Christ would have him live. But I do know that when he came to our church he experienced forgiveness. And if we meet again, we will meet as friends.

❑   ❑   ❑   ❑   ❑

The Blue Blanket

For months the blanket had been kicked around, stepped on and over by kids, and used to wipe up stains and drips around the van. The blanket, once bright blue and clean, was now torn, crusted with dirt and oil, and had long since lost its color. Should've been thrown away long ago! But someone saw its value as an all-purpose rag used to keep the van clean.

One early morning as I started on my rounds for the day I noticed that the blue blanket had been moved from its regular place under the front seat. Finally someone dumped the thing in the garbage! I thought.

I had just shifted the creaking van into first and started down Westfield Avenue when I heard an unusual noise behind me. I ignored it as I turned the corner. The sound persisted. So I pulled the van to the curb, put on the brake, and cautiously moved toward the back of the van, craning my neck to see what lay behind the final seat. To my consternation there lay the tattered blue blanket, now dirtier than ever and covering an equally dirty eight-year-old, Nyhiem Jones, asleep. Even the starting and stopping of the van had not disturbed the exhausted child.

Unhappily this is not a story about a boy who wanted to play a prank. Finding a place to sleep is a nightly event for Nyhiem. The rest of his story is just as sad. Nyhiem has not been in school for three months. His mother is usually gone most of the day from their shabby two-room apartment trying to make her own desperate way, leaving Nyhiem on the streets to fend for himself. He spends his days scrounging for chocolate bars and french fries to fill his stomach. His social worker is so inundated with other cases that she only gets to check on Nyhiem every two months—that is, if she can find him. At eight years old, Nyhiem's future is being decided for him. He has no real home, he will have no education, and he probably will end up in jail at a very early age. Nyhiem is becoming another painful statistic of the inner city. And there he lay, innocently asleep in our van.

Recently, there has been a lot of hype in our city about change. A new aquarium has been built that is supposedly going to attract new businesses and jobs. It is hard to get too excited about change when at a very human level we see children like Nyhiem who are falling through the cracks of society and will become sixteen (if he's not dead) with no education, no job skills, and no family support systems. How is a city to change if the people within that city are not changing? How can we begin to pretend that bringing a few new businesses to a city is going to affect the crucial elements influencing people's development, such as family, spirituality, and education? Change must begin with individual people. The cycle of poverty will be broken only when individual lives are transformed and changed. It is a single changed life that will go forth to change the lives of others, and ultimately cities.

Happy Birthday, Hasan

I walked down the dreary, narrow hallway toward room 4B. The door had taken a few knocks over the year. Paint was chipped and there were greasy finger marks around the doorknob.

I gave the door a little rap. My knock seemed to spring off the door and bounced down the hall from wall to wall finding nothing to absorb its echo. I didn't dare knock too loud. The last thing I wanted was to awaken the other tenants to come see the stranger in their hall.

Slowly the door opened. In the shadow of the door stood a rather small woman. Her eyes did not lift to meet my own. She may have been embarrassed, or perhaps she was trying to hide something. Regardless, she motioned me into the room.

"Is Hasan ready to go?" I asked the woman, Hasan's mother, who had already found her way back to a broken couch that had been propped up by a couple of books. Glancing across the barren apartment, I saw my little friend staring blankly at a small screen, black-and-white TV. The reception was so poor that I could hardly make out the image on the screen.

"Hasan! Hasan! Hasan!" yelled his mother.

The little boy snapped out of his trance, walked toward his mother, and gave her a kiss. The door closed behind us and together we shuffled back down the corridor.

"Hasan, did you do anything for your birthday today?" I inquired. "I mean, did you have a birthday cake, or a party, or presents?" I asked, trying to clarify my question.

"No, noth'n like that," replied Hasan with a note of sadness in his voice. It was hard for me to put myself in the shoes of a little boy who just spent his tenth birthday staring blankly at a TV in a dreary, one-bedroom apartment. No cake, no gift, and no friends. Just a dreary little room with a mom who could hardly pull herself off the couch.

Hasan and I got in the car, drove up Kaighn Avenue, and finally arrived at my home. The house was still. The only sound was the creaking of the back door as we entered. Hasan took the lead, opening the door to the kitchen. Then it happened. The lights went on and a mighty roar went forth.

"SURPRISE! HAPPY BIRTHDAY, HASAN!!"

Hasan buried his head in his hands and ran into the crowded room. The seventy staff workers who jammed themselves in the kitchen hugged and kissed him and showered him with gifts. The blank stare had disappeared. Hasan's eyes sparkled with life, and he couldn't hide his smile. He felt special. Hasan felt like a child of God.

❑   ❑   ❑   ❑   ❑

A Shroud of Prayer

Her smile is big and bright. Her teeth are pearly white, reflecting light in all directions. If you see her preparing to smile, get ready, because you are in for a treat. She is always courteous, thankful and appreciative of what the counselors do for her. But most of all, this little girl loves to sing. Whenever there is music, her smile increases twofold. It's as if the first note starts a chain reaction that tells her body to celebrate. The eyes begin their dance, and the mysterious aura of joy fills her face.

Needless to say, twelve-year-old Summer is one of the children who make my job worth continuing. Every time Summer shows up, God somehow uses her to reinforce my conviction and calling to ministry. God reminds me there is no other work in the world that could top what I do. To think that I get to share and experience the joys of children on a daily basis is an incredible privilege. The fact that I get to worship God daily with a host of children who sing and dance to God's glory with passion, freedom, and beautiful childlike innocence makes me one of the wealthiest men in the world.

To my dismay, however, Summer disappeared from our program this summer. It was odd that she stopped coming. Summer seemed to live for club and other events we sponsored. I called and dropped by her house, but each time I was turned away by whoever answered the door. She was not allowed to leave the house. I missed my little inspirational friend very much.

Then, a few weeks ago, Summer showed up to Sunday school. I was elated! It did not take long, however, to notice that Summer was not mixing with the other children. She ate her pancakes alone and seemed to have lost all the enthusiasm she had once carried to church.

Fortunately one of the staff noticed her. Before I knew it, they were engaged in serious discussion. I had a feeling that Summer needed a listening ear. I was glad to see that one of the staff had picked up on her need.

Later that day I inquired about the conversation. The staff worker told me that when the talk had turned to the topic of family, tears had welled up in Summer's eyes as she shared that she had not been able to come during the summer months because she had had to take care of three babies. Her nineteen-year-old sister, supporting a cocaine habit, had abandoned the babies to Summer and her mother. Summer's mother had to work, so Summer got the call to look after the children.

But the story continued. Partway through the summer, the sister had returned home for money. When Summer's mother walked in to find the sister ransacking the house, mother and daughter had collided in an ugly battle. The mother was left with enough razor blade slashes on her body to require over three hundred stitches. It had all happened in front of Summer.

I wrote this little story about Summer three years ago and sent it to some of the churches and friends who support our ministry. One of the people who received the letter was moved by the story and decided to post it on the church mission board so that others could read it and pray for the situation. Time passed and I completely forgot about the letter. Summer had returned to the programs, her mother healed well, and their family was able to move to a better neighborhood. Things had really made a turn for the better.

Then, about a year ago I received a letter from a middle-aged woman in Canada. The name was not familiar to me, and I had no idea why she would be writing me. As the letter unfolded, I learned that this woman had read the story about Summer two years prior. She wasn't on our mailing list, but she had seen the letter tacked to the mission bulletin board at her church. She decided that she would commit Summer and her family to prayers. Every day for the past two years, she had prayed for this child and her family. Now she was writing a letter because she was curious as to how Summer was doing.

I finished the letter and sat back in amazement. Out of all the hundreds of children and teens with whom we work, Summer is the teenager who most stands out as one who is committed to Christ. She now serves on our leadership council, sings in the choir, is committed to church, has a heart that is sensitive to the things of God, and is eager to grow in her faith.

I have to wonder where Summer would be today if some unknown woman 5,000 miles away had not been on her knees every morning for this youngster. There is no doubt that God has been faithful to the persistent prayer of a saint who sacrificially went to God on behalf of another. There is no doubt that little Summer is who she is today because of the shroud of prayers that enveloped her during these crucial years of her life.

Chapter 2

Camden:
The City Invincible

Raw statistics about the city of Camden are shocking, but statistics cannot communicate to the rest of America the growing sense of hopelessness and devastation that pervades the city. However, in spite of this, the numbers still tell us a great deal.

In Camden, New Jersey, a city that is connected to Philadelphia by a couple of bridges, the facts and figures are depressingly stark. Unemployment in Camden has soared to 25 percent, and among teenagers and older youth it reaches a staggering 65 percent. The vast majority of births are to teenagers out of wedlock.[1] Many of these young mothers are so messed up by drugs and alcohol that birth defects are common. One doctor at a Camden hospital remarked in an interview, "It's reached a point where we celebrate if a baby is born with all his parts."

Of those teenagers who enter high school as freshmen, only 30 percent will graduate. To add insult to injury, of those who graduate, one third will do so as functional illiterates. In one of the government housing projects where youth workers who are part of our ministry team faithfully serve, drug lords rule the streets and violent death is an everyday occurrence. When interviewed by a reporter from *Time,* a young resident in his early twenties said, "All the kids I grew up with are either dead, in jail, blown away by drugs, or freaked out on Jesus."[2]

I was glad to hear that this young man was aware that, for some of his friends, Jesus had proven to be a live option. Being converted to Jesus has been the exit route from despair for hundreds of kids who have found themselves trapped in such desperate settings. But for every one of them

who is rescued, there seem to be ten new victims who fall prey to the diabolical social forces at work in such neighborhoods.

Those committed to urban youth ministry are often tempted to experience a sense of futility about what they do. Day by day, as they pick up
the individual casualties of a pathological social system, there is a growing awareness that what they are doing is not going to turn the tide
against despair. They realize that it is not just individuals who have to be
changed. Sooner or later, the social system itself must be changed so that
it doesn't turn out so many victims.

There is no difficulty getting church people on board to support the
efforts to rescue and restore the broken young people that the political-economic system spews out with painful regularity. But organizing
for the kind of social action that is required to challenge those who
maintain the oppressive social system raises all kind of questions for
them. When questions are raised about the strategies of corporate
executives whose decisions cripple local economies and leave
uncounted workers without any jobs, some people wonder whether
Christians are messing around with things that are none of their business. When labor unions are challenged for discriminating practices
that keep African-Americans or Latinos from having a fair chance at
high-paying blue-collar employment, there are those who say that we
are butting into situations where we just don't belong.

There is no doubt in the minds of most church people that we are supposed to address the personal sins of those who live in urban ghettos, but
when we begin to address the sinful ways in which institutions and corporate structures can be demonic instruments for perpetrating injustice
and oppression, we run into trouble. When we clergy types address such
"systemic evil," we are often told that we are not "preaching the gospel"
anymore and we may find that we are turning off the very people who
provide financial support for our ministries.

In the past I may not have been so sure that trying to change social
structures was an integral part of the Christian missionary enterprise. But
nowadays it all seems very clear. To attack the evils that have taken hold
and pervaded urban social structures is obviously a part of the church's
mission. I have seen the ways in which Satan has used the "principalities
and powers" which dominate urban life to wreak havoc in lives and bring
devastation to once-proud cities. I have watched as evil social forces have
organized to turn the city streets on which carefree kids once played into
dangerous places. I am now absolutely convinced that the church that
does not address the systemic evils that are eating up the cities of Amer-

ica is not living out its calling. Our task, says the scriptures, is to "destroy the works of the devil" (1 John 3:8), and those works seem nowhere more evident than in the politics and economics that are at work destroying our "alabaster cities."

To give some concrete expression to what I am trying to say, allow me to tell you about what happened to a neighborhood in Camden where some of my relatives once lived. It was a blue-collar community, with block after block of row houses. A good number of the people who lived there made a decent living in two large factories and a shipyard, which were, for most of them, within walking distance of their houses. The many high-paying semi-skilled and unskilled jobs available at the end of World War II gave Camden the lowest unemployment rate in the nation. There was a bustling and vital downtown shopping district with an array of shops and department stores that drew patrons from miles outside the city. It was a solid, stable little city made up of ethnic whites. Hot summer evenings were marked by the laughter and shouts of children playing street games and people sitting on the front steps of their homes talking to neighbors about politics and sports. Churches were alive and well, and the YMCA was packed with people playing and learning. Carved in stone along the front of the city hall was a line of Walt Whitman's that seemed to express the collective consciousness of Camden: "I Dreamed I Was a City Invincible."

Unfortunately, good times for Camden would not last. As early as 1939 there were forces at work that would wreak havoc in the city. That was the year they completed the mighty Benjamin Franklin Bridge connecting the city to Philadelphia. It was, for a short time, the largest and longest bridge in the world, and its massive structure still dominates the city. Before the bridge was built, there were ferryboats connecting the two cities. But the growing flow of traffic back and forth to Philadelphia made the ferries inadequate. A bridge was needed and a bridge was built. Everyone knew that the bridge would change the city, but few people guessed how much.

With the building of the bridge came the expanding of Highway 30, the road leading to the bridge. Highway 30 cut right through the center of town. At first it was just a busy four-lane street, but as bridge traffic increased, the highway had to be widened, and by the 1950s the highway had become a "natural barrier" dividing Camden in half.[3] The city would never be a whole city again. The people on the north side of the barrier were cut off from the stores, the jobs, and the people who lived on the south side. For all intents and purposes, Camden became two separate communities.

But there were other things going on in the city that would have even more painful consequences for its people. RCA, a company that had provided them with thousands of jobs, was gradually moving its operations out of Camden. The shipyard, another major employer, would close down shortly after World War II. And Campbell Soup, which owned the other large factory in the city, would dramatically scale down its operations and move much of its production to another part of the country. In a little more than a decade, a city that once boasted more jobs per capita than any other city in America had lost its economic base. Today there are few good-paying jobs available for the low-skilled workers who live in Camden.

Still other things happened to Camden to further hasten the city's decline. Out in Cherry Hill, a suburb of the city, a huge shopping center opened up. The Cherry Hill Shopping Mall had ample parking. The post World War II era was marked by just about every family having a car of its own, and old cities like Camden were not built with cars in mind. The managers of the large department stores and other merchants soon realized that, with people using cars to do their shopping, the life of downtown Camden as a commercial center was quickly coming to an end. There just wasn't ample parking space in the city. Instead of people taking buses to come into the city to shop, they were driving to the suburban mall. Even the people of Camden were going out there to shop. Camden business owners knew that they had better move their stores out to the mall too if they were to have any kind of a future at all. Soon most of the good stores of the city were closed down. Suddenly boarded-up stores seemed omnipresent. Without warning, the shoppers disappeared from the sidewalks. The city was looking increasingly seedy, and everyone knew it was dying.

As I have been going over the history of Camden, you are probably thinking that such developments are unfortunate for those who have a vested interest in the city, but they hardly seem like the works of some malevolent "principalities and powers" or demonic forces. Maybe not! But more was at work destroying this city than first meets the eye. I want you to consider how once-decent urban neighborhoods became slums, seemingly overnight, because of the manipulations of those who controlled the real estate and banking businesses of the city. Real estate speculators can be clever people, and in Camden some of them came up with a scheme that enabled them to make some quick money by playing on the racial fears of those who lived there. When a black family moved into North Camden, there were rumors that it had been deliberately arranged to "break the block" to pave the way for other blacks to move in. Prejudice and myth took over from there. The racism that pervaded the neighborhood was the basis for the panic selling of some houses, and it wasn't long before people were saying things like, "There goes the neighborhood." Real estate agents encouraged this panic selling. One of them told my uncle, "You'd better sell now and get out while you can. Soon the value of these houses will be down to nothing."

My uncle didn't sell, but his neighbors did. Their racism worked against their economic self-interest because they were willing to underprice their homes just to make quick sales and get away from what they believed was going to be an onslaught of blacks moving in, further depressing real estate values and making the streets unsafe. For Sale signs went up everywhere, and real estate dealers were making a fortune on commissions.

In some cases, real estate agents found even slyer ways to make money. Because of people's fears, some real estate agents were able to buy up houses for themselves at prices well below what the market warranted. They then turned around and sold these same houses at relatively high prices to immigrant black families who were part of the mass migration movement from the South that marked the postwar period. The African-American families being drawn to the city with the promise of jobs needed places to live, and they were ready to pay relatively high prices to get them.

The banks of the city also did their part to help destroy the city. They "red-lined!" If you are not familiar with this jargonized expression, then imagine a map in the bank president's office. The bank president realizes that real estate values in certain sections of the city have become destabilized. Furthermore, this bank official knows that if the bank lends money for house mortgages in these troubled areas and people default on their loans, the bank eventually could be left with worthless property on its hands. And so the president takes out a red crayon and draws a line around those parts of the city that are in the throes of racial change. From that time on, his bank will arrange no mortgages for people to buy homes in those "red-lined" neighborhoods.[4]

The consequences of red-lining are easy to figure out. Few people are able to come up with cash when purchasing a home, and if they cannot get mortgages to buy in a red-lined section of the city, they will just have to buy somewhere else. To the would-be sellers in the red-lined neighborhood, that means potential buyers disappear. From then on the law of supply and demand takes over. With the number of buyers dramatically dropping, the prices for houses also drop. In the case of Camden, houses that were selling for $20,000 one year dropped in price to less than $10,000 the following year.

In the worst possible scenario, some houses prove to be unsellable at any price. When this happens, many families simply move out and leave their former homes abandoned—but not before stripping them. Plumbing fixtures, copper pipes, encased wiring, window casings, doors, heating systems, mantel pieces, stoves, lighting switches, and whatever else could bring a few dollars from junk dealers are torn out, leaving only shells of houses behind. It isn't long before gutted buildings are omnipresent throughout the city. Obviously, these gutted shells on a given city block destroy whatever value the other houses may have.

The social consequences of abandoned houses pose a more sinister threat to the neighborhood than just the loss of property values. Nowadays, pimps and drug pushers look at these houses as havens for their dirty work. Some of them become crack houses. They often become places where cocaine is "cut," mixed with baking soda and then cooked into the brown crystals called crack. This relatively inexpensive drug has become the major scourge of the poor. It sells for as little as $10 a fix, and it is even more addictive than cocaine itself.

Crack houses are easy to find in Camden. Everybody seems to know where they are, except the police. The kinds of people crack houses pull into a neighborhood make walking the streets a dangerous thing to do. Crack addicts will burglarize and break into parked cars to take what can be pawned. They are not above killing just to get a few dollars to nurse their habits. Then, there are pathetic women, and even girls, who hang out around crack houses ready to turn some tricks for another fix. The soiled mattresses used for such degradation can be found in the back rooms of most of the deserted houses of Camden and give painful evidence of what goes on in them nightly.

We must also consider those leeches called "slum landlords." They find it profitable to buy up houses in a deteriorating neighborhood, and then rent them at exorbitantly high prices. I know, because our missionary organization rented one of them in 1987 to house some of our staff workers for a few months. The rent for a dilapidated shack with one tiny bathroom was $650 per month. In order to make the place safe, we had to put bars on the windows. And in order to make the place livable, we had to get work groups from suburban churches to come in and do basic repairs. There was no chance of getting the landlord to do anything.

I am sure you are wondering why the rents in a slum can be so high when the living conditions are so poor. The answer is the welfare system.

Huge numbers of families in Camden are on public assistance, and the welfare system approves rent allowances for these people. But the money is available only for renting—not for buying. And the real estate lobby has seen to it that it's going to stay that way. There are fortunes to be made in renting slum housing to welfare families, and housing brokers pull all the political strings they have in order to protect this gold mine.

If any systematic inspection of the rental units were to be made by the city's building inspectors, most slum rentals would be condemned. But that doesn't happen. Some say it's because the city is close to bankruptcy and doesn't have the funds to hire enough inspectors to get the job done. However, my limited experiences with the building inspectors have led me to believe that in some instances bribes may be the reason for the city's indifference to what is happening to these rental units. There are rampant rumors that some slum landlords pay off the inspectors to keep from being cited for violations. I think about this whenever I read in the paper that one of these firetraps has ignited and some children have been burned to death.

Sometimes fires are deliberately set. It is common knowledge around Camden that when the slum landlords can't get any more money out of their rental units, they hire "specialists" who will set them on fire so that insurance money can be collected. It is hard to go anywhere in Camden without seeing what professional arsonists have done.

Burning abandoned houses has also become a sport in Camden. Kids are starting fires just for the fun of it. A couple of years ago there were more than eighty major fires burning simultaneously on the night before Halloween.[5] The youth of the city decided that for their version of Mischief Night they would set fire to any abandoned houses they could find.

I hope you are able to picture what Camden looks like today. The bombed-out cities in Europe during World War II had nothing on this city so far as destruction is concerned.

It is shocking to learn that the disintegration of Camden was significantly encouraged by official government policies that were set in place following World War II. A grateful nation granted to war veterans the benefits of what has come to be known as the GI Bill of Rights. This package of benefits provided a host of blessings for those who had given up part of their lives to defend the country and to stop the spread of fascism. For some veterans, educational grants available through the GI Bill made possible a college education that otherwise would have been unattainable. Special loan arrangements gave others the chance to start their own businesses. Most important, the GI Bill included a housing plan that enabled returning veterans to buy homes with no down payments and low-interest mortgages.

What was not immediately recognized was that buried in the bill were stipulations for home mortgages that encouraged *de facto* racial segregation and hastened the demise of the older cities of America. These unchallenged conditions on mortgages would have dire consequences for the future of Camden. The stipulation with the most detrimental impact on the city was that the GI Bill would grant those low-interest, no down payment mortgages only for "new and detached" homes in what were considered to be "homogenous" neighborhoods. Giving that the best possible spin, it could be said that the requirement that the homes be new and detached was designed to encourage the massive and necessary building of new housing units. However, this requisite inadvertently made it impossible for veterans to buy any of the old row homes in cities like Camden. Consequently, many new housing developments were built outside the city limits, and the suburbanization of America was put into high gear. The mass production of homes in such housing developments as the Levittowns outside Philadelphia and New York was replicated by other builders across the country. The young families of this post World War II decade who might have given vitality and support to America's cities were encouraged to locate in the "burbs."

The city of Camden was among the serious victims of this government-induced process of suburbanization. Given the guidelines for mortgages in the GI Bill, many of Camden's finest young adults who returned after the war had little practical alternative but to establish their new homes outside the city. The loss of this young, upwardly mobile middle-class cohort would impact inner-city Camden for years to come.

Adding insult to injury, the GI Bill also expressed the racism of the times and encouraged the practice of *de facto* segregation which still haunts cities like Camden today. As I stated earlier, housing purchased under the GI Bill had to be in "homogeneous" neighborhoods. Racial homogeneity was clearly what was being proposed. The government was saying to African-American war vets, "Stay out of the new lily-white suburbs that are being built with taxpayers' dollars. Either go back to picking cotton on southern plantations or find yourself a home in the crowded ghettos of northern cities." Most African-Americans chose the latter of the two alternatives, and it was not long before the "doughnut effect" became evident. Cities like Camden became home to impoverished people of color (Hispanic and African-American) and were surrounded by a ring of middle-class white suburbanites.

With Camden, as with many cities, the "doughnut effect" has had far-reaching ramifications. Cities are shortchanged when funds are appropriated for schools because white suburbanites are generally unwilling to vote subsidies for the education of urban African-American and Hispanic children. When decisions are made concerning gun control, the politically conservative whites who live in the suburbs usually protect their "right to bear arms" without much regard to what the easy availability of guns means to those who live in poor urban neighborhoods. Attempts to get guns registered are resisted, and even efforts to keep attack weapons off the streets are opposed, making police work in the cities more and more dangerous. Last year, murders committed with guns cost the city of Philadelphia $58 million and the city of Camden more than $10 million.[6] The loss of human lives cannot be measured in dollars.

The reaction of the conservative whites who live out in the ring of the doughnut has been to call for more repressive measures. "Build more jails!" they say. "Lock up those delinquents and throw away the keys!" These suburbanites demand that the criminal justice system get tougher on "them." Even as they call for such policies, these same white suburbanites usually refuse to support increased funding for the courts of the city or the appropriation of money to build the additional jail space that carrying out such measures would require.

The growing political power of the suburbs along with the declining political power of the cities enables and encourages state legislators to do such things as mandating that more jails be built and creating criminal justice systems that are tough on those who use guns in committing crimes. But the same politicians usually fail to provide the fiscal means for carrying out such mandates. Thus, they can look like they are tough on crime without their actions costing their constituencies a dime. Such unfunded mandates have helped bankrupt Camden. The city has been required to spend money to build more jails and hire more judges but denied the funds that would enable it to meet those demands. To make matters worse, cities like Camden often find themselves threatened with legal suits by the American Civil Liberties Union (ACLU) and other rights organizations when, in order to get tough on crime, they overcrowd the jails or delay the trials of those who are incarcerated.

Today, the city of Camden is bankrupt or on the verge of bankruptcy most of the time and is unable to pay the bills for essential services like adequate police and fire protection. This dire financial situation is due in part to corrupt and incompetent city officials. But a larger part of the problem results from the way in which tax dollars are used and who pays for what. In trying to understand the fiscal plight of Camden, significant attention must be given to the taxing arrangements whereby those who live in that city have to pay a huge price to provide benefits and services for people who do not live there. As a case in point, the widening of Highway 30 took vast amounts of land out of the tax base of the city. Property tax dollars that Camden sorely needed were lost when buildings were torn down to make way for this expanded thoroughfare. Highway 30 was expanded in order to facilitate, with a minimum of inconvenience, the travel through the city of Camden for the suburbanites of South Jersey on the way to their jobs in Philadelphia. Highway 30 has provided no improvement in the quality of life of the people who live in Camden, nor has it given them any significant economic benefits. It can be argued that by routing traffic away from the downtown streets of the city, the highway has contributed to a loss of sales in stores and to the collapse of Camden's business district.

A more recent instance of the sacrificing of Camden's tax base to provide services for people who do not live there can be found in the new aquarium and concert center just built along the city's waterfront. A couple of hundred acres of prime real estate which could have been developed into high-tax-yielding condos and/or apartment buildings were taken out of the tax base of the city in order to make space for "culturally enriching" structures that pay the city almost nothing. A survey of those who have gained employment through the jobs created by these new facilities reveals that they are people who, for the most part, do not live within city limits.[7] Similar negative fiscal consequences have resulted from the huge expansion of the Camden campus of Rutgers University and the large new state prison that has recently been built along the waterfront of North Camden.

The levying of increased wage taxes on those suburbanites who work in the city in order to make up for lost tax revenues won't solve the problem. Such wage taxes too often have the effect of driving the few remaining tax-paying businesses out of the city because their workers do not want to work where they pay additional taxes.

Since policies put into place by the federal government had a significant role to play in creating the social and fiscal problems of cities like Camden, it seems legitimate to expect that the federal government would do something to help out these cities. And for many years, they did. In the late 1960s, Richard Nixon, a Republican president, joined with a Democratic Congress to create a revenue-sharing plan that helped America's urban communities through many of their financial struggles. Nixon had no difficulty getting his revenue plan through Congress because Congress was dominated by urban-based Democrats whose constituencies would benefit most from the plan. Under Nixon's plan, federal tax dollars would be returned to cities to help finance their operations.

The funds that were given to the cities from Washington over the next couple of decades were not always properly spent, but there is no question that they kept many big city governments from going under. However, political winds began to change in the '80s with the election of Ronald Reagan. This president ushered in a new era of political and economic conservatism that was hard on cities like Camden.

Under the Reagan Administration, even funds that were voted by Congress to be used to help urban communities were not delivered. While almost all facets of city life and all departments of city governments were affected, the most dramatic consequences of this changed federal attitude toward cities were evident in the low-cost government housing projects. Hundreds of thousands of housing units were constructed during the '50s and '60s to provide low-cost housing for economically disadvantaged families. Camden was a city in which 5,000 units were constructed. HUD, the Department of Housing and Urban Development, funded the construction of these units and was responsible for overseeing their maintenance.

There is little question but that the design of these "projects" left much to be desired. High-rise buildings especially proved to be less than functional for the lower socioeconomic family units that lived in them. Inadequate toilet facilities led to children urinating in elevators because they could not get up to their apartments in time. Poor lighting and concealed hallways created opportunities for muggings and rapes. Liberal political action groups destroyed the means that residents originally had to keep out undesirables (for example, people with poor references or/and those with criminal records). By the late 1970s, most of the government housing projects in U.S. cities had become dilapidated and dangerous places in which to live.

Camden provides some prime examples of how a government housing program could go astray. Such housing projects as Westfield Acres and Morgan Village rivaled any of the horrors of Cabrini Green in Chicago or Richard Alan Homes in Philadelphia. Drugs, teenage pregnancies, high school dropouts, crime, and unemployment became omnipresent. But as bad as things were, they were doomed to become even worse during the Reagan years. For the eight years that President Ronald Reagan was in office, absolutely no money was given to help maintain government housing units, and by 1988 a significant proportion of these units had fallen into such disrepair that they were abandoned and boarded up.[8]

Still tougher days were ahead, not only for those who lived in the government housing projects of cities like Camden, but for all of those urbanites who looked to Washington for help. In the elections of November 1994, a landslide victory enabled the Republicans to gain control of both houses of Congress and to finish what Reagan had started—a revolution in government policies for the urban poor.

Determined to cut spending and to balance the federal budget, Congress curtailed a host of government programs aimed at ameliorating the problems of cities. I saw the effects of those cuts in Camden. Youth workers who served with Urban Promise, a faith-based program that I helped to establish, found that funds were no longer available for a much needed summer jobs program. That program had been an incredible help in keeping teenagers gainfully employed over the summer months instead of hanging out on street corners and getting into trouble.

Today, what worries me more is that the future looks even less promising. The shift of power into the hands of the Republicans since the congressional election of 1994 has meant a shift from a party that has been urban-based to a party that draws most of its strength from suburbanites. Suburban voters demand lower taxes, cuts in the federal budget, and the paying off of the national debt. Believing, with some justification, that cities have misused and squandered federal funds in the past, suburbanites are quite ready to vote for less money going into urban programs and more dollars staying in their own pockets.

It is not just that the old urban Democratic political machines are no longer in control of the majority of votes in Congress; they also have lost the leadership control that they had as chairpersons of the various committees of both the House and the Senate. These chair positions had formerly enabled the "old" city bosses like Chicago's Dan Rostenkowski to get all kinds of favors for urban programs from less urban-oriented politicians in exchange for allowing legislation that they desired to get out of committee and on to the floor for discussion and voting. The bargaining power of the city bosses is now gone, perhaps forever, and cities like Camden are feeling the absence of it.

Given this brief overview of some of the forces at work in the ongoing destruction of Camden, I hope that you can concur with my assessment that the struggle to reclaim this city involves a battle against suprahuman "principalities and powers," even as we read in scripture:

> For we wrestle not against flesh and blood, but against principalities, against powers, against the rulers of the darkness of this world, against spiritual wickedness in high places. (Eph. 6:12)

It is not just that there are some evil people who need to be converted to Christ; there are entire political and economic structures which must be challenged. The system of blockbusting for profit in the real estate business must be challenged. The way banks structure their loans and investments must be changed. The system of slum landlords must be abolished. And the international drug cartel that controls the drug trade must be destroyed by creatively challenging and changing federal policies. These and other "principalities and powers" have become the instruments whereby demonic powers bring evil and destruction to a city like Camden.

We are dealing with what sociologists have labeled "systemic evil"— social, economic, and political structures and policies that, once created, seem to have a life of their own. I am talking about institutionalized social systems that, although created by people, have the capacity to *re-create their creators*. We humans are the makers of these "principalities and powers," but although they are generated by human ingenuity, they are capable of controlling our behavior and even leading us into practices that we know will have destructive consequences.[9] Regardless of where they come from, these suprapersonal "principalities and powers" do the work of the demonic and pose a major problem for those of us who want to see a city like Camden become even a limited manifestation of God's kingdom on earth. There is much to overcome in the effort to help Camden live out the words cut in stone on its city hall—"A City Invincible."

Chapter 3

Partnering with Government

Getting government out of handling the social welfare problems of urban America is viewed by many as one of the best things that could happen. Without denying that those who have tried to make the government into the great physician for urban maladies have had good intentions, these usually politically conservative critics of failed government policies claim that government just can't do what needs to be done to solve urban problems. Charles Murray, whose book *Losing Ground* became a bible for urban policymakers in the Reagan White House, makes the case that the Great Society antipoverty programs of the Johnson Administration made matters worse for the very people that the programs were supposed to help.[1]

With a host of statistical tables, Murray sets out to prove that these government-sponsored welfare programs only created dependency among the poor and encouraged a lethargy that rendered many welfare recipients unwilling to work for a living. Murray claims that the Great Society programs did more harm than good. But upon reading through his book, *Losing Ground,* there is one nagging question that begs an answer: What does he suggest that we put in place of the welfare system? As Murray carefully explains why each and every possible attempt to reform the welfare system is doomed to failure, the reader looks anxiously for what he proposes as an answer to the social mess that has resulted from the liberal ideas and "giveaway programs" that marked the Johnson era and the Great Society initiative. Murray does answer the question, but his answer took me somewhat by surprise. He proposes

47

nothing! He contends that as hard as it may be on the poor initially, the only way for America to escape what he considers to be the horrors of the welfare state is for us to stop the welfare system "cold turkey."

When I first read Murray's book, I thought to myself, *It will never happen.* The American people would never tolerate an abrupt end to the welfare system and leave millions of their fellow Americans without a safety net. Well, I was wrong. I had underestimated the growing resentment of the vast majority of middle-class Americans toward what the media has described as "the emerging underclass."[2] The stereotypical images of crime-bent, drug-using, uneducated, promiscuous "welfare queens" having babies that they expect working people to support have had their effect on the general populace. With a little help from the Radical Right, who made it appear that welfare was un-American, if not socialistic, the voters of the country let it be known that they were fed up with the system and demanded change. Consequently, in 1996, President Clinton signed into law a welfare reform bill which, by his own admission, ended welfare as it had been. The government got out of the welfare business and we have yet to see how this will impact the cities of this country.

Looking at Camden, the effects of this change might appear to be negligible. Some of the people who have been pushed off the welfare rolls had no right collecting government dollars in the first place. They are the ones who had jobs that enabled them to earn unreported income and collect welfare at the same time. A good number of them worked as domestics, gas station attendants, and baby-sitters. They could collect cash from such work while pretending to be unemployed and illegally collecting welfare benefits.

On the other hand, some people who *should* be on welfare have lost desperately needed benefits because they are emotionally or mentally impaired and failed to show up for appointments with welfare workers. Still others have disappeared from the welfare rolls without anyone knowing what happened to them. What we do know is that rescue missions and shelters for the homeless have registered dramatic increases in the numbers of people who are showing up at their doors for help.[3]

The full consequences of the end of the welfare system on the city of Camden are just now being felt. All of those who were on welfare when the new bill took effect have lost their benefits. The bill stipulated that persons on welfare could receive benefits for up to two years for any given period and for a total of five years in a lifetime. The first two-year period has expired and thousands of uninformed, inadequately prepared welfare recipients are no longer receiving checks. Most of them probably do not know what hit them.

Those Christians who make up the Religious Right claim to have an answer for the poor who fall between the cracks with no societal welfare safety net to catch them. They propose that the church step in and take care of these people. It is their belief that caring for the poor has always been the responsibility of the church and that the church was in error in abdicating this responsibility to the state. They say that the time is at hand for the church to assume responsibility for the poor and to reestablish its compassionate ministries to them.

The most prominent advocate of this strategy has been the editor of *World* magazine, Marvin Olasky. In his book, *The Tragedy of American Compassion,* Olasky not only echoes the conclusions of Murray about the welfare system, but also proposes a strong response from religious institutions as the only good way to address the problems of the truly disadvantaged.[4] Tapping into American church history, Olasky gives multiple examples of the effectiveness of the church's response to the needy in the days before the government stepped in and created the welfare industry. Olasky's book became must reading for the new members of the 103rd Congress who came to Washington convinced that they had a mandate to end social liberalism. Olasky's Christian commitment makes him a person who recognizes the biblical admonition to care for the poor, but his political conservatism leads him to believe that this care should be exercised by the church rather than the government.

There is much to commend Olasky's proposals. Going back to the middle of the nineteenth century, there is the example of Charles Finney, the Billy Graham of the era, who called the Christian community to social responsibility. To Finney, a primary precondition for a national spiritual revival was to create justice for the poor and oppressed. The evangelist was more than just talk in this respect, in that he became a primary force in the antislavery movement and provided much of the impetus of the emerging feminist movement.[5] But a little-known part of his many efforts to achieve social justice is that he put together a significant response by wealthy Christians to the sufferings of the poor of America. Working together with the socially conscious Tappan Brothers of New York City, the founder of the Bache Wall Street investment firm, Finney was able to bring together an array of Christian philanthropists who contributed vast amounts of money to faith-based social welfare programs. At its peak, this group of wealthy patrons of the poor contributed moneys that equaled half of the national budget.[6]

Needless to say, we are not living in the middle of the nineteenth century, and the simplistic solutions to the needs of the poor and oppressed that worked so well back then probably would not work as well in our complex mass society. It can be argued that even in the day of Charles Finney, charity by the Christian community was less than what was needed to meet the needs of the socially disinherited who wandered aimlessly on the streets of our cities.[7]

I think that one of the prime weaknesses of Olasky's argument is that he believes that the church will do more than many social analysts think it is willing or able to do. In one report from the *New York Times,* it was pointed out that it would take every church in America increasing its giving to the poor by $150,000 per year to meet the needs of the people who are presently being cared for by government-sponsored social programs.[8] Such generous giving is hardly likely to be forthcoming from American churches, given the inward-looking attitude that characterizes most of them.

But Olasky does not expect the church to do *all* that the government does. Instead, he proposes that only the *deserving* poor be helped, and he is fairly specific about who is deserving and who is not. The principles guiding his thinking are as follows:

1. *Affiliation:* When material help is needed, charities should try to raise it from relatives and others with personal ties instead of appropriating funds from the taxpayers.

2. *Bonding:* When applicants are truly alone, there should be bonding with volunteers, who in essence become new family members. This requires personal involvement with the needy.

3. *Categorization:* Charity organizations should not trust everyone equally and should help only those who are "Worthy of Relief"—who are poor through no fault of their own and unable to change their situation quickly. Other applicants are to be placed in other categories such as "Needing Work Rather than Relief," or "Unworthy, Not Entitled to Relief" or "Confirmed Intemperance," etc.

4. *Discernment:* Charity workers must learn that well-meant interference, unaccompanied by personal knowledge of all the circumstances, often does more harm than good and becomes a temptation rather than a help.

5. *Employment:* Able-bodied persons must accept available jobs rather than be made into charity cases. Even when charity is given, some labor for the community must be required of the recipients.

6. *Freedom:* The opportunity must be given to work and worship without government restrictions. Welfare benefits are not to be viewed as a right by people in a free society.

7. *God:* True philanthropy must take into account spiritual as well as physical needs. Leading people into a religious commitment must be part of helping them, if the help is to have any lasting significance.[9]

I have a hard time accepting the idea that only "the deserving" should be helped. I believe that the gospel is a call to imitate a Jesus who reaches out to the undeserving. That, to me, is what grace is all about.

Perhaps the most realistic hope for the immediate future is a partnership between the state and the church. It is obvious from research that faith-based programs accomplish far more than government-sponsored programs, and do so for just a small fraction of the cost that government pays. As a case in point, Teen Challenge, a faith-based drug rehabilitation program started by the Pentecostal evangelist David Wilkerson, is far more effective in helping addicts than any government-sponsored program. Teen Challenge has an 81 percent "cure" rate. Most other programs come nowhere near that level of effectiveness.[10] Urban Promise, the ministry in Camden founded by our own EAPE/Kingdomworks organization, spends about $10 per month to engage a child in daily after-school programming that includes tutoring, character building, and recreation. A similar government-sponsored program would probably require ten times that amount per child and, in all likelihood, its results would not measure up to what the spiritually motivated Urban Promise workers achieve.

Calling on churches and other faith-based organizations like EAPE/Kingdomworks to expand their outreach programs to the hundreds of thousands who will be abandoned by government agencies is probably a great idea. However, there are many questions being raised about whether such an idea can be a comprehensive solution to the problem.

The most serious question being raised is where these faith-based organizations will get the necessary funding to increase their programming. To most people, it is far-fetched thinking to believe that America's churches will come up with $150,000 per congregation each year.

Then again, miracles are the stuff that created the church in the first place. Realism, however, requires that we face the discouraging fact that since the new welfare bill has been enacted there have been very few signs of a ground swell of new financial support for ministries to the urban poor from the church or anyplace else. Many of those organizations that have made helping the poor their *raison d'être* have been complaining that it is actually getting *more* difficult to raise the needed funds to keep their programs going. The Salvation Army, for one, has sent up clear warning signals that it is not prepared to take on the challenge of replacing government-financed welfare programs with programs sponsored by charitable organizations.

What many leaders in government and in the faith communities are beginning to see as one hopeful response to the needs of the truly disadvantaged poor is some kind of partnership between the state and the church. Attempts at such a partnership are already under way. For instance, President Clinton has helped to make it possible for up to 50,000 young people to work in faith-based social service agencies as part of his Americorps program. If they have student loans, these young people get deferments on those loans. What is more, the government pays the interest on those student loans during the borrower's time of community service. In the President's speech at the Summit on Volunteerism in Philadelphia on July 4, 1996, he supported this program by declaring that no young person should have to be financially penalized for serving other people.

Not only will opening up the Americorps program to include faith-based ministries free thousands of young people who take time off to serve others from worrying about paying off their student loans, but it also will help them to pay for their educations. At the end of each year of service, the Americorps program will provide a $4,500 educational grant to each one who serves.

What could be the most significant boost for faith-based ministries to the urban poor is the legislation that is being proposed by Senator Dan Coates from Indiana. Senator Coates wants the IRS to give an annual $500 tax credit to each American taxpayer, which can be applied to any officially recognized social service agency of his or her choice, faith-based or otherwise.[11] If passed, this legislation would be a bonanza for faith-based social service agencies and might just provide what is needed for them to meet the challenges being laid on them by those who share Olasky's views.

Regardless of what special arrangements our government makes to undergird faith-based efforts to meet the needs of the victims of welfare cuts, both conservatives and liberals within the church are recognizing that the Christian community must do something. Already Call to Renewal, a political action organization that offers itself as an alternative to the Christian Coalition and the Religious Right, has brought together evangelicals from across the political spectrum to explore possible responses to the cuts in welfare benefits. Rejecting the old dichotomies that have polarized the Christian community into Democrats and Republicans, the Call to Renewal contends that the old answers to the social problems of our times proposed by both conservatives and liberals have been proven inadequate.[12] This new political action group has been holding Evangelical Roundtables, which have enabled representatives from all political persuasions with a common commitment to evangelical Christianity to unite in finding ways to cooperate in addressing the crisis that looms for families on welfare. Christian political action groups as diverse as the Sojourners Community on the left and the Family Research Council on the right are coming together at these Roundtables in an endeavor to find some common ground on which to minister to the economically disadvantaged. At a press conference following one of the Roundtables, Richard Cizik of the National Association of Evangelicals declared, "When it comes to responding to the needs of the poor, let it be known that the old war between the conservatives and the liberals in the church is over. We're together in this thing!"[13]

One of the most promising plans to come out of this unusual coalition is a scheme whereby churches will "adopt" welfare families to help them out of their plight. Following the war in Southeast Asia, churches cooperated with government to handle the huge number of refugee Vietnamese and Cambodian families arriving on America's shores. The Call to Renewal has proposed a similar plan to provide for our own nation's welfare families. Organizations that are part of the Evangelical Roundtable are being urged to get their churches to adopt and take responsibility for specific welfare families and help them to get decent housing, jobs, education, and health care. The plan is to get as many as 10,000 such families "adopted" in this fashion, with churches doing all that an ideal welfare system could ever hope to do—and more. It is proposed that such an effort would start a trend so that other religious organizations would get into the act. Thus faith-based social action could make a major contribution in solving the pressing problems presented by those leaving the welfare rolls with no place to go. It remains to be seen just how realistic this proposal will prove to be.

Some of our college-aged EAPE missionaries assigned to Camden decided to reach out to one of Camden's devastated drug-infested neighborhoods. A team of six women and two men, committed to being change agents for Christ, moved into one of the newly deserted houses. It was a small row house, given to them by a man who could not sell it. With the help of a youth group from a suburban church, they fixed up the place.

The first night the team slept in the house, there was a murder on the pavement across the street. Bullets were flying not more than twenty yards away from where they lived. The screams of a mortally wounded man filled the air. The sirens and the flashing strobe lights of police cars created a surreal scene that lasted until daybreak. This wasn't the worst of it. Our new "mission station" was next door to the hangout of a major gang that was into dealing drugs. Seedy-looking people came and went from the house in endless succession. But this gang's control of the neighborhood did not go unchallenged, and the night following the murder another gang showed up to take over. A battle broke out, and while our frightened staff stared in disbelief, young hoods battled each other using chains, baseball bats, knives, and zip guns. The violence ended as quickly as it had started, and the armies dragged away their wounded to nurse them in secret. The alien gang was beaten back and the next-door "neighbors" still reigned supreme.

It was what happened the third night that forced us to give up and move the team out. Sometime around two o'clock in the morning, three thugs tried to smash down the front door of the house to get at the young women who were part of our ministry team. The two young men who also lived in the house were sleeping in the front living room when the attack started. They rushed to the front door and threw their weight against it, but they knew they couldn't keep the would-be intruders out for long. One of them was able to push an old sofa against the door to reinforce it. Upstairs the young women both prayed and screamed out the windows for help. Lights went on in the neighbors' homes and people across the street started yelling at the thugs to leave our threatened missionaries alone. And then, before it was too late, the police arrived.

The next morning we moved our ministry out of the neighborhood. We had to give up on our plan to establish an evangelical service center in that needy community. The risks were too great.

But there are worse stories to be told. The drug business has been internationalized, with supplies coming out of Colombia and para-military units from Caribbean nations controlling the distribution. Recently a drug lord up from Jamaica moved into a burnt-out slum in Camden to take over a lucrative trade in crack. He forced an elderly couple in the neighborhood to open their home to him. The drug lord knocked on the door, and when the old man opened it to see who was there, the Jamaican pushed his way in and announced that from then on he would live there and that they had better shut up about it if they wanted to live. He took over the front bedroom and made the old lady cook his meals and wash his clothes. He made life a living hell for those two elderly people.

That old couple had been left behind when the neighborhood changed. When the other middle-class people had moved out, they couldn't afford to do it. All they owned was their little row house, and all the money they had was a small pension and a monthly Social Security check. They didn't have the means to do anything else except tough it out and stay in the house that had been their home. With the coming of the drug lord, that home became their prison, and they were reduced to being the slaves of an obscene criminal who lacked even the slightest trace of human pity.

Other people who lived on the block knew what was going on but didn't do anything about it. They knew what happened to anybody who reported such things. Jamaican drug lords are not challenged without dire consequences. Even the police are afraid of them. But eventually the frightened neighbors did act when this evil man took to raping the old lady. The screams from the little house were more than they could bear. Hearing the old lady begging to be left alone while her 79-year-old husband sat on the front steps of his house sobbing uncontrollably drove even the terrorized neighbors to action. They called the police and the drug lord was arrested. The story made the papers, so the police, for public relations purposes, posted a couple of officers to guard the neighborhood. But everyone knows that the police won't stay forever, and people wonder what will happen when they leave.

In the face of such overpowering diabolical social forces, a lot of people have fled. Many who once lived in Camden drive through their old neighborhoods from time to time and usually offer simplistic explanations for what has happened.

"It's because of *them* that Camden went down," they say. "When the blacks moved in, *they* ruined everything! It used to be a nice town until *they* moved in."

But it wasn't *them* that destroyed Camden. The race of the new residents had little to do with the devastation of the city, and blaming it all on a people who have already endured unbearable discrimination is only one more work of the devil.

But the church stays on in the city. Across Camden there are faithful pastors who stand fast and refuse to give up. Their congregations have diminished to mere handfuls of people. The money they need to keep their social programs going just isn't there. Their buildings are covered with graffiti and in disrepair, but these servants of God refuse to walk away. These pastors and their churches are the final hope of the city. They need our help and our encouragement. They cannot do what must be done to save Camden unless those of us who do not live there make some bold and daring moves. They will fail unless there is a new strategy for saving the city.

This book is about how we can ensure that those brave souls, who even now are dreaming of a resurrection, will not be disappointed.

Chapter 4

The Church as
the "Lead Institution"

Talcott Parsons, the onetime dean of American Sociology, defined a "lead institution" as that institution which controls the process of change within a given societal system. A lead institution determines the functions and structure of all other institutions as well as exercising power and influence over the behavior of individuals.[1]

In times past, one institution or another has played this role and controlled the destiny of America. As a case in point, Franklin Delano Roosevelt once said, "So goes General Motors, so goes the nation." In that declaration, he acknowledged that the future of America was tied up with the industrial economy and, specifically, with the automotive industry.

Roosevelt was well aware of the fact that the functions and structures of all the other social institutions of America were shaped by heavy industry. What the leaders of these industries chose to do or not do would spell the life or death of the towns and cities in which their factories were located. The decision to keep their mills and factories in place or move them elsewhere would determine the destinies of countless numbers of people. Such decisions would determine what would happen to everything from school life to family life. If factories closed in a given town, the unemployed would be likely to move to other places in search of work, while those who remained behind would show the social and psychological effects of unemployment in their lifestyles. Family breakdown would become common. Young people in these communities would give up on the American Dream. The emotional despair and sense of powerlessness that always goes with being the victims of such corporate decisions would affect everyone.

In hard-hit communities, churches would lose their base of support, and the disheartened folks who remained would become harder and harder to reach with claims that there was "good news" in the gospel for them. The small businesses in such towns would close down one by one, because there would be neither the money nor the clientele to support them. Such power over people and the communities in which they lived made heavy industry the lead institution during the years of the FDR Administration.

More recently, the lead institution of society has been the government. It can be said that the whole idea behind the New Deal policies of the 1930s was to have government controlled by the people, rather than big business determining what goes on in America. The New Deal ushered in a new era that, for better or worse, meant that pure *laissez-faire* economics was at an end and that, in the future, government would increasingly control what business and industry could and could not do. To the founders of the New Deal, it seemed obvious that the corporate community, motivated by the profit motive, could not be expected to make decisions in the best interests of the public good. It was assumed that government had to step in and become the lead institution for the benefit of society as a whole. In the New Deal, banks would be controlled by the FDIC. The stock market would be regulated by the Securities and Exchange Commission. And the corporate world would be increasingly regulated by Washington. With the New Deal of FDR, it was determined that the future of America would no longer be left to the wiles of the so-called "Invisible Hand" of economics.[2] Instead, America would be guided by the dictates of big government for what was claimed to be the good of "all the people."

It is now increasingly clear that we are facing a situation in which neither big business *nor* big government can be counted on to be the lead institution. To many of us, it is becoming more and more clear that if the cities of America are going to be saved, another institution must take the lead. Many of us believe the time has come for the church to fulfill that role. If the blight and destruction that is growing like a cancer in the old cities of the nation is to be eradicated, we believe that the church must step forward and recognize that its hour to be society's lead institution is at hand. Many of us are convinced that the time is at hand for the church to step up and assume the mantle of change agent and to recognize that it is for just such a task that the church is now being called by God.

One obvious reason for the church to assume this crucial role is because "it's there!" Most other institutions have faded and some even have disappeared from city life. Business and industry have followed the flight of the middle class to the greener grass of suburbia. Malls have replaced downtown as the place where people shop. Even recreation and the arts have moved outside the city line.[3]

While everybody and everything seems to have moved to the suburbs, any tour of urban neighborhoods will reveal that there are still a lot of churches left. When we take a look at what is left in urban America, we find a growing mass of underclass people surrounding a significant number of abiding churches that, for one reason or another, refuse to give up the city. Some of these churches are huge stone structures with towering steeples that hark back to another time. All you will find in some of these old churches are small gatherings of white-haired people who remember the glory days when their churches were packed with Sunday worshipers. Now those who remain do so for a variety of reasons. Some stay because of a deep sense of allegiance. They were baptized and married in those churches, and they fully expect to be buried by them. Others stay out of a sense of calling to carry on ministry to the new people in their communities. Still others stay (and this is the worst of possible reasons) because they think they *own* these churches.

While many of these remaining inner-city churches seem to be hanging on for dear life, others still have some dynamic life left in them. Good leadership and vision have kept them vital. They still have critical masses of members and are able to carry on some solid programming. My son Bart and his family belong to such a church. Sitting in West Philadelphia on the edge of what is called University City, their church has a good Sunday School and a strong youth program. There are many young couples with children who attend this church, and they find with each other the friendship and activities that dispel the alienation that often marks life in the big city.

Remaining behind in the city are also the ethnic churches. These are churches that often boast large memberships and multiple staff members. The members of these churches are not all from their immediate neighborhoods, but also include people who drive in from the suburbs. Many African-American churches fall into this category. My own church, Mt. Carmel Baptist in West Philadelphia, is one of them. Our two Sunday morning services are packed by hundreds of faithful worshipers who are favored each Lord's Day with some of the best choir music and preaching in America. Members come from all over the Philadelphia

region, and a significant number of them (many upper-middle-class professionals) drive long distances to be a part of this great church situated
in a quickly deteriorating neighborhood. Mt. Carmel, in spite of its location, is presently having some of its best days of ministry. Our pastor, Dr.
Albert F. Campbell, is one of the city's most influential personalities, and
the sheer size of his congregation guarantees that our church exercises
great influence in the neighborhood.

Still another type of church that we find in urban America these days
goes by the name Pentecostal, or charismatic. Churches of this type seem
to have appeared out of nowhere over the last decade or so and often show
signs of dramatic growth and vitality. Drawing together not only the
socially disinherited but a significant number of zealous, highly educated
young adults, these churches defy all sociological expectations. Their congregations are usually racially integrated, and they often draw members
from across the socioeconomic spectrum. The worship services at these
churches are marked by long periods of singing what has come to be called
"the new worship music."

These Pentecostal and/or charismatic churches are usually committed
to reaching out to their immediate neighborhoods. Church members
seem willing to do anything, from door-to-door visitation evangelism to
street-corner preaching. While their gospel tends to be highly personal-
istic in content, these churches are increasingly aware that sharing the
gospel with the people at their doorsteps requires a sensitivity to their
social and economic needs.

These categories by no means cover all the kinds of churches that
remain in our dying cities. There are storefront churches that offer a
haven for defeated and discouraged people who do not feel at home in
other kinds of churches. There are a variety of neighborhood Roman
Catholic churches that serve enclaves of ethnic Christians from southern
and eastern Europe. The list of types of churches could go on and on. I
believe that together these churches have the potential to become the
lead institution for the renewal and redevelopment of the blighted cities
of America.

Many of the churches in the inner city are already making major contributions to their neighborhoods and to society at large. But more is required
of them, and too often they do not see the larger role that they are being
called on to assume. Seldom do they realize that the Church is called to
be the lead institution that can govern the direction and the character
of social change in urban America. Rarely are they aware that the hour
has come for them to step out of their societal background and claim con-

trol over the destiny of America's cities. Often these churches already have the human and material resources to get the job done. They must be made to realize that to whom much is given, much is expected.

What I want to do in this book is to lay out a scenario for the way in which inner-city churches can achieve this high calling to become the lead institution for urban renewal. It is a scenario that has emerged out of my personal reflection and conversation with some knowledgeable people, and my somewhat limited reading and research. Everything I am about to suggest has been successfully tried by somebody, someplace. In that respect, all the components of the plan have been empirically validated. But the various parts of the whole have not yet been put together in one unified scheme. Consequently, there is no way of knowing whether the whole thing will work. What I am hoping is that some charismatic church leaders will study what I am about to outline here and be sufficiently convinced of its viability to give it a try. Then and only then will it be possible to have some evidence to validate this scenario.

When I use the term charismatic leaders in this context, I am *not* alluding to the use that has become increasingly common in many religious circles. I am *not* using the term to necessarily suggest that what is needed are some leaders who have had a Pentecostal experience wherein they are filled with the Holy Spirit. Instead, I am using the term in the way in which it was used by the great German sociologist, Max Weber.[4] I am referring to those who belong to that unique "ideal type" of leadership that Weber believes is capable of initiating dramatic new social movements. I am pointing to those people who have an alternative vision of the future, who are able to inspire a following. Specifically, I am referring to those who convey a sense that they have a mandate to lead that comes from beyond themselves. When the charismatic leaders conform to Weber's ideal type, they communicate clearly to all who hear them that they are *called* to their roles as leaders and that, since their leadership has some kind of trans-human legitimization, they cannot fail. Under the influence of such leadership, ordinary people are convinced that they can change the world. Charismatic leaders generally offer a plan that is easy to understand and which their followers can readily believe is workable. Charismatic leaders define their schemes for changing the world with such force that they enable their followers to believe that success is guaranteed. As they declare their visions for change, the plans of such leaders seem obviously workable, and those who follow them are convinced that what is envisioned is as good as done. It is in the context of such inspiration that those who join movements can be certain that their labor is not in vain. Only charismatic leaders can inspire the kind of all-out commitment from their followers that any movement needs to succeed.

Charismatic leaders, according to Weber, cannot be created via rational means. There is no training program that will produce them. They are not educated or academically prepared for this role. They *emerge.* They seem to come out of nowhere at a time of crisis. They possess an authority that does not come from some credentialing organization. They possess a unique kind of authenticity. When they speak, those who follow believe that they are hearing something that rings with the authority of God.[5]

His extensive knowledge of religion enabled Weber to find charismatic leaders throughout the Bible, especially in the book of Judges. As Weber surveyed biblical history he saw that, when Israel was in a time of crisis, Yahweh would raise up a charismatic leader with extraordinary powers. Such leaders inspired hope in times of despair. For the Jewish people, they were seen as instruments of deliverance from their enemies and agents of God who would help them to create a new social order that they labeled, "The Kingdom of God."

Such are the times in which we live—at least so far as urban America is concerned. The conditions among the growing underclass in the blighted neighborhoods of our cities can only be described as desperate. What is needed are charismatic leaders with an inspired alternative vision for the cities of our country, along with plans for translating their vision into concrete reality.

What is needed are men and women who will respond to the crisis of urban America with charismatic leadership. Jesus called on us to pray that His Father would raise up such leaders as well as to pray for an army of committed followers. He told us that "the fields . . . are white already to harvest" (John 4:35).

Today, the cities of our country are that ripe and ready field. The time for the church to reap a harvest for the Kingdom of God is at hand. Therefore, we ought to be praying that the Lord of the Harvest will raise up charismatic leaders with both a vision and a plan. In biblical language, it is "the fullness of time" for the church. If there are no leaders with vision raised up, and if the church does not respond to the urban challenge, then the church will become an irrelevant social force in American history instead of realizing its call to greatness.

Chapter 5

Getting the Church
into the World

The good urban pastor will get the people of the church into the community. Jesus got things going by sending out his disciples door to door and instructing them to minister to any who would receive them. That is a good model for the church today. We don't have to go beyond the Bible for directives. All of this is recorded in an unforgettable passage in the Gospel according to Luke:

> After these things the Lord appointed other seventy also, and sent them two and two before his face into every city and place, whither he himself would come. Therefore said he unto them, The harvest truly is great, but the laborers are few: pray ye therefore the Lord of the harvest, that he would send forth laborers into his harvest. Go your ways: behold, I send you forth as lambs among wolves. Carry neither purse, nor scrip, nor shoes: and salute no man by the way. And into whatsoever house ye enter, first say, Peace be to this house. And if the son of peace be there, your peace shall rest upon it: if not, it shall turn to you again. And in the same house remain, eating and drinking such things as they give: for the laborer is worthy of his hire. Go not from house to house. And into whatsoever city ye enter, and they receive you, eat such things as are set before you: And heal the sick that are therein, and say unto them, The kingdom of God is come nigh unto you. But into whatsoever city ye enter, and they receive you not, go your ways out into the streets of the same, and say, Even the very dust of your city, which cleaveth on us, we do wipe off against you: notwithstanding, be ye sure of this, that the

kingdom of God is come nigh unto you. But I say unto you, that it shall be more tolerable in that day for Sodom, than for that city. Woe unto thee, Chorazin! woe unto thee, Bethsaida! for if the mighty works had been done in Tyre and Sidon, which have been done in you, they had a great while ago repented, sitting in sackcloth and ashes. But it shall be more tolerable for Tyre and Sidon at the judgment, than for you. And thou, Capernaum, which art exalted to heaven, shalt be thrust down to hell. He that heareth you heareth me; and he that despiseth you despiseth me; and he that despiseth me despiseth him that sent me. And the seventy returned again with joy, saying, Lord, even the devils are subject unto us through thy name. (Luke 10:1–17)

Visiting door to door is where we have to begin. If we are going to turn things around in urban America, we have to make contact with the people in the neighborhoods that surround our churches. As simple as this seems, it is seldom done. When pastors of inner-city churches are asked if they or their members have visited the people who live within a mile of their churches, they generally answer, "No!" I hear inner city-pastors explain how the people who once supported their churches have moved away and how their neighborhoods have changed. And I hear them complain that the new people who have moved into their neighborhoods just don't come to their churches. Seldom do I find that these pastors have gotten their members to join them in reaching out to these new people and personally inviting them to be a part of their churches.

I am often told by urban pastors that the doors of their churches are always open to any new people who may want to *come*. But Jesus did not tell his disciples to wait until people came to them. Instead, he commanded his disciples to *go* out into the world and *invite* people to come into his church (Matthew 22:9). His words to those who would claim to be his followers are these:

Go ye into all the world, and preach the gospel to every creature. (Mark 16:15)

Following this directive of Jesus is the first step in the scenario I am proposing for the church if it is going to be a major player in transforming urban America. Church leaders have to mobilize the members of their congregations to join them in going door to door in their own neighborhoods with the express purpose of carrying out The Great Commission that this verse prescribes.

The reasons that pastors give for failing to carry out this simple directive to do door-to-door visiting are manifold. Some pastors agree that it has to be done but say that over the years their churches have lost so many members that those who remain are tired. They claim that, in years gone by, people worked hard in their churches. But the remaining members are older now, a bit worn-out, and no longer have the energy that a visitation program would require.

A second explanation that I often hear for their failure to visit is that many pastors are intimidated by the task. The people in their neighborhoods are frequently hostile to any would-be callers—whether they be encyclopedia salespersons or people from the local church. Visiting door to door is often hard on the ego. Those who answer have been known to shut their doors in the faces of even the most gracious callers. It takes a great deal of motivation and self-discipline for pastors to do this "grunge work" of the ministry. Consequently, many urban pastors find something else that needs doing, leaving door-to-door visitation for some later time when their churches are ready "to do it right." Such procrastination probably means that these pastors will never get around to visiting, especially in light of the fact that urban pastorates tend to have remarkably short tenures. While sometimes lethargic and sometimes emotionally immobilized inner-city ministers are playing a delaying game, the Jehovah Witnesses and Mormons are hard at work knocking on doors right under their noses, and these competitors are achieving remarkable results.

Third, there are pastors of inner-city churches who don't get into door-to-door visitation because they are, pure and simple, "burned out." They have labored long and hard in the city vineyards, often going at it alone. Lacking the support they need to carry out their dreams for vital and effective ministries, these pastors often become discouraged. Feeling that their efforts have produced little in the way of significant fruit, these pastors settle into a routine style of ministry. They go through the motions, but the spark they once had seems gone. They are on a survival course, doing what has to be done to keep their churches alive, but they have long since lost their passion. These pastors have settled into doing church maintenance. They preach their sermons, they visit the sick, they run church business meetings, and they keep an array of committees functioning. But the dreams and visions that once generated zeal have all but completely evaporated. One burnt-out inner-city pastor told me that he had been disillusioned and hurt far too many times to go on putting his heart and soul into his ministry. He talked about all the times he had made heavy investments of love, time, and energy in young people, only to find that his efforts seemed to amount to nothing. In spite of his hard work, the girls in his youth group still got pregnant and the boys still got into drugs and crime. He said that he stays in his church because he believes it is his God-given duty to stay. But this man readily admits that he long ago gave up believing that much would come from his efforts. When I talked to him about revitalizing his church through a visitation evangelism program, he simply shrugged his shoulders and said, "I really don't think that it would accomplish much."

Finally, there are those urban pastors who could fairly be labeled as losers. Dying inner-city churches are often where denominational executives dump those ministers that no other churches want. Preachers who can't preach, pastors who have a hard time getting along with others, and those ministers without organizational skills are all too frequently the ones who are assigned to struggling inner-city churches. In more cases than not, those ministers who fall into this category don't have an entrepreneurial bone in their bodies. To expect such pastors to inspire the laity to do door-to-door visitation is to expect more than they are capable of delivering.

Concerning urban pastors, however, it's not all bad news. There is one new source of urban clergy that is increasingly providing some of the most qualified and dynamic church leaders now occupying inner-city pulpits. I am referring to the recent array of women who are graduating from seminaries. As a side effect of the feminist movement, more and more women are standing up and letting it be known that they want to use their gifts in the gospel ministry. Unfortunately, prejudices against women ministers are still so great that most of them do not get the opportunities to pastor the larger and more desirable churches, usually located in suburbia. Too often congregations prefer to settle for a male minister of lesser talent rather than take a chance on a woman preacher. An exception to that tendency was evident when Dr. Roberta Hestenes, the former president of Eastern College, resigned to pastor a large church in Southern California.[1] Those of us on the Eastern faculty greeted her resignation with mixed emotions. On the one hand, we were saddened for Eastern to lose one of the most creative college presidents in America. On the other hand, we were happy to learn that she had accepted a call to be the senior pastor of one of the largest and most prestigious churches of the United Presbyterian Church (U.S.A.). Seldom does a woman get to serve such a prominent church, even when she has the abilities and vision of a Roberta Hestenes. In reality, a significant proportion of highly qualified women clergy find it difficult to get any church at all.

A consequence of this unjust discrimination against women has been that some top-notch women end up pastoring urban churches that many men of equal ability would readily shun. While all of us should deplore any discrimination against women, we must simultaneously note that a growing number of weak and fiscally strapped city churches are being blessed with women ministers of great ability and vision.

I am convinced that female church leaders will be among the primary agents of God in the coming renewal of urban churches in the twenty-first century. I also believe that it is likely that women will play a prominent role in leading the urban church into becoming the lead institution for social change in the next century.

In addition to a growing supply of quality women pastors for inner-city congregations, there are other hopeful signs that the dearth of dynamic and effective leaders for these churches can be overcome. For instance, more and more of our brightest and best young people are looking to become pastors in urban settings. Efforts to set forth the challenge and importance of urban ministry by seminaries and speakers at missionary conferences such as the triennial missions conference staged by Intervarsity Christian Fellowship at Urbana, as well as the impressive success of urban ministries like the Brooklyn Tabernacle, Deliverance Tabernacle in Philadelphia, and the Mariners Church of San Francisco, are attracting many outstanding candidates to urban ministries. My only fear is that urban ministry is being described in ways that make it unrealistically attractive.

What those who accept this calling must realize is that, most of the time, inner-city pastorates are not very glamorous. Those who imagine that the role of urban pastor will make them into bold prophets railing against evil principalities and powers are likely to experience a come-down when they are confronted with the mundane realities of what is really involved.

There is a lot of routine and difficult work that goes with serving city churches. Ministry in urban neighborhoods begins with getting out and getting to know people face to face. Knocking on doors like a salesperson is anything but glamorous. But there is really no other way of connecting with neighborhood people apart from visiting them door to door.

Ideally, pastors need to get their own people to "turn on" and join them in this ministry of visitation. Probably the best time for them to try to do this is right at the beginning of their pastorates. The first six to ten months of a pastorate, usually referred to as the honeymoon, is the period when church members will be most likely to volunteer for a visitation program. During those first few months, congregations usually seem more willing to do whatever the new minister asks of them than at any other time. New pastors should capitalize on that and get the laity involved in visitation programs early on, making door-to-door evangelism a defining characteristic of their new pastorates.

Regardless of when people are challenged to this task, the laity must be led to see that visitation evangelism is at the core of what urban ministry is all about. Preachers must preach sermons that call people to give themselves to this urgent task. Voices from the pulpits must convince those in the pews that visitation evangelism is a calling from God and not just a marketing program for their churches. Do not underestimate the power of preaching. The Word of God, properly delivered in the power of the Holy Spirit, is sharper than any two-edged sword. Ministers should be prayerfully prepared to use their pulpits to inspire their people about the great things that God can do through ordinary people through visitation evangelism. The "seventy" sent out by Jesus to visit people door to door with the Gospel were amazed at what happened to them. They found that they were able to speak with an authority they never suspected was theirs. These ordinary folks realized that they were endowed in ministry with extraordinary powers. The Bible says that "the seventy returned with joy" (Luke 10:17).

Ministers who have gotten their people involved in door-to-door personal evangelism will tell great stories about the results. I love one such story told to me by my friend Will Willimon, Dean of Chapel, Duke University.

> In my last congregation, we decided that we needed to grow. We voted to launch a program of evangelism. Evangelism—you know what that means. It's the "'We-had-better-go-out-and-get-new-members-or-we'll-die syndrome.'" Beginning in the sixties, our church had begun a two-decade decline in membership, so we figured that a little church-growth strategy was in order.
>
> We studied a program from our denomination telling us how to get new members. Among other things, the church-growth program advocated a system of door-to-door visitation. So we organized ourselves into groups of two and, on an appointed Sunday afternoon, we set out to visit and to invite people to our church.
>
> The teams went out, armed with packets of pamphlets describing our congregation, pamphlets telling about our denomination, fliers portraying me, the smiling, accessible pastor, inviting people

to our church. Each team was given a map with their assigned street.

Helen and Gladys were given a map. They were clearly told to go down Summit Drive and to turn right. That's what they were told. I even heard the team leader tell them, "You go down Summit Drive and turn right. You do hear me, Helen and Gladys, that's down Summit Drive and turn right."

But Helen and Gladys, both approaching eighty, after lifetimes of teaching elementary school, were better at giving than receiving directions. They went down Summit Drive, and they turned left, venturing right into the housing projects. We told them to turn right, but they turned left.

Which meant, of course, that Helen and Gladys proceeded to evangelize the wrong neighborhood, and thereby ran the risk of evangelizing the wrong people.

Late that afternoon, each team returned to the church to make their report. Helen and Gladys had only one interested person to report to us, a woman named Verleen. Nobody on their spurious route was interested in visiting our church, nobody but Verleen. She lived with her two children in a three-room apartment in the projects, we were told. Although she had never been to a church in her life, Verleen wanted to visit ours.

"This is what you get," I said to myself, "when you don't follow directions, when you don't do what the pastor tells you to do. This is what you get, a woman from the projects named Verleen."

The next Sunday, Helen and Gladys proudly presented Verleen at the eleven o'clock service, along with her two feral-looking children. Verleen liked the service so much that she said she wanted to attend the Women's Thursday Morning Bible Study. Helen and Gladys said they would pick her up on Thursday.

On Thursday, Verleen appeared, proudly clutching her new Bible, a gift of Helen's circle, the first Bible Verleen had ever seen, much less owned.

I was leading the study that morning on the lectionary for the coming Sunday, Luke 4, the story of Jesus' temptation in the wilderness. "Have any of you ever been faced with temptation and, with Jesus' help, resisted?" I asked the group after presenting my material. "Have any of you refused some temptation because of your Christian commitment?"

One woman told about how, just the week before, there was some confusion in the supermarket checkout line, and before she knew it, she was standing in the supermarket parking lot with a loaf of bread that she hadn't paid for.

She said, "At first, I thought why should I pay for it? They have enough money here as it is." But then I thought, "No, you're a Christian." So I went back in the store and paid them for the loaf of bread.

I made some sort of approving comment.

It was then that Verleen spoke. "A couple of years ago, I was into cocaine really big. You know what that's like! You know how that stuff makes you crazy. Well, anyway, my boyfriend, not the one I've got now, the one who was the daddy of my first child, that one, well, we knocked over a gas station one night—got two hundred dollars out of it. It was as simple as taking candy from a baby. Well, my boyfriend, he says to me, 'Let's knock off that 7–11 down on the corner.' And something in me, it says, 'No, I've held up that gas station with you, but I ain't going to hold up no convenience store.' He beat the hell out of me, but I still said No. It felt great to say No, 'cause that's the only time in my life I ever said No to anything. Made me feel like I was somebody."

Through stunned silence, I managed to mutter, "Well, er, uh, that's resisting temptation, all right. That's sort of what this text is about. And now it's time for our closing prayer."

After I stumbled out of the church parlor and was sitting out in the parking lot, helping Helen into her Plymouth, she said to me, "You know, Pastor, I can't wait to get home and get on the phone and invite people to come next Thursday! Your Bible studies used to be dull. I think I can get a good crowd up for this!"[2]

Getting people involved in door-to-door ministry is the hardest part of the job. But once people are willing to act, knowing what to do and how to do it is not very difficult to figure out. Pastors can develop their own visitation program materials, or they can utilize materials, developed by others. D. James Kennedy, a Presbyterian minister from Ft. Lauderdale, has developed one of the most thorough and effective programs for visitation evangelism. It is called Evangelism Explosion.[3] He also provides excellent training seminars for those who want to employ his well-developed plan for reaching neighborhoods with the gospel. And if his theology and social ideology, as it comes across television, is too conservative for some, it should be noted that churches and pastors from a broad spectrum of religious commitments, some quite opposed to his, have been well served by his Evangelism Explosion program.

Declaring the salvation story is not all that needs to be accomplished through door-to-door neighborhood visits. A second purpose of such house calls is to get church members to *listen* to the people of the neighborhood. Actually, the listening may be the most important part of what goes on in this program. Listening should always come first, with the sharing of the gospel being a response to the felt needs of people as discerned in the listening. Not to make listening an essential part of house calling is to create situations in which people feel "preached at" rather than "cared for."

Listening is also an essential means for getting to know the personal and social needs of neighborhood people. Listening enables the church to find out what is going on in people's private lives. The visitors should be sensitive with each house call to discern if there might be

- a son on drugs who needs a referral to a rehab clinic;
- a single daughter who is pregnant and looking for a good arrangement for an adoption;
- an alcohol problem in the family;
- someone in the family in need of a job.

With careful sensitivity, referrals can be made. Any survey of what goes on in urban communities will reveal that there are a host of well-staffed and effective social service agencies available which are only sparsely used because people just do not know about them. Social service agencies are notoriously poor when it comes to marketing what they have to offer. It is amazing and sad to discover that there are people with desperate needs unmet while those who could help them are just around the corner. Connecting people with problems to those who are able to help them is one of the most necessary ministries that churches can offer in urban neighborhoods. But an effective referral ministry is only possible when church people get to know what is going on in the lives of those who live in the immediate vicinity of their churches.

There is one more very important purpose to be served by a door-to-door visitation program. In addition to learning about people's personal needs, it is also important to learn what social problems exist in their neighborhoods. A good visitation program can provide the church with answers to such questions as

- Are there drug pushers on the street corners?
- Are the schools failing to educate children?
- Are the streets unsafe?

- Is the trash and garbage being properly picked up?
- Are there enough stores for convenient shopping?
- Are the banks red-lining?
- Is there a need for good recreational programs in the area?
- Is public transportation ample?
- What can be done to solve the unemployment problems of the neighborhoods?

These and other problems can be solved only through cooperative action as neighborhood people come together. Once the church grasps what problems need to be addressed, it has a basis for calling neighborhood people together to talk about what they themselves can do to solve those problems. I do not want to get ahead of myself in the development of this suggested scenario for urban social change, but at this point I must allude to the role of churches as conveners of "town meetings."

It must be stated early on that churches cannot get the job of urban renewal done alone. They must mobilize and help to empower all segments of the population and bring all kinds of people together into a movement. Door-to-door visitation is a primary means of making this happen. During visits, as people talk about how their neighborhoods can be saved from deterioration, blight, and fear, the church has a golden opportunity to be a catalyst for community organizing. The visitors can use such occasions to invite troubled people to get together with other concerned neighbors to talk about what can be done to change things. When such gatherings, or town meetings, are held in the church, people become aware that the church is socially concerned and perhaps, for the first time, think of the church as relevant to their pressing concerns.

Town meetings that enable people to experience the synergy which comes from intensive interactions with like-minded neighbors generate enthusiasm for positive social change. At such meetings people begin to feel that they can do something about what is happening around them. In a well-run town meeting, people feel a sense of power that annihilates their mind-set that they are victims of forces beyond their control. But such meetings are not likely to happen unless church people get out and meet their neighbors where they live, listen to their concerns, and bring them together to become a collective force for change. Visitation by church people is a good place to begin the process of saving a city.

Chapter 6

The Acceptable
Year of Our Lord

Before the nature and possibilities of church-sponsored town meetings are discussed any further, it is important to digress and offer some hope for those pastors and churches that believe they lack the human resources to even attempt such an extensive door-to-door neighborhood visitation program. They may say, "It is all good and well to hope that God will raise up dynamic charismatic church leaders who can motivate people to get out into their communities, but some of us need outside help if we are going to get into such an effort.

"To tell the truth, it takes all the people-power and energy we've got just to keep our churches going. Where would we ever get the extra human resources to do this kind of neighborhood outreach?"

I love to tell the make-believe story of a tour group going through an oil refinery. On the tour, they are shown all the complicated machinery and piping that the refinery uses to process petroleum. The various stages of refining petroleum are described, and good explanations are given as to how the refinery workers get their work done. As the tour ends, one of the group asks the guide if they can visit the shipping department.

"Shipping department!?" he exclaims, "We don't have a shipping department."

"What do you mean, you don't have a shipping department?" asks the incredulous visitor.

"Well, you see," answers the tour guide, "all the petroleum energy produced in this refinery is used up keeping the refinery going."

Some urban churches are like that. Burdened with huge buildings to maintain and an array of established church programs to sustain, these churches exhaust their resources just trying to keep themselves in business. They may have viable congregations, ranging from a hundred to a couple of hundred members, but they are churches which are programmatically structured for maintenance rather than for outreach. Their pastor may long to reach out to the community but isn't sure they have what it takes to get into an extensive door-to-door visitation program. It is tempting for outsiders to conclude that such churches should abandon their old structures, sell their buildings, and downsize—even as many corporations are doing these days. But churches change slowly, and besides, we will see later on that those old church buildings, especially their educational plants, can be very useful for programs related to our scenario for urban renewal.

In response to these realities, allow me to propose a suggestion. Some of us have initiated a new youth movement in America that just might jump-start such urban churches into greater community involvement. It is a movement involving college students. Presently, we are recruiting hundreds of these young people, asking them to take a year off school, either during or following their college education. During this year of service, they will be assigned to specific urban churches to carry out just the kind of door-to-door visiting that we've been talking about. This program is called Mission Year, and it has the potential to exercise a revolutionary impact on the ways in which urban churches connect with their neighborhoods. Young people who become part of Mission Year will impact urban churches to become the lead institutions that can change the character of our nation's cities.

Mission Year is a program created by EAPE/Kingdomworks. Since 1965, this organization has helped to create and nurture into independence universities in Third World countries, a network of small schools among the poorest of the poor in Haiti, an alternative school for disadvantaged children in Philadelphia, and an array of programs for "at-risk" urban children and teenagers in cities across the country.

In 1996, EAPE/Kingdomworks began developing Mission Year, with the specific goal of engaging college-aged young people to strengthen the ministries of inner-city churches. Those of us who work with EAPE/ Kingdomworks believe in the local church. We are convinced that whatever good parachurch organizations such as ours may be able to accomplish, their impact is limited. We believe that unless there are local congregations that will integrate into their memberships those persons who have been transformed by the gospel, much of the good accomplished by parachurch organizations will be lost.

For many years, EAPE/Kingdomworks has run after-school programs for thousands of children in Philadelphia and Camden. Utilizing large numbers of collegians who have volunteered their summers without pay, we have sponsored summer camps, sports programs, cultural enrichment activities, and a variety of programs in Christian education. These programs have targeted boys and girls who otherwise might have been bored and gotten into trouble on the asphalt streets of the city. But experience has taught us that unless the children and teenagers that we lead to Christ become intensely involved in local churches, many of the benefits of our work seem to be short-lived. Volunteers come and go, but local churches stay put. Parachurch organizations are great at reaching children and teenagers and doing evangelism, but too often they lack the ability to provide the ongoing nurturing that children and teenagers need if they are to become mature Christians with lifelong commitments to the cause of Christ's kingdom.

The Mission Year program was developed by EAPE/Kingdomworks because of what we learned about the importance of local churches in the lives of those we have evangelized. It is a program designed to support those inner-city churches that are committed to staying in the city and serving urban neighborhoods. As I explained earlier, we have gone across the country recruiting young people between the ages of 18 and 29 to take off a year from whatever they are doing and spend that year in urban missions. While taking young people from all walks of life, we have concentrated especially on recruiting college and university students. Enlisting students when they are getting ready to graduate is especially desirable, but we do not hesitate to get them into the Mission Year program while they are still in the midst of their collegiate education. For students who haven't got a clue about what to do with their lives, it can be a defining experience to take a year off from school and get involved in a ministry that brings them into constant contact with some of the most socially disadvantaged and oppressed people in America. Time and time again, listening to and praying with people in need helps these students to grapple with what their own lives mean. In more cases than not, unfocused young people come away from this year of missionary service with clarity about their vocational choices. Many of them gain from this year of ministry a vision of urban missions as a life vocation.

When speaking to groups of college students, I often challenge them to consider whether their lack of a clear sense of calling in life results in

their wasting the huge investment of time and money that a college education has cost them. Generally, I say, "How many of you, if you had to
take the final exams of the courses you took last year right now, would
pass them?" Usually the students smile back at me with grins that let me
know that there would be a fat chance of them getting decent grades in
such a testing. I then ask, "What did you do with your textbooks from
last year?" There is almost always an acknowledging chuckle followed by
admissions that they sold them. I go on to say, "Fine! You forgot what
you learned, and you sold your textbooks—and you call this *higher education?* You need to drop out of school for a year and figure out what the
point of going to college is all about!" Then, appealing to their higher
motivations, I say, "If the Mormon kids can take off *two* years of their
lives to do missionary work, I want to know why you won't take off one
year—and give it in service to God and to those God calls you to serve?"

The response to this challenge has been very encouraging. We are getting thousands of inquiries and already have placed teams in cities
stretching across America.

The young people we recruit for Mission Year are organized into teams
of six, and each team is assigned to work with a carefully chosen inner-city
church. The churches we select for them must have a strong commitment
to reaching neighborhood people with the gospel and to socially transforming their communities. The members of these churches must be
ready to work along with team members when they are needed, and they
must be open to allowing Mission Year team members to use their gifts to
participate in church life as Sunday School teachers, youth workers, and
choir members. In return, Mission Year churches receive thousands of
hours of service from our collegiate missionaries.

Mission Year missionaries live together in what has been called "inten-
tional community." Each team resides in a home or an apartment located
close to the church that is its base of operations. Insofar as it is possible,
they try to live out the lifestyle of the early church:

> And the multitude of them that believed were of one heart and of one
> soul: neither said any of them that aught of the things which he pos-
> sessed was his own; but they had all things common. And with great
> power gave the apostles witness of the resurrection of the Lord Jesus:
> and great grace was upon them all. Neither was there any among
> them that lacked: for as many as were possessors of lands or houses
> sold them, and brought the prices of the things that were sold, and
> laid them down at the apostles' feet: and distribution was made unto

every man according as he had need. And Joses, who by the apostles
was surnamed Barnabas, (which is, being interpreted, The son of con-
solation,) a Levite, and of the country of Cyprus, Having land, sold it,
and brought the money, and laid it at the apostles' feet. (Acts 4:32–37)

These young people learn about the kind of fellowship (*koinonia*) that
Christians can enjoy when they become a family in the Spirit. They can
experience that mystical communion so often shown by brothers and sisters in Christ as they come to bear each other's burdens, help each other
to overcome their personal faults, and try to live out a common commitment to Christ and to one another. We want our Mission Year missionaries to have every opportunity possible to taste the joy and excitement
of this kind of community before they go back to the individualized
nuclear families that have come to mark life in the modern world in
which they normally live.

We expect the pastors of these churches to give significant time and
energy to mentoring the young recruits we send their way. These pastors
must be prepared to conduct regular Bible studies and lead discussions
with their teams, so that the Mission Year workers can get the encouragement and direction that they need to effectively relate to neighborhood people and to remain faithful to their service commitments. They
must be sufficiently knowledgeable to spot any signs of psychological and
social maladjustment among the young people in their care, and be
courageous enough to step in and help when necessary. Without careful
supervision, it is easy for young people to fall apart emotionally and spiritually, given the kinds of stressful situations that are characteristic of
urban ministry.

In each city where we establish our programs, we try to place as many
as twelve teams. This is because for each city program we appoint a full-
time city director to look after things and to make sure that any problems
are quickly and properly addressed. The city director must see to it that
each pastor is faithfully caring for the Mission Year workers who are serving in his or her church. Also, each city director has to check into the
behavior of the young missionaries and constantly be asking a host of per-
tinent questions:

- Are they living consistent Christian lives?
- Are they being sufficiently careful and not taking any unnecessary
  risks on the city streets?
- Are they getting along well with the pastors and the church people with whom they are working?

- Are their social and economic needs being met?
- Are they staying healthy?

Each Mission Year volunteer is required to do forty hours of ministry a week. Twenty of these hours are designated for door-to-door visitation. Whenever possible, members of the churches they are serving are asked to go along on these visits. When church members fully respond to this challenge, there are six groups of two going out each afternoon and evening to make calls on neighborhood people instead of just three teams, which would be the case if the Mission Year missionaries did the work all by themselves.

Following a biblical model, they go out two by two, asking for nothing more than to be a blessing to those whom they visit. Jesus established their methodology when he told his disciples:

> These twelve Jesus sent forth, and commanded them, saying, Go not into the way of the Gentiles, and into any city of the Samaritans enter ye not: But go rather to the lost sheep of the house of Israel. And as ye go, preach, saying, The kingdom of heaven is at hand. Heal the sick, cleanse the lepers, raise the dead, cast out devils: freely ye have received, freely give. Provide neither gold, nor silver, nor brass in your purses; Nor scrip for your journey, neither two coats, neither shoes, nor yet staves: for the workman is worthy of his meat. And into whatsoever city or town ye shall enter, inquire who in it is worthy; and there abide till ye go thence. And when ye come into an house, salute it. And if the house be worthy, let your peace come upon it: but if it be not worthy, let your peace return to you. And whosoever shall not receive you, nor hear your words, when ye depart out of that house or city, shake off the dust of your feet. Verily I say unto you, It shall be more tolerable for the land of Sodom and Gomorrah in the day of judgment, than for that city. (Matt. 10:5–15)

When our Mission Year workers knock on a door and get an answer, they simply say:

> We're from the church down the street, and we've made a commitment to pray for every family in the immediate neighborhood. We very much want to pray with you and to ask God's blessing on you and on those who live with you. We're not selling anything or trying to get you to come to our church—though if you would come, we'd be very happy. We're not even trying to convert you to anything. We just want to pray *for* you and with you. Can we do that? We don't

have to come in or anything like that—we can pray God's blessing on you right here on the steps of your house.

The surprised and sometimes skeptical neighbor usually says, "Yes." Even if he or she is of another religion or an agnostic, there usually is a guarded but positive response like, "I suppose it wouldn't hurt!"

There is then a follow-up question: "Are there any special needs or concerns that you or those who live with you have that we should hold before the Lord as we pray?"

At that juncture, many of them will open up and share what is on their hearts and minds:

- "I have a son who was just busted on drugs and is in jail, and I don't know where to turn for a lawyer."
- "My daughter's pregnant and she needs help."
- "My youngest is failing in school and wants to drop out, and I don't know what to do."
- "My husband is out of work and can't find a job."

Then the visitors pray and ask God's help and blessing on the home.

This is exactly what Jesus asked his followers to do 2,000 years ago. He simply told them to go door to door blessing the houses they visited. When our Mission Year missionaries ask what they should say if they are asked difficult questions, I simply point out that Christ's early disciples must have asked the same question because he instructed them:

> But when they deliver you up, take no thought how or what ye shall speak: for it shall be given you in that same hour what ye shall speak. (Matt. 10:19)

There is another side effect that this visitation ministry has on the lives of the young missionaries themselves. Over the course of their year of service, these young people get to really know the Bible. Most of them develop a fairly sophisticated biblically based theology. As they encounter difficult situations and listen to people during their daily rounds of door-to-door visitation, they are often asked questions. And it is in answering those questions that these novice missionaries are driven to find out what the Bible really has to say about the burning issues of life. For instance, when confronted by a desperate mother who wants to know why her little girl was just killed by a stray bullet from a drive-by shooting, a young missionary might stumble through the Bible looking for some comforting verse—once! The next time this Mission Year worker is ready. In one way or another, the verses that speak to real needs of such a hurting person will be found and memorized.

The Bible is learned best in such existential situations, and what is learned is unlikely to be forgotten. By the end of a year of trying to give the gospel to needy people, Mission Year missionaries are ready to give answers about the faith that lies within them. At the end of a year, there is good reason to believe that we will be sending back to their home churches biblically literate young people who know not only what they believe, but how to use the Bible to back it up.

This visiting is not as easy as it appears in this brief description. When our young recruits ask how they should handle it if they get doors slammed in their faces—and in some instances they will—I again tell them that Jesus provided his followers an answer:

> And whosoever shall not receive you, nor hear your words, when ye depart out of that house or city, shake off the dust of your feet. Verily I say unto you, It shall be more tolerable for the land of Sodom and Gomorrah in the day of judgment, than for that city. (Matt. 10:14–15)

In more modern language I jokingly suggest that they simply mutter to themselves, "Oh, man! You're in trouble now! You just slammed the door on a messenger from God!"

If the Mission Year missionaries did nothing else but pray with people, they would have rendered a crucial and precious ministry in their respective neighborhoods. Activist Protestants know how to pray for their ministries by asking God to provide workers and material resources to make their programs effective. But unlike many mystical Christians, especially those in the Roman Catholic and Orthodox traditions, they seldom recognize that praying, all by itself, can be a very fruitful ministry. Mystics know that in prayer they can become conduits through whom the Holy Spirit flows out toward the world around them, changing everything. They know that more things are wrought through prayer alone than this world will ever know.

Mission Year missionaries are also expected to spend ten hours a week serving in church-sponsored programs. Supporting the already existing programs of the church is of great importance. We do not want to create programs that are dependent on our workers and might collapse should they leave.

We especially seek out churches that have established after-school programs. Such programs are desperately needed in most urban neighborhoods. The boys and girls who live there need extra help if they are to survive in the public school system. So many inner-city children lack a support system for learning at home and require extra tutoring just to meet the minimal requirements of being functionally literate. For some children, these programs provide the only environment they have that is conducive for doing homework. Just providing a place where they do not have to listen to blaring television sets can make a dramatic difference in their school work. But there is much more to our after-school programs than that. People who care are there to listen and to help. Studies done by social scientists give ample evidence that after-school programs like ours dramatically enhance the academic achievements of children simply because of the extra attention they receive. In one program sponsored by EAPE/Kingdomworks, a seventeen-year-old ninth grader improved so quickly that in just one year he was moved all the way up to the twelfth grade. Today that young man is in college.

In addition to the academic assistance that they give to children, these church-sponsored after-school programs also provide opportunities for personal counseling and evangelism. They offer such children their only chance to unburden themselves of the problems and difficulties that they face in their everyday lives. Mission Year missionaries are never allowed to forget that they are primarily missionaries and, as such, should endeavor to use the relationships they develop with children to introduce them to Christ. It is only by the grace of God and the empowerment that comes through the Holy Spirit that many of those children have any possibility of overcoming the negative influences in their environments.

The final ten hours in the workweek of each Mission Year missionary is spent serving in a variety of community service programs such as AIDS hospices, soup kitchens, and Habitat for Humanity programs. Great emphasis is put on working in the public schools. These missionaries often assist teachers as tutors and provide special attention to troubled children. They come alongside of inner-city teachers as helpers, even as these teachers struggle against incredible odds in their attempts to be effective educators. Sometimes they give their time and energy to helping the too-often defunct Parent-Teacher Associations redevelop into the kinds of organizations that can give to teachers the support they need to get their jobs done. Strong PTAs get parents involved in their children's education in ways that translate into dramatic academic improvement. When helped by tutors, children show great improvement in their schoolwork. But when those tutors are parents, the achievements of children go off the charts.

On top of their required working schedule, Mission Year missionaries are expected to be actively involved in the life and activities of their base churches. After all, other church members who aren't missionaries usually have to do their church work in addition to a forty-hour workweek. Why should the Mission Year missionaries be any different? It would be setting up a false understanding of what it takes for the laity to be involved in church activities if the time Mission Year missionaries spent serving in their churches was out of their forty-hour work schedule.

We are concerned about the spiritual and intellectual growth of our missionaries. Therefore, we work hard to help them to maintain a daily schedule for study and reflection. A special study guidebook has been developed for our Mission Year workers. It contains daily prescriptions for Bible readings and carefully selected readings in the sociology of the city. The study guide provides directions to help the missionaries analyze specific aspects of the character of the neighborhoods in which they serve. It helps them to study such things as the role of the police and the ways in which politicians function in their communities. There are also guidelines for analyzing the economic forces that are at work shaping the destinies of their neighborhoods. Guidance is given for developing a necessary cultural sensitivity to the people who live around them, minimizing possible offensiveness and helping them to see the world through their neighbors' eyes. Great effort and significant financial investment have been put into this study guide because we realized early on how important it was that our missionaries have the kind of help that would enable them to understand what goes on both in their own personal lives and in the neighborhoods they serve.

We want each Mission Year missionary to develop a strong social conscience. We want our workers to become sensitized to the ways in which evil social structures can overpower individuals in the urban setting, leaving them little freedom to realize their God-given potential and sometimes coercing them into patterns of behavior that can lead to their destruction. Our workers must become aware of the ways in which social institutions that God created to do good can become demonic and end up oppressing and destroying people. I found a good example of this in a story told by urban theologian Robert Linthicum about the evil social structures he encountered as he tried to carry out God's work on the streets of Chicago.

> It was 1957, and I was working among black teenagers in a slum in a large city of the United States. Our youth ministry included a spec-

trum of recreational and athletic activities centered around Bible studies. A fourteen-year-old girl (whom I will call Eva) began to attend one of these Bible study groups.

Eva was an exceptionally beautiful teenager, physically mature for her age. She became even more radiant when she received Christ as her Lord and Savior. I began discipling Eva, building her up in the "nurture and admonition" of the Lord.

My academic year was drawing to a close and I was looking forward to returning home for summer vacation. Just before I was to leave my teenage "parish," Eva came to me greatly troubled.

"Bob," she said, "I am under terrible pressure and I don't know what to do. There is a very large gang in this slum that recruits girls to be prostitutes for wealthy white men in the suburbs. They are trying to force me to join them. I know it's wrong. But what should I do?"

I gave Eva all the appropriate advice I had learned in church and college about how if she resisted evil, it would flee from her. I urged her to stick with her Bible study group and not to give in to this gang's demands.

Then I left for my summer vacation.

Three months later, I returned to school and to the ministry in which I was engaged in that city. Eva was nowhere to be found. When I asked about her at the Bible study, the other youth told me she had stopped coming about a month after I had left.

I went to Eva's home. She answered my knock on the door. As soon as she saw me, she burst into tears.

"They got to me, Bob," she said. "I've become a whore!"

"Eva, how could you give in like that?" I unsympathetically responded. "Why didn't you resist?"

"I didn't give in," she responded. "I was forced." Then she told me a story of terror.

"First they told me they would beat my father if I didn't become one of their 'girls.' I refused, and they beat him—bad. Then they said my brother was to be next. He ended up in the hospital. Then they told me that if I didn't yield, they would gang-rape my mother. I know they meant it, and I had no alternatives. So I gave in and became one of their whores."

"But, Eva," I said, "why didn't you get some protection? Why didn't you go to the police?"

"Bob, you honkey," Eva responded. "Who do you think are in that gang? It's the police—the police are running the prostitution ring!"[1]

To help our Mission Year missionaries bring together their experiences and make some sense out of them we plan a special conference to be held at the end of their year of service. We ask them to meet and discuss the following kinds of questions:

- What did the people you encountered teach you about the problems of their neighborhoods, and what answers to these problems did *they* propose?
- How viable were their answers and to what extent do you agree with them?
- What social policies do you believe should be put in place to address these problems?
- What can you do when you return to your home churches and your colleges to make these policies a reality?

Consciousness-raising and commitment to being change agents come out of the Mission Year experience. In the best sense, the things that our young missionaries have heard and learned on the city streets make them mad. Righteous indignation is the stuff that radicalizes young people and inspires social movements. We do not have speakers at the weekend conference because our purpose is not to indoctrinate. Instead, we bring in a facilitator who can draw out of our young missionaries the concerns and insights they have gained in their urban ministries.

The whole Mission Year program has been developed in cooperation with Call to Renewal, an evangelical political organization that came into existence to promote a new kind of participatory democracy. Believing that neither the old political left nor the new political right have the answers to the pressing social problems that face the nation, those who created Call to Renewal have called for an "evangelical round table" that will bring together Christians of good will from across the political spectrum. Those who participate in the roundtable endeavor to create a consensus about what can be done together to ameliorate the horrendous pathologies that plague our society. So far, what Call to Renewal has carried off has been impressive. Several roundtable discussions have created significant unity as to what can be done to help get people off welfare, re-create strong families in the inner city, create jobs for the unemployed, build affordable housing, and provide care for the homeless. We want our Mission Year workers to bring to this movement the considerable knowledge they have picked up in their year of urban ministry. To achieve that, we plan our year-end conferences to run in conjunction with the roundtable meetings of Call to Renewal. We believe that it is important for our missionaries to participate in creating economic and political policies that can implement the values of the Kingdom of God within the context of contemporary societal situations.

Finally, and most important, as they go door to door to make their calls, our Mission Year missionaries are told that in their daily rounds they meet *more* than neighborhood people. These young people have to learn that in their encounters with those in need, they often meet Jesus himself. Our workers must realize that, in their ministry, they are not so much taking Jesus to where he is not as they are meeting Jesus where he already is. Jesus always precedes us, wherever we go. No matter where we travel, he is there waiting for us, and our Mission Year workers soon learn this. In the sometimes strange encounters that they have while making their daily rounds, they meet more than they expect. They sometimes entertain angels unaware, and if they are prepared, they may even meet Jesus himself. I always tell the young people who work in our ministries to look carefully into the eyes of the people they meet because they can never know when Jesus will be staring back at them through those eyes.

I believe in what St. Francis once tried to explain to the world when he claimed that God uses people sacramentally. Francis meant that God uses the ordinary people we encounter on life's journey as a means of grace. If we are ready to receive him, Jesus comes *through* such people to us, especially through those who are called "the least of these."

To convey this truth, I sometimes tell our young recruits about something that happened to me one day as I was walking down Chestnut Street in downtown Philadelphia. Coming at me was a schizophrenic man. He was one of those dirty street people who make me feel so uncomfortable that I often pretend not to notice as I pass by. This particular man was usually yelling at an invisible presence, and his tirades were filled with the "F" word, as though that were the only adjective in his vocabulary.

On this summer day, however, there was something different about him. He had in his hand a Styrofoam cup filled with coffee from McDonald's. As he approached, he screamed at me, "Hey mister! Ya wanna' drink some of my coffee?"

Needless to say, I gave him a patronizing smile and said, "No, thank you."

No sooner did we pass each other than I felt this strange impulse. I got about ten steps or so past him when I felt compelled to turn around and yell, "Yo, mister! I've changed my mind! I really would like a sip of your coffee."

I walked back to him as he held out the cup with his arm at full length. I took the cup and sipped a little of the coffee. Then with an inquiry meant to be cordial I asked, "How come you're giving away coffee this morning? You're getting extra generous, aren't you?"

He answered, "Well, the coffee is especially good this morning, and I figure that when God gives you something especially good, you ought to share it with people!"

I was blindsided by his answer and asked, "Is there anything I can give you?"

I thought he might hit me up for five dollars. Instead he answered, "Yeah! You can hug me!" Actually as I looked at him, I thought that I would have preferred the five dollars.

As I hugged him on that busy street, I realized he wasn't going to let me go. People passing us stared at that bum hugging this embarrassed establishment-looking man. Then, slowly, I became aware of something mystically wonderful. I gradually sensed that this was no bum I was holding in my arms. Instead, I grasped the reality that I was holding in my arms the one who once said, "Whatever you do to the least of these—ye do to Me!" He was in my arms.

As our Mission Year volunteers go out onto the streets, as they knock on doors, as they talk to people—especially people in need—I tell them that they should always be prepared to meet Jesus. Such strange and wonderful encounters change our young missionaries—often dramatically—and most of them are never the same again.

Funding this program is a major undertaking. EAPE/Kingdomworks is constantly working to raise the funds to cover operating expenses, but most of the needed funding is raised by the missionaries themselves, usually from their home churches. We call on these churches to provide $600 a month to cover room, board, and health insurance for each young person they send to work with us. Churches should be more than willing to lend this kind of support to their young people. Mission Year has to be one of the best "bangs-for-the-dollar" available for churches that take missions seriously. Compare Mission Year to those two-week tours that provide a taste of missionary work in some Caribbean country, or an equally brief but exciting "urban plunge" in a U.S. city. Such short-term experiences usually cannot offer young people the opportunity to do any missionary work of lasting value. Mission Year is *real* full-time missionary work. Our missionaries hit the field running. They do not require years of language training to communicate with indigenous peoples. These young people already know the language of those whom they serve. In all probability, because of their untamed zeal and energy, they are doing more direct evangelism and social justice work on a daily basis than do most veterans in the field.

There is a theological rationale in getting the local church to be the sponsor of the Mission Year missionary. Biblically, a missionary is described as a part of the church which all the members are called on to support. The work of a missionary is an expression of the ministry of a local church. This is made abundantly clear in 1 Corinthians 12. In the last part of that chapter, Paul tells us:

> Now ye are the body of Christ, and members in particular. And God hath set some in the church, first apostles, secondarily prophets, thirdly teachers, after that miracles, then gifts of healings, helps, governments, diversities of tongues. Are all apostles? are all prophets? are all teachers? are all workers of miracles? Have all the gifts of healing? do all speak with tongues? do all interpret? But covet earnestly the best gifts: and yet show I unto you a more excellent way. (1 Cor. 12: 27–31)

Of all the functions of the body of Christ, the ministry of being an apostle (i.e., missionary) is listed as primary. That being the case, the missionary is at least as deserving of the prayerful and financial support of the other members of the body as is the pastor. A missionary must not be viewed as some individual who has had a private calling from God. Instead, the missionary ought to be understood and have a self-understanding that defines him or her as being called, commissioned, and sent by the home church. Such was the case in the earliest days of Christianity, as was evident when Barnabas and Paul were sent out by missionaries from the church at Antioch (Acts 13:1–3). Then, the missionary was the responsibility of the home church in every way. So it should be today.

A further benefit of this arrangement is that when the gifts from the home church are what maintains the missionary in the field, the members of that church become much more likely to support the missionary with constant prayers. When the Bible says that where your treasure is there will your heart be also, it establishes a guarantee that where church people put their financial support, they will put their loving prayers.

By assuming the financial burden for the missionary, the home church has an additional basis for being the accountability group that holds the missionary responsible for what the Mission Year worker does during his or her year of urban ministry. The missionary is made aware that responsibility is not to EAPE/Kingdomworks but to the sending congregation.

Recognizing the sacrifices that the people back in the home church are making to keep him or her on the field can generate a diligence in labor born out of a sense of obligation.

EAPE/Kingdomworks has worked hard to make things easy for financially pressed young people to be a part of Mission Year. Special arrangements have been worked out with the government so that they will not be held responsible for making payments on their student loans during their year of service. What is more, legislation is now in place so that the government will pay for any interest accumulating on those loans. At the Summit for Volunteerism held in Philadelphia in April 1997, President Clinton made special reference to Mission Year and pledged to work for the passage of this legislation. He has followed through on his promise.

For those who come to us from very small or poor churches which would have difficulty coming up with the $600 per month for support, we have a commitment from a charitable foundation to put up matching funds to cover up to half of the needed amount. This particular arrangement is especially important to ensure that people of color are strongly represented on Mission Year teams. It is safe to say that financial considerations should not be a barrier to anyone who wants to be a part of the Mission Year program. EAPE/Kingdomworks is committed to doing everything it deems possible to ensure that dedicated young people get a chance to be part of this vitally important urban service program.

Chapter 7

How to Have
a Town Meeting

P articipatory democracy in America was one of the things that fasci-
nated Alexis de Tocqueville. This brilliant French journalist came
to America in the early part of the nineteenth century to figure out why
democracy had worked so well in America while it had failed so miser-
ably in his own country. The American Revolution had produced a society free from totalitarian controls, while the French Revolution, though
born out of the same lofty idealism, had ended in dictatorship.[1]

De Tocqueville found part of the answer to his question in the New
England town meetings. In villages and hamlets across these Northeast-
ern states, he observed people coming together to discuss and solve their
community problems. In those early days of America, people did not look
to the federal government to address their local concerns. Instead they
looked to themselves, convinced that with their Yankee know-how they
could find ways to resolve their neighborhood conflicts, cure their social
pathologies, and meet their communal needs. Controlling crime, providing good education, regulating commerce, and building roads were all
viewed as the responsibilities of the local townspeople. It never occurred
to them to look to Washington for help. Engineering an improved community was a task that neighbors undertook for themselves. Town meetings, often held at the largest church on the village green, were the places
where concerned citizens came together to talk things over and seek out
solutions to their collective problems. These were meetings where everyone had a chance to be heard and where the power of persuasion was the
only power allowed to be exercised. It was at town meetings that people

experienced the exhilaration of exercising their right to make the decisions that would determine their own social destiny.

Things have changed over the years. Town meetings, for the most part, have become things of the past. A few of them still linger on in some New England communities, but for the most part, people have allocated the caring for the public good to higher governing powers on the state and federal levels as they have pursued increasingly private agendas for themselves. Also, the mobility that goes with living in our fast-paced urban industrial society does not lend itself to such community gatherings, and the few town meetings that remain seem like quaint remnants of another time in American life.

We get a glimpse of the workings of town meetings from the movies. In the book *Peyton Place,* the decisive scene where public opinion is changed takes place at a town meeting. And in *Jaws*, it is at a town meeting that the communal decision is made as to what to do about the giant shark that is threatening the town's tourist trade. But for most Americans, town meetings are not the way things are done today. People across the nation have allowed political power to slip out of their hands. More and more, Americans believe that it is up to elected officials, who function in distant places outside of public view, to provide answers to the social problems that perplex us. Every year we go to the polls and elect "them." Then we go about the business of our personal lives and expect "them" to take care of things for us.

Democracy has come to be seen as little more than having the opportunity to choose those who make decisions for us. No longer do people in neighborhoods, especially urban neighborhoods, view themselves as decision-makers and implementers of social policies. Instead, we tend to leave it all up to "them," the politicians, to decide what happens to us. When things go wrong, we blame "them" and vote "them" out of office. And when the new politicians also fail to live up to our expectations, we cynically complain and say, "Politicians! They're all the same." Such cynicism leads many Americans to give up on politics altogether. Convinced that it doesn't do any good to try to change the system, more and more Americans simply fail to show up on election day, resigning themselves to whatever may happen as a consequence of this so-called democratic process.

Any survey of opinions in depressed inner-city neighborhoods will give all the evidence necessary to support the claims that the people who live there are, in numbers disproportionate to the rest of the population, non-voters who don't really believe that what happens in the realm of politics is going to make things any better for them. In this alienated condition, they are sure that politicians want only their votes and that, once elected, politicians will forget all about them and their problems. Especially with the urban poor, the last thing in the world they believe is that they matter and can make any real difference as far as the political and economic destinies of their neighborhoods are concerned. Hence, the poor often fail even to register to vote, and their underrepresentation in the U.S. Census every ten years usually results in government spending for social programs in their neighborhoods being less than these communities deserve because it is done on a per capita basis. Churches could do a lot of good for their neighborhoods if they simply worked on getting people registered to vote, thus increasing their entitlements and building up their importance to vote-seeking politicos.

If de Tocqueville returned to America today, he would wonder what has happened to the participatory democracy that he observed almost a hundred and seventy years ago. He would be dismayed over the noninvolvement of people in the process of making those decisions that control their societal destinies. He would be saddened that people on the local level have let power slip out of their hands to Washington. It would be hard for de Tocqueville to believe that the American people have resigned themselves to letting unknown bureaucrats spend their tax dollars on programs that will supposedly solve their own neighborhood problems, even though they know that those bureaucrats haven't a clue as to what is really going on in those neighborhoods. Furthermore, de Tocqueville would warn us that unless we wise up and once again take charge of what is happening in our own communities, the viable solutions to neighborhood problems are not likely to be found and implemented. But the church can change all of that.

Town Meetings as an Opportunity for the Church

Bringing people together in town meetings is crucial if the urban church is going to assume its role as the lead institution for social change. Through the town meeting, the inner-city church can rekindle participatory democracy in its neighborhood. The discussions, exchanges of ideas, and problem-solving that can come out of such community gatherings have the potential to empower people once again to assume control over their own social environments. Furthermore, in the context of the town meeting, the church has an opportunity to give witness to the good news of what God intends for its community, without coming across as either preachy or sectarian. By giving respect to each person who rises to speak, the church enhances the dignity of those individuals and affirms their importance. And by supporting the collective decisions that lead to curtailing the evils in the community, the church can make known a God who is at work changing the world through ordinary people. After making sure that other groups with other beliefs have been respectfully heard, those in the church should not be reluctant to state what they believe and give the biblical basis for their beliefs. Respect for others earns respect in return, and church people ought not to be ashamed of the gospel of Christ as they participate in discussions.

In all of this, it must be remembered that the *process* is just as important as the *product*. How the church goes about organizing these town meetings and how it goes about conducting the proceedings when the people get together are every bit as important as any good that will come out of these meetings.

Before the town meeting can be called, a great deal of research has to take place. It is not enough simply to advertise and get a lot of neighborhood people together. Every effort must be made to ensure that all the *real* community leaders are in attendance. Saul Alinsky, the man who made such meetings an instrument of urban renewal in "the Back-of-Yards" section of Chicago in the 1950s, made it clear that to have any kind of effective community organization, it is essential to bring together those who actually are the key people in the neighborhood. Alinsky was particularly uptight about "liberals" who seem able to deal only with those who share their ideology.[2] It may be that those who are the real leaders in a given community will prove to be racists, homophobes, and male chauvinists. They may not be people who share the values that liberals hold dear or embrace any kind of a biblical morality. But if town meetings bring together only those who are like-minded, they are unlikely to be representative of the entire neighborhood, and the discussions at the meetings will probably not include vital perspectives on what people really think is wrong or actually needs to be done to set things right. Too often, town meetings end up with people simply preaching to others who agree with them while those with contrary points of view are never heard because they are not there. People can go home from such meetings congratulating each other for having dealt with the problems of their neighborhoods when, in reality, they have simply been part of a mutual admiration and affirmation society. The plans for action that come out of such gatherings of like-minded liberals are seldom realized because they leave a large segment of the population out of the decision and planning processes. Those who don't agree with their perceptions of why things are amiss in the community or concur with their proposed plans for "improving" things have not been heard.

As a case in point, this is what happened to President Clinton's initiative on race and the town meetings that he sponsored.[3] There has yet to be an honest discussion about race in most neighborhoods because some conflicting points of view, many of them considered "un-American," have no representation. In private, people express their discontent and prejudices, but white people seldom get to hear what black people really think about what is happening on the streets. And black people do not usually get up-front honesty from white people as to what they really think about black people or what they think black people are doing to the neighborhood. In most public gatherings, people bend over backwards trying to say politically correct things that will cast them as fair, open-minded, and socially enlightened citizens. The truth is that African-Americans are fed up with the dishonesty of such discussions and know that any consensus that comes out of them is make-believe.

An effective town meeting allows for all kinds of people to say what is really on their minds. Only then can neighbors come to know and understand one another. Archie Bunker types must be heard and understood, even as the followers of Louis Farakhan are entitled to be given serious consideration. It is the church's job to moderate town meetings so that there can be honesty without anyone being shouted down or silenced. Alinsky found that, in spite of all of their prejudices and shortcomings, people were usually able to arrive at a consensus as to what should be done to address community problems, as long as public discussions were open and forthright.

When a town meeting is called, it must be inclusive. The committee people from both the local Democratic and Republican parties must be there. All the religious groups, from the synagogues to the mosques, must be represented adequately. Storekeepers, police, teachers, and school administrators need to be there. Union leaders as well as managers of local industries must be invited. It is imperative that all of those voices that determine what goes on in the neighborhood have the opportunity to have their say. That may include the local drug dealers.

The church, as the convener of the town meeting, must spend a lot of time and effort getting to know the movers and shakers of the neighborhood. This means talking to people in coffee shops and even bars. It involves finding out who really exercises influence and controls opinions in the neighborhood. There are risks in seeing to it that all the leaders of all segments of the neighborhood are present and able to express themselves at the town meeting, but anything less will be a sham.

Alinsky cautions that there are likely to be self-appointed "leaders" who loudly claim to be spokespersons for this group or that group in the neighborhood, yet have no real following at all. Special care must be given to avoid being taken in by those who make a profession out of speaking for "their people" but in reality speak only for themselves. In my own experience in community organization work in Philadelphia, I have found that the same people have a way of turning up as spokesperson for one group after another, especially if there is grant money to be given out. A lot of government dollars have disappeared because such "professional" leaders have learned official-sounding jargon and used hot rhetoric to create high-paying jobs for themselves.

Before the church convenes the town meeting, it had better have a good handle on who speaks for whom and know the opinion groups that exist in its particular community. This process can take many months, and it is one of the benefits that can come from an extensive door-to-door visitation program. Merely *announcing* the town meeting will not ensure that people will come. The church must sell the benefits of such a meeting to the neighborhood. People must be assured that they will be heard and their opinions seriously considered. In return, the church needs to know that these leaders will show up and bring their supporters along. Making sure that the right people turn out for the town meeting takes the same kind of organizational effort and strategizing that a ward politician gives to getting out the vote on election day. It is a good idea for church people to meet with various interest groups in the community prior to the main town meeting. For example, they should meet with the precinct leaders of each of the political parties and tell them why their participation in the town meeting is so important. Going to the service clubs that exist in the neighborhood (for example, Rotary, Kiwanis, and Lions) is a good move.

Personal meetings with all of the various religious group leaders is essential. Be ready to seize any opportunities to address their congregations.

Talking to gang leaders as well as to those at the local police stations about why they should be involved in a town meeting is critical. A town meeting ought not to be called until you have touched base with all of the neighborhood organizations and given serious attention to each of them.

Setting the Agenda
and Maintaining Order

The agenda for the town meeting should be defined well in advance. People do not come to meetings just to hear other people talk. They need to know that what is going to be discussed will be of vital concern to them. Developing the agenda is a crucial part of selling the town meeting to those leaders whose presence is essential for a real and effective discussion. One-on-one conversations will give community leaders the opportunity to provide input for the agenda. Leaders need to know, and be able to assure their people, that their particular concerns about the neighborhood will be heard in the overall give and take of the meeting.

Usually, the night of the first meeting will be tense. There will be a great deal of suspicion, and the church that convenes the meeting will be well aware that its reputation in the community is at stake. Things must not be allowed to get out of hand. The moderator of the meetings must be a strong leader who can keep order and make sure that no one voice or point of view is allowed to dominate. If the church does not have a person with the charisma and experience to lead the meeting, it would be a good idea to bring in an experienced moderator from the outside. It is not difficult to imagine that there could be chaos and disaster without the right person to lead the meeting.

Rules for discussion must be outlined clearly before the discussion starts. How often and how long people will be allowed to speak need to be precisely delineated. A sergeant-at-arms must be available and able to act. Everything must be done, as the Bible says, "decently and in order" (1 Cor. 14:40). A stated time when the meeting will adjourn should be announced when the meeting starts, and the meeting must be ended exactly at the appointed hour.

As the discussion unfolds, use an overhead projector or some other means to list salient points and make them visible to everyone present. An appointed recorder should keep track of what is said and proposed so that comprehensive reports of the proceedings can be made available to all concerned.

Insofar as it is possible, keep the press out! If the press is visible at the meeting, it may stifle discussion or result in people speaking for the benefit of the news media rather than to one another.

A simple agenda might begin with half an hour given to going over the agenda and listing the problems that will be under discussion. In this initial period, additions or comments from the floor should be entertained. Insofar as it is possible, no one should be left with the sense that things are being railroaded without his or her consent. After the issues to be discussed are agreed upon and prioritized, the floor should be opened to those who want to speak.

The hardest job of all will be to keep people on the subject. Speakers often get carried away with their own rhetoric. Name calling should be forbidden! There must be a Herculean effort by the moderator to keep the discussion focused on ways to solve the problems, rather than allowing people at the meeting to condemn each other for what has gone wrong in the community. Remember, the town meeting is supposed to help neighbors come up with answers to their common problems. It is not a time for promoting personal ideologies and self-aggrandizing speeches.

As people propose ways of dealing with neighborhood problems, there should be one principle guiding them. The human and material resources needed to carry out any proposed solution should be available within the community itself. Solutions that rely on outside funding or depend on those who live outside the neighborhood should, as much as possible, be avoided. The idea is to guide people to think about what they themselves, with their own resources, can do to address what they see wrong in their immediate community. For example, it may well be that the inadequate educational system in the neighborhood schools requires more funding from city and state government. People may agree that efforts must be made to lobby for that funding. That is all good and well, but at the town meeting attention should be focused on what the participants themselves can do to make the schools better. Is there a way to get community people involved in serving as teacher's assistants? Can neighborhood churches, mosques, and synagogues set up after-school tutoring programs? Is it possible to build up the involvement of parents in the PTA and to get them otherwise involved in the educating of their children? Can community people police the neighborhoods and turn in truants? Are there ways that people can work together to make the schools drug free? Problems like these can be addressed using local people and the resources that already exist in the community.

Solving the Crime Problem

The problem that is most likely to come up in discussion at any urban town meeting is crime. Few city neighborhoods are safe these days. The poverty and prevalent drug use that mark most inner-city communities put neighborhood crime near the top of any list of concerns. Again, the moderator of the town meeting must guide people to seek solutions that will tap the people and resources that are locally at hand.

In a tough Boston neighborhood, a gang chased after a teenaged boy from a rival gang as he ran into a Sunday morning church service seeking sanctuary. There, in front of the worshiping congregation, the gang shot the teenager to death. In response to this horror, one of the pastors of the community, the Rev. Eugene Rivers, remarked, "If the church doesn't go out onto the streets to meet people in their needs, then it shouldn't be surprised that the people on the streets invade the church."

Out of the shocked concern generated by this killing, the people of the neighborhood came together for a town meeting to figure out what they could do to put an end to the senseless murders that were becoming increasingly common on their streets. After much thought and a town meeting, the people came up with what has been called The 10-Point Program, which includes the following:

1. To establish four or five church cluster-collaborations that sponsor "Adopt a Gang" programs to organize and evangelize youth in gangs. Inner-city churches would serve as drop-in centers providing sanctuary for troubled youth.

2. To commission missionaries to serve as advocates for black and Latino juveniles in the courts. Such missionaries would work closely with probation officers, law enforcement officials, and youth street workers to assist at-risk youth and their families.

   To convene summit meetings between school superintendents, principals of public middle and high schools, and black and Latino pastors to develop partnerships that will focus on the youth most at risk. We propose to do pastoral work with the most violent and troubled young people and their families. In our judgment, this is a rational alternative to ill-conceived proposals to suspend the principle of due process.

3. To commission youth evangelists to do street-level one-on-one evangelism with youth involved in drug trafficking. These evangelists would also work to prepare these youth for participation in the economic life of the nation. Such work might include preparation for college, the development of legal revenue-generating enterprises, and the acquisition of trade skills and union membership.

4. To establish accountable community-based economic development projects that go beyond "market and state" visions of revenue generation. Such economic development initiatives will include community land trusts, micro-enterprise projects, worker cooperatives, community finance institutions, consumer cooperatives, and democratically run community development corporations.

5. To establish links between suburban and downtown churches and front-line ministries to provide spiritual, human resource, and material support.

6. To initiate and support neighborhood crime-watch programs within local church neighborhoods. If, for example, 200 churches covered the four corners surrounding their sites, 800 blocks would be safer.

7. To establish working relationships between local churches and community-based health centers to provide pastoral counseling for families during times of crisis. We also propose the initiation of abstinence-oriented educational programs focusing on the prevention of AIDS and sexually transmitted diseases.

8. To convene a working summit meeting for Christian black and Latino men in order to discuss the development of Christian brotherhoods that would provide rational alternatives to violent gang life. Such brotherhoods would also be charged with fostering responsibility to family and protecting houses of worship.

9. To establish rape crisis drop-in centers and services for battered women in churches. Counseling programs must be established for abusive men, particularly teenagers and young adults.

10. To develop an aggressive black and Latino history curriculum, with an additional focus on the struggles of women and poor people. Such a curriculum could be taught in churches as a means of helping our youth to understand that the God of history has been and remains active in the lives of all peoples.[4]

Wrapping Up the Meeting

There must be discernible positive accomplishments coming out of town meetings, or people will regard them as a waste of time and support will be lost. People get tired of talk that is full of fury but signifies nothing. If they are to continue to believe in the participatory democracy that the town meeting is supposed to facilitate, people must be able to see something significant come from their investment of time and energy. To assure that such results are forthcoming, the following questions must be answered *before the town meeting is dismissed:*

1. *What is going to be done?*

2. *How is it going to be done?* A specific course of action has to be agreed on by the participants. The more specific the plan, the better. Defining what resources are needed and where they can be secured is very important.

3. *Who will be responsible for carrying out the plan?* Designating who will be in charge and getting broad support for that person's efforts is essential for success.

4. *When will the program or plan be in place?* Specific target dates must be established. A timetable and deadline for each step of the process needs to be discussed and finalized.

Nothing should be left hanging in an indefinite state. Not to have answered these questions by the meeting's end is to have failed in some significant ways. And finally, the last thing that should be agreed on before the meeting is ended is the date, time, and place for the next town meeting.

If the church can make this process work, it will have defined itself as an important change-agent in the community and established its relevancy to what is really important to people in their everyday lives. As the convener of the town meeting, the church will have taken on the role of Jesus as a servant-leader. It will be a church that does not dictate its own answers to problems but instead helps people to struggle with the perplexing concerns of their own community—a church that does not seek power for itself but instead empowers the people of the neighborhood to increasingly control their own social destiny. Such is the church that God willed when the Holy Spirit was sent on the day of Pentecost to bring the church into existence.

Chapter 8

The New Politics

There is still a larger context in which the town meeting should be understood. For many of us the town meeting is an expression of the new politics that people throughout America are longing to see. From coast to coast there is a growing sense that the old politics of both the Democrats and the Republicans has failed and that something new is needed.

Republicans saw the outworking of their conservative ideology in what happened following the Civil War. From that time up to the Great Depression years, their philosophy of *laissez faire* government and economics produced huge profits for a handful of industrialists and financiers. During those same years the huddled masses that came to America from Europe's teeming shores became the huddled masses in urban tenements. Left to the goodwill of the more affluent and their private charitable organizations, the tens of thousands of pathetic homeless children that wandered aimlessly on the streets of New York City experienced little aid and comfort. While robber barons of the Gilded Age amassed huge fortunes, their lauded benevolence did nothing to eliminate the long lines at soup kitchens or provide alternatives for those who had to make their homes in urban shantytowns. Ultraconservative journalists, like Marvin Olasky, give glowing reports of how successful private faith-based charitable mission work was during this era.[1] But the reality was that millions of desperate urban Americans were forced to live in conditions that could aptly be described—as they were for those who lived in the slums of Manhattan—as "Hell's Kitchen." The government that governed least did not govern best, as some Republicans these days try to claim that it did. The Republicans who think that all was just hunky-dory before big government got its hands on things have little sense of history.[2]

Then, the Democrats had their opportunity at solving the socioeconomic problems of the nation, and specifically, the problems of urban America. From the beginning of the Roosevelt New Deal through the Great Society years of Lyndon B. Johnson, big government in Washington prescribed solutions to the problems that had become endemic to city life. But while the well-intentioned plans of liberal sophisticated social engineers consumed vast amounts of taxpayers' dollars, they failed to deliver the expected and hoped-for results. A case can be made that, instead of eliminating the problems, they made matters worse. Critics in such conservative think tanks as the American Enterprise Institute have contended that these government-sponsored programs, instead of curing the sickness of urban America, have become one of it worst diseases. The government "projects" that were supposed to provide decent housing for low-income families have become disintegrating slum ghettos where we starve a despairing, socially disinherited underclass. The welfare system that was supposed to provide a safety net for those who were temporarily unemployed has created a personally destructive form of dependency. And the public assistance that was supposed to be a panacea for the poor and oppressed has spawned huge social service bureaucracies that have become legendary for high costs and scandalous inefficiencies.

By the time the Ronald Reagan years rolled around, the American middle class was ready to exercise a great deal of the "benign neglect" toward the poor. Daniel Patrick Moynihan had proposed this twenty years earlier—especially with regard to the urban blacks who seemed to him to be particularly troublesome.[3] Through the 1980s, urban problems were increasingly ignored in the hope that they just might go away. Money that was appropriated for social programs by a Democratic Congress was often left unspent by a Republican administration. This was especially true with respect to sustaining the urban housing projects that had been built in the 1950s and early 1960s to provide low-income people with places to live. In Philadelphia and Camden, absolutely no money came to the housing authorities of these cities for maintenance. Inefficient social bureaucracies began to wind down—and it should be noted that the HUD programs were the most notorious in this respect.

The response of the Reagan Administration to the growing horrors of the city was to find ways that the private sector might be encouraged to invest in urban economic development. The program they believed held the greatest promise toward that end was the creation of what they called "enterprise zones." Certain areas in designated cities were set aside to be used for new businesses and industries that, it was hoped, would create jobs for the urban unemployed and get money circulating in urban neighborhoods. To lure investors to establish businesses and industries in these inner-city enterprise zones, a variety of tax incentives and low-interest loans were provided. It seemed like a good idea, but it didn't work. One of the main reasons was that the kind of skilled employees who were needed in the increasingly high-tech production systems of the day did not find working in the city very desirable. While there might be tax breaks for their corporations, workers did not want to have jobs in cities like Camden and Philadelphia because they would have to pay high city wage taxes. Also, cities frightened people. High crime rates were a deterrent to suburbanites who did not fancy driving into high-risk neighborhoods. And moving into the city just did not seem like a desirable thing for Americans who had been sold on the dream of the good life in suburbia.

This, and other schemes to make the free enterprise system work to stem the tide of growing urban blight and poverty, had limited success. While the urban working class and the new growing underclass being spawned by the de-industrialization of America were being pushed beneath the poverty line, the middle class of the country went on a spending spree.

In the midst of these years of middle-class euphoria, lip service was paid to the mounting national debt. A nation that had already overspent its financial resources by trillions of dollars during the Vietnam War did not hesitate to spend trillions more on "defense" as Reagan determined to outspend Russia and to bring down that "Evil Empire." And as the national debt reached catastrophic dimensions, talk radio, the most underrated instrument for opinion formation in America, found a ready scapegoat in the poor. "It's the welfare system that's bleeding this country dry," dissident radio voices screamed at us. And it was Christian talk radio that hammered away at this theme the most. All too many Americans believed what they heard. No matter that only five cents of every tax dollar was being spent on the poor, both domestically and abroad, while fifteen cents of the tax dollar was spent on arms. Americans were still ready to blame their huge national indebtedness on the poor, and politicians of both parties were all too ready to balance the budget on the backs of the poor.

The urban poor were among the most serious victims of these emerging attitudes. Without proper funding, urban schools lost their capacity to educate. Family life deteriorated as single women in their early teens had children they did not know how to raise. Stores that had been robbed once too often closed down, and job-sustaining businesses moved to the suburbs. Urban housing units deteriorated and were often left abandoned. Drug dealers claimed whole sections of the city as their territories, and increasingly violent teenaged gangs roamed the streets. The ruling establishment responded to the increasing crime by adopting a "get tough" policy that required hiring more police and building more prisons—the only housing program that got more funding.

As things fell apart in the cities, people grew disillusioned with the politicians who had promised more than could be delivered. It was not that the politicians were necessarily corrupt (though some were) or insincere about their commitments to make things better; it was simply that politicians did not know how to turn things around. Neither the salvation formulas of the big government Democrats nor the solutions of the little government free enterprise Republicans seemed to have any viability when it came to addressing the developing urban crisis. The old politics that were being served up to inner-city people provided very little to give them hope. Neither party seemed to have any answers.

The Rise of the Religious Right

The Christian community was not indifferent to what was going on, and its members were ready to do something to save America. Evangelicals had some idea what was wrong. Most of them were convinced that the urban crisis had been caused by something more than just socioeconomic forces. They believed that the urban crisis was really the result of an overall moral crisis in America, and they were looking for leaders who could mobilize godly people to take America back from those seemingly demonic forces that had hijacked their country. It was in this context that the Religious Right got its start. Evangelical Christians, who had always been quiet politically, found in the televangelist Jerry Falwell a voice that could articulate their concerns and an organizer who knew how to mold them into a powerful political pressure group. Seemingly coming out of nowhere in the late 1960s, Falwell organized huge numbers of Christians into the now famous Moral Majority.

At first Falwell's movement capitalized on the moral discontent of Christians who were outraged over the legalization of abortion and the demands for rights being made by the emerging feminist and gay rights movements. But the Moral Majority soon broadened its agenda to embrace economic and political concerns as well. This made it a natural ally of the conservative wing of the Republican Party. By 1980 the Moral Majority was sufficiently powerful as a political force in America to claim a great deal of the credit for electing Ronald Reagan. From then on, the Religious Right served notice that it was out to claim the Republican Party as its own and through the Republican Party to "reclaim America."

While the Moral Majority had become a force to be reckoned with on the American political landscape, few were able to envision the power that the Religious Right would soon exercise through the successor to the Moral Majority, the Christian Coalition. This later organization would, by the middle of the 1990s, replace the Moral Majority as the lightning rod through which politically conservative evangelicals would express their discontent with the direction in which the country seemed to be heading. Taking over the organizational structures and personnel from Pat Robertson's failed campaign for the presidency, Ralph Reed, the onetime head of the Young Republicans, made the Christian Coalition into the most powerful political action lobbying group in America. With effectiveness and commitment, the members of the Christian Coalition soon gained total control of the Republican Party organization in a third of the states, while exercising a dominant influence in at least another third of them. By 1996, the Christian Coalition was in a position to dictate much of the platform of the Republican Party and control the agenda for Bob Dole, the party's candidate for the presidency.

But not all evangelical Christians were in harmony with the designs of the Christian Coalition. There were leaders outside the Religious Right with more moderate leanings who were committed to policies that were at odds with some major positions of conservative Republicanism. Ron Sider, the founder of Evangelicals for Social Action (ESA), and Jim Wallis, the founder of the Sojourners Community in Washington, D.C., were prominent among them. In late 1995, along with several other evangelical leaders who opposed the hegemony that the Christian Coalition was threatening to exercise over evangelical Christianity, Wallis gave leadership to the creation of a countervailing movement that has come to be known as Call to Renewal. I have already discussed the role of Call to Renewal in our mission year program in chapter 6.

This new organization worked hard to keep from being labeled as politically left. In fact, it was the simplistic dichotomy of left and right in American politics that troubled its members. Those who joined Call to

Renewal were convinced that neither the politics of liberal Democrats nor that of conservative Republicans provided substantial answers to the problems of America, and especially to the urban poor. While sharing a number of moral concerns with the Christian Coalition, Call to Renewal movement has points of significant difference with their politically conservative brothers and sisters.

Call to Renewal leaders have been especially concerned about the changes in the welfare system that have been supported by the Christian Coalition. While recognizing that the old established welfare system needed radical changes, they are upset over the harshness of the program created via a Republican Congress and signed into law by a Democratic president. They believe that the new law ends welfare too abruptly for millions of Americans without providing adequate vocational training or job creation for the people involved. They complain that forcing single mothers to work without adequate provisions being made for child-care programs is unconscionable. The dominant conviction motivating the leaders of Call to Renewal is that God expects the government as well as the church to care for the poor and champion the rights of the oppressed.

There are other differences that have set Call to Renewal people at odds with the Christian Coalition. They have been troubled by the Coalition's refusal to raise questions about political candidates who support the tobacco industry. They are upset with the Coalition's strong opposition to effective gun control, its willingness to dismantle laws that protect the environment, and its plan to eliminate the Department of Education.

Bottom-up Politics

A very important difference between the Christian Coalition and Call to Renewal is that the latter is offering a new way of doing politics. Instead of organizing to get candidates elected to office, Call to Renewal seeks to get people involved in participatory democracy on the grass-roots level. Instead of supporting candidates whom they hope will take over the apparatus of government and implement "Christian" policies from the highest office of the nation on down, they have advocated a "bottom-up" approach to facilitating social change. Call to Renewal advocates the creation of town meetings (such as those described earlier) as a means of bringing people together and empowering them to solve community problems on the local level. Their kind of grass-roots approach to politics aims at getting people to take charge of neighborhoods and to solve their community problems through face-to-face decision making and strategizing.

The politics of Call to Renewal is based on the belief that ordinary people must be involved personally in political debate. Democracy is more than the right to vote. It also involves people speaking out with the hope of changing other people's minds, as well as listening to what others have to say.

When Ross Perot, in his run for the presidency, suggested that buttons be put on every television set in America so that people could register their opinions on political issues after hearing discussions from the floor of Congress, he missed the point of what democracy is all about. In a true democracy, people have a chance themselves to participate in the give and take of the discussion. Democracy requires a process of interaction so that individuals feel respected and each has a chance to mold public opinion and define the options under consideration. That is why Call to Renewal has promoted the town meeting as its key instrument for involving people in the political process. Ideally, according to those promoting Call to Renewal, there will be churches all across America which will call together the various peoples in their respective communities for such discussions and exchanges of ideas. It is hoped that out of these town meetings will come initiatives that will address the problems troubling these communities.

A very positive result of these town meetings is the way in which people tend to work toward a consensus. The ideological differences that divide Democrats and Republicans slowly disappear as people look for practical and workable solutions to the social problems that confront them on the local level. Instead of liberal or conservative answers to a question like "What do we do about the drug pushers hanging around the local high school?" the participants look for pragmatic answers. Rather than asking whether the Democrats or Republicans offer the best answers, solutions are judged according to their viability.

It must be emphasized that town meeting politics does *not* mean that what goes on in Washington is irrelevant to local community affairs. Decisions made in the nation's capital have dramatic consequences for city neighborhoods. It is just that those associated with Call to Renewal believe that the people in the halls of Congress cannot really know what is happening in specific urban communities. They say that only those who live in those communities day in and day out are capable of providing the kind of analysis that tells what is really going on, why it is happening, who is responsible, and what can be done about it. Eventually those in the town meeting will have to be in touch with those on the state and national levels of government to enlist legislative help and financial support. To bring about the needed changes in any urban community will eventually require altering the ways in which that community is functionally related to the larger societal system in which it is set. However, the new politics advocated by Call to Renewal contends that policies should be developed locally by the indigenous people of a neighborhood, with the resources of the higher echelons of government being tapped later to undergird the local initiatives. The responsibilities of those "higher up" powers must be to ensure the rights of *all* persons in local communities against any form of local tyranny and to integrate what goes on in local problem-solving into the plans of national government. This is politics from the bottom up, rather than from the top down.

For far too long, well-meaning people in far away Washington have established policies and guidelines for solving problems in neighborhoods about which they know nothing. In this new Call to Renewal kind of politics, those at the top will be informed by those in local situations, and policies at the top will be constructed in response to the discussions of neighborhood people at their own local town meetings.

This model for neighborhood politics being proposed by Call to Renewal provides the kind of arrangement that sociologists have long known is essential for the preservation of individual freedom and true democracy. Town meetings, with their neighborhood politics, create what sociologists sometimes call "intermediate power blocs." Sociologists from Auguste Comte[4] and Alexis de Tocqueville[5] to Emile Durkheim[6] have recognized that such intermediate power units are essential to serve as countervailing checks on the totalitarian tendencies inherent in all governments. These sociologists all noted that the kings in the *ancien régime* of France had their totalitarian tendencies checked by the church, the aristocracy, and the guilds—each of which served as a buffer against the arbitrary use of power that kings might otherwise be tempted to exercise. Together these intermediate power blocs had sufficient strength to prevent the kings from acting with total disregard for the way in which their actions would impact lesser people in the kingdom.

When the French Revolution led to the beheading of the aristocracy, the obliteration of the role of the church in the affairs of state, and the breaking of the power of the guilds, totalitarianism became inevitable. It makes no difference that slaves can elect their masters if, once elected, those masters exercise unchecked control over the people as though they were slaves. That is what happened in the early French Republic. Those who ruled in the name of the people totally controlled the people because there were no intermediate power blocs to check their totalitarian tendencies.

Comte wanted to create a new church built on his "positivistic philosophy" that would substitute for the old Roman Catholic Church and serve as such an intermediate power bloc. Durkheim imagined that subculture social units which would unite people of similar vocations might assume this countervailing role against totalitarianism.

Later, social scientists such as E. Digby Baltzell and John Kenneth Galbraith also saw the need for such intermediate power units. Baltzell talked about the need for a contemporary aristocracy made up of a self-recognized elite that critiqued and stood against any autocratic tendencies it saw emerging in government.[7] Galbraith, in his classic work, *The Affluent Society*, argued that following World War II, America had strong unions, big business, and big government functioning as countervailing powers that kept each other under control.[8] Any two of those power units, according to Galbraith, could combine to counteract the totalitarian tendencies of the third. If unions got too uppity, the government with the help of business was able to bring them back into line. That is just what happened with the Taft-Hartley bill.[9] On the other hand, if big business moved toward exercising monopolistic control over society, the unions and government could get together and put a halt to it. Antitrust legislation attests to that arrangement. Finally, the government's power could not be exercised in detrimental ways as long as unions and business were powerful enough to call it into responsibility. Unions and business together had the obvious means to control a government that might be tempted to get out of line.

In today's world, with unions on the wane and big business becoming part of a gigantic political-economic complex, some new countervailing check is needed to keep government from becoming a self-serving institution and to make it more responsive to the needs of people on the local level. The town meetings can fill that void, and churches, as the conveners of the town meetings, can serve a requisite role in creating this new balance in politics. This is an ideal role for churches to play because it enables them to become politically involved without becoming politically partisan. It is a way for churches to create a new political order without imposing any of their own self-serving agendas on their communities.

Bill Bradley, the popular and effective senator who once represented New Jersey, decided not to run for re-election because he felt that the federal government had gotten out of touch with people and had, consequently, lost its ability to respond effectively to their needs. He said that government was "broken" and had to be reinvented in a way that would allow local communities to express their concerns and get government to act on their behalf. He saw the need for some institutional means to provide the ordinary citizen a way to exercise political power.[10] It was no surprise that, when introduced to the politics of Call to Renewal, Senator Bradley said that this was what he was looking for and that he wanted to be a part of it.

That the church should be involved in politics was never a question with those who founded Call to Renewal. They were all of the mind that the Jesus of Scripture is Lord of all, and that all spheres of societal life should be under his domain. They were convinced that Christ's mandate was to join him in extending his kingdom over all "principalities and powers" (Eph. 1:20–23) to the end that the kingdoms of this world might become the kingdoms of our God (Revelation 11:15). Creating that kingdom required that political systems be made into instruments of God's will so that they could be used to bring about this societal transformation. The concern of those in this new movement has been how the church could play a role in all of this without becoming triumphalistic. All of those working with Call to Renewal were concerned lest the church become a political power itself, imposing its will on the rest of society.

They believed the church was called to assume the role of "servant," not master, and that when the church did try to exercise its will on others through the use of coercive powers it was being unfaithful both to its calling and to its Lord. As Call to Renewal founders considered the ways in which the Christian Coalition was functioning, they were increasingly concerned that Coalition members were carrying the church into just this erroneous role. They heard much triumphalism in the rhetoric of the Christian Coalition as some of its leaders talked about "taking this country back for Jesus" and "making America into a Christian nation again." Those in Call to Renewal feared that behind such words was a plan to elect Coalition candidates to office and then impose a Christian social order on the rest of the nation. They already had witnessed the takeover of school boards and local party structures of the Republican Party by the Coalition. While many of the social changes that Christians had been able to bring about through this exercise of power might seem desirable to some, those in Call to Renewal were disturbed with the ways in which these changes were being imposed on people in various communities. They were concerned about the increasing evidence of book censorship, school curriculum that favored a Christian worldview over other perspectives, and threats of discrimination in hiring for teaching positions people whom some Christian Coalition members believed to be detrimental to the well-being of their children (for example, homosexuals). To organize a voting bloc that would use its power to impose what its members believed to be a Christian agenda on the rest of the community was a way of doing politics that those in Call to Renewal believed violated the essential nature of Christianity.

The new politics of Call to Renewal prescribes a different way of impacting the political order. Instead of voter guides that rate *candidates* as to how Christian they are (and it is sometimes hard to see how opposing gun control, dismantling the Environmental Protection Agency, building up a stronger military and ignoring the evils of the tobacco industry are necessarily Christian) those in Call to Renewal simply raise issues which they believe that Christians should study prayerfully, consider and discuss as they prepare to vote.

Call to Renewal members do admit to one particular bias: for the poor and the oppressed. They confess that they make deliverance from the curse of poverty a major focus of their politics, because they believe that a bias for the poor is at the heart of the message of Jesus.

The major difference between Call to Renewal politics and the politics of the Christian Coalition is that the former is not out to elect specific candidates or to support a particular party. The Christian Coalition undoubtedly would make the same claim. That goes with their claim that they are a non-profit organization deserving of giving tax deductions to their donors. But the way in which they develop voter guides, their omnipresence at the Republican National Convention, and their absence from the Democratic National Convention belies that claim. Call to Renewal, instead, tries to establish a new kind of politics wherein the church does not seek power for itself, but endeavors to empower all peoples in society, especially politically silent poor and oppressed minorities, to express themselves within the political process. Town meetings, which Call to Renewal believes should be convened by churches everywhere, are designed to give *all* people, regardless of religion, race, political affiliation or social status, a voice in determining their own political destiny. Call to Renewal is made up of people who contend that the role of the church in this process is not to dominate or dictate the agenda, nor to organize people to do its will. Instead, it is to play the role of a servant that calls people together so that they might participate together in resolving the issues that concern them and come up with a collective course of action to address these concerns. Those who lead Call to Renewal believe that along the way the church can speak to these issues as a participant in the community discussion, interjecting its understanding of the biblical perspective on issues under discussion, and bathing the entire process in prayer. This is a more humble role for the church to play than the triumphalistic role which many in the Religious Right seem to suggest, but the leaders in the Call to Renewal movement believe that it comes closer to the servant role that the Lord would have them play.

Chapter 9

When Work Disappears

As people in truly disadvantaged neighborhoods express their concerns and needs in town meetings, there is almost certainly going to be one overarching plea. It will be a call for jobs. It is easy to trace most of the other problems of inner-city neighborhoods to the disappearance of viable employment opportunities for the low-skilled workers who live there.

Joblessness is related to the gangs of young men who hang out on street corners. It contributes greatly to the breakdown of the family that is so typical of ghetto life. The flourishing drug trade and the array of robberies that plague the troubled sections of American cities are interrelated with the disappearance of decent-paying, legitimate employment for the poorly educated, untrained people who live there. Undoubtedly, the low educational aspirations of young people in the public school systems of our cities are conditioned by their failure to see much in the way of job prospects in the vicinity of their neighborhoods. Even a superficial knowledge of inner-city life will lead to the conclusion that unless something is done to create massive numbers of jobs for the semiskilled and untrained people who live in disadvantaged urban neighborhoods, the problems that trouble these communities will not go away.

My city is Philadelphia, a city which has lost 165,000 jobs in twenty years. In the 1980s alone, Philadelphia lost 55,000 jobs that required low levels of education.[1] And the question has to be asked, "What happens to a city when work disappears?" More specifically, "What happens to a city when good-paying semi-skilled jobs disappear?" In the changing employment

113

opportunities of urban America, there are a host of new jobs being created daily for those who have the know-how to run computers or the skills needed for other high-tech work options. But what happens when those without the ability or the training required for sophisticated jobs are left without viable employment options?

In many inner-city ghettos, more than half of all adults are without work in a given week, and I am not talking about the kind of people who are able to meet the requirements for the new jobs in America's white-collar business world. If those who live in such neighborhoods were to hold town meetings, it is exceedingly likely that they would express there the fact that their most pressing community need is the need for jobs. Neighborhood people are very much aware of the consequences of unemployment on their everyday lives and the life of their community. They know, from personal experience, that most other social problems in their community are, in one way or another, connected with their own joblessness and the joblessness of their neighbors. The most obvious effect of joblessness is poverty. As the unemployed are pushed off the public welfare rolls by the repeal of the old welfare system, most are simultaneously pushed below the poverty line and will lack the means for earning a decent living.

About half of all the poor in America are people who live in urban neighborhoods. This is a significant increase from 1959, when only one third of America's poor were trapped in urban poverty.[2] Because inner-city ghettos are increasingly home for minority groups, the problem of poverty has huge implications for race relations in this country. As my city of Philadelphia has become increasingly African-American during the last twenty-five years, it has simultaneously lost 64 percent of its manufacturing jobs, leaving hundreds of thousands in the black community with few options for semiskilled employment. Since the well-educated African-American middle class has moved to the suburbs along with their white middle-class counterparts, America's inner-city ghettos have increasingly become concentrations of uneducated poor African-Americans, along with other people of color who suffer similar socioeconomic hardships.

Other major cities have not fared much better during the last twenty years, with Chicago losing 60 percent of its manufacturing jobs (326,000), New York City losing 58 percent (520,000), and Detroit losing 51 percent (108,000).[3]

When jobs leave a city, a lot more leaves with them. Banks and other businesses also leave. Restaurants close down. Cleaners, convenience stores, service stations, and supermarkets go out of business. The constant threat of robberies, common in neighborhoods with high unemployment, along with the riot-related high cost of insurance, drive essential storekeepers to give up on the inner-city and find other places to earn a living.

Those who arrogantly claim that people who want to work can always find jobs are not aware of the changes in the economic structure of our cities over the past quarter of a century, nor are they aware of what hurdles today's unemployed people have to face, compared to those who went job hunting just a generation ago. With the suburbanization of employment that has gone with businesses and industries relocating in industrial parks outside city limits, urban dwellers find great difficulty in locating jobs. If they do find them, they may discover that it is too expensive to get to those jobs because public transportation has gone through a rapid decline in metropolitan areas everywhere. The cost involved for city people to get to and from suburban workplaces often makes taking all but high-paying jobs unfeasible. As a case in point, my secretary has to spend $30 per week in round-trip fares so that she can travel between her home and our suburban office. Add to that the fact that she has to spend three hours a day in transit, and you can see that a low-paying job with such a travel requisite can make working something that is less than worthwhile. Buying a car is not a good option for a low-paid worker because the cost of car insurance can range from $5,000 to $8,000 a year for anyone who gives a city address as a place of residence. Getting to and from workplaces in the suburbs is so difficult and expensive for inner-city people that even going for job interviews requires more of them than most can handle.

Those who say that people who really want to find jobs can always do so have not been in the position of most ghetto dwellers. Often, employers do not even advertise in city papers because, for a variety of reasons, they don't want to attract ghetto dwellers. One way employers keep ghetto blacks from applying for jobs is to fail to advertise those jobs in the newspapers that are accessible to them. Thus, employment notices are printed in suburban newspapers or in newspapers that serve only certain "desirable" neighborhoods. William Julius Wilson of Harvard University has conducted studies which provide ample evidence that most employers regard ghetto dwellers as being lazy, dishonest, threatening, and more trouble than they are worth.[4] Such opinions are held not only by white employers; African-American employers are even more prone to hold those opinions about ghetto people, according to Wilson. As we shall see, the culture of ghetto dwellers has nurtured traits in people that give some credibility to these seemingly biased opinions.

Perhaps contributing even more to the failure of ghetto dwellers to find jobs is that they are not networked to find employment. Most people who find jobs do not even use the newspapers to locate them. Instead, neighbors, friends, and relatives tell them about available jobs. Actually, most employers prefer to get new workers through such an informal means of advertising because it gives them more assurance that they are getting the kind of people whom they deem desirable. But such networks, in most cases, do not exist for ghetto dwellers. It is not likely that those who live in urban government housing projects will get hot tips about job options from their next-door neighbors, since there is a high probability that their next-door neighbors will be unemployed, too. The relatives and friends of ghetto people are not the kind of people who are likely to have the connections that make finding jobs easy. When it comes to job hunting, most urban ghetto people haven't a clue as to where to start.

Joblessness and Family Life

Joblessness has a devastating effect on the family life of the urban poor. High levels of joblessness are correlated with high levels of social disorganization, and the institution most affected is the family. This phenomenon affects African-American families most of all. Only one third of black families in cities consist of husbands, wives, and children living together. In those census tracts that are predominantly African-American and where 40 percent or more are living below the poverty level, only 16.5 percent of the families are intact. There are ghettos in Chicago where 47 percent of black mothers have never been married and only 6 percent of expectant fathers marry the women they get pregnant.[5]

Some social workers suggest that we shouldn't make negative judgments in the light of such facts, but it is not racist to claim that there are socioeconomic forces, rather than genetic factors, which are responsible for these dysfunctional familial conditions. These horrendous realities are the direct result of the growing unemployment among black males since 1960.

Back in 1967, Elliott Liebow noted the impact of unemployment on ghetto black males in his classic study, *Tally's Corner*.[6] Liebow discovered that unemployed young black men abandoned the women that they got pregnant for a variety of reasons, the most likely of which was shame. Realizing that they were unable to financially provide for them, they deserted these women rather than openly admit that they were unemployable and poor. The welfare system being what it was, these young men without jobs saw that the women were probably better off without them being around. That way, the women could get the full benefits of food stamps, health insurance, and Aid to Families with Dependent Children (AFDC).[7]

The benefits derived from the welfare system are hardly a bonanza for the single mothers who are left to live off them. Consider the fact that in 1993 a single welfare mother who had never been married had a median income of $9,272, compared to $43,578 for a married couple. Consider the fact that welfare benefits have less purchasing power today than in 1975. Between 1975 and 1995, the real cash value of AFDC fell 37 percent.[8] Some benefits have been cut while others have not kept pace with inflation. The present Republican Congress seems committed to making matters worse by giving tax breaks to the rich that they would pay for by cutting back on programs that help the poor. Given the figures cited above, welfare benefits hardly provide for subsistence let alone offer any motivation for having children in the first place. Incidentally, studies have shown that getting welfare benefits plays no significant role in determining which women have out-of-wedlock births.[9]

Another consequence of joblessness for families in the ghetto is that children get out of control. Failure in employment, and the poverty that goes with it, undermines the self-confidence of parents, leading them to doubt their own abilities as child-rearing agents. The children of the unemployed often lose respect for their parents and find it easy to defy their directives. Add to this the substantial evidence that when unemployment and poverty become pervasive in a neighborhood, community supervision of neighborhood children breaks down. People become disconnected from each other and increasingly private. Those who live in ghetto communities learn that "minding your own business" is a survival technique. Hence, people learn to ignore the negative behavior of other children in the neighborhood, paying attention only to their own.

Older people in urban neighborhoods remember with nostalgia the days when any adult in a neighborhood could correct any misbehaving child, even employing corporal punishment. They like to recall a time when no words uttered were more threatening to a would-be delinquent than "I'm going to tell your parents."

This breakdown of informal controls on the behavior of the young has opened a Pandora's box, and a host of evils have come out of it. In many ghetto communities, teenagers now control the streets, deciding who can and cannot walk on them. Drug dealers have been able to exploit this reality by bringing teenagers into their trade. Drugs in general, and crack in particular, have wreaked incredible destruction in urban neighborhoods. Addicted girls often become prostitutes and addicted boys regularly become drug runners. The dealers know that the police are not prone to touch youngsters on the streets out of fear of serious accusations, and even if those youngsters are arrested, their punishment is likely to be extremely light. Too many youngsters ask, "Why go to school and work hard to get some low-paying job when there's a lot of money to be made in drugs? You don't learn anything in school anyway!"

With the drugs come the guns, so that guns now seem omnipresent on city streets. In Newark, New Jersey, 22 percent of teenagers own guns and 12 percent carry them all the time. The number of homicides among black youths has exploded. In 1984, there were 80 homicides per 100,000. In 1992, just six years later, the rate had soared to 180 per 100,000. Guns have created an atmosphere of fear in many urban neighborhoods so that people are afraid to go out. Consequently, attendance at everything from church to PTA meetings drops off and community solidarity further disintegrates.[10]

The Religious Right comes across as a white middle-class political movement that is unconcerned about inner-city black people when it stands opposed to gun control. Their rhetoric about guns not killing people—criminals do—just does not wash in the face of social reality. In societies wherein guns are controlled (for example, New Zealand, Hong Kong, Singapore, and the Scandinavian countries), there is a decided reduction in violent crime.

Not many urban dwellers, especially the usually politically conservative police, oppose gun control. Those who live in the ghettos know what the proliferation of guns has done to their neighborhoods. Where unemployment has diminished self-respect and denied men any status in the mainstream society, young men seek respect by carrying guns. If they can't get from the rest of us the respect that they think they deserve, they at least try to elicit fear with guns. Unfortunately, they succeed!

Among all of the horrific consequences of unemployment in urban ghettos, perhaps the most subtle are the spiritual and the psychological. Work is more than a means to make money; it is a way of life. Without work, people lose faith in themselves, in the social system, in their neighbors, and even in God. Those who think that unemployment and poverty make people more religious have not done their research. What unemployment and poverty really generate is a deep sense of apathy. So pervasive is that apathy that people end up not taking advantage of the few opportunities that are available to them. Unemployment has far-reaching effects and can wipe out positive possibilities even for those of coming generations.

Those who would make the apathy and lethargy of black people in the ghetto into a racist issue ought to consider the study made by Marie Jahoda, Paul S. Lazarsfeld, and Hans Zeisel of the town of Marienthal, Austria. In this town of solid Germanic stock, unemployment generated the same kind of apathetic attitudes toward life that have come to characterize those who live in black ghettos. The town of Marienthal was organized around one huge factory, and when that factory closed, the entire town was made dependent on the government welfare system.

The people in the town slowly lost their sociability. Although they once gathered in public places to discuss the goings-on in the world, there was little in the way of such get-togethers after unemployment had had its effects. Not even politics could generate any kind of discussion. People no longer participated in community activities, and the town seemed to lose any sense of what once had been cohesiveness or feelings of belonging.

There was a gradual loss of "self-sufficiency," said Jahoda, Lazarsfeld, and Zeisel, as people seemed unable to define any steps that they might take to improve themselves or their town. They also lost their "self-efficiency"—they lost confidence in their own work skills and came to define themselves as incompetent people incapable of doing anything worthwhile with their lives. Particularly evident was the loss of self-efficiency that parents had in respect to raising their children. They saw themselves as powerless when it came to child rearing.[9]

Jahoda, Lazarsfeld, and Zeisel pointed out that the people in Marienthal seemed to have forgotten how to hurry. Their lethargy was a painful thing to behold. Without jobs life becomes disorganized and people experience anomie. Jobs provide a rhythm to life, prescribing when we get up, when we eat, and even when we go to bed. Our jobs define our places and our status in a society. Without jobs, there are no patterns for our lives, nor is there much in the way of expectations. People lose a sense of identity and become lazy. In short, they tend to fall apart. What was wrong with the people in Marienthal is exactly what we are likely to find among the unemployed African-Americans who live in our urban ghettos. Joblessness has effects on people which ought not to be defined as racial characteristics.

Christian scholars have given much thought to developing a theology of work, and in the context of that theology, they ought to be able to easily figure out what unemployment can do to people. They say that our God is a creative god and that we live as creatures in the image of God when we engage in creative work ourselves. If that is true, what does it say about those who have been denied creative labor through unemployment? Do they not feel that they have lost something they deemed godly about themselves?

There are those who have theologized that it is through the work we do that we express the essence of our humanity and achieve that sense of spiritual fulfillment that gives us joy. If that is the case, does it not mean that those who lose their jobs find their humanity diminished and their joy of living painfully curtailed?

Any pastor who has served a church in a community plagued with massive unemployment can give ample testimony to the consequences it has for people. Every social pathology from drug use and alcoholism to suicide becomes accentuated. Support of voluntary organizations, including the church, drops off, and, worst of all, a spiritual and psychological malaise permeates the community.

In such a setting, it becomes difficult to preach any "good news" about what God is doing in the world. It becomes hard for people to believe that there is much in the way of biblically prescribed hope for them

What the Church Can Do

It is obvious from all that has been said that any town meeting in a neighborhood depressed by unemployment will be likely to focus on what can be done about finding people work. And if churches are to play the role of servant in such settings, they should be ready to respond to the cries of neighborhood people and meet their need for jobs. Some specific things that urban churches can do in the context of all this are:

1. *In conjunction with others in the neighborhood, urban churches can challenge people to develop a "town watch" to make the streets safer.* Businesses are more likely to flourish in the context of safety, creating more jobs.

2. *Urban churches can network with the business community and with suburban churches to find out where jobs are available.* City churches need to be affiliated with suburban churches that have members who are well connected for placing people who need employment. A concerted effort can be made to bring together those who need jobs and those who know where to find them. Often the people who own what businesses still do exist in a given urban neighborhood live in the

suburbs and are not connected to the people in the neighborhood. These owners would find it useful to employ people from the immediate vicinity of their businesses and would probably do so if the neighborhood churches would recommend trustworthy and reliable workers. Businesspeople know that it is always good business to have the goodwill of the neighborhood and that such goodwill can best be gained by employing neighborhood people. Networking facilitated by inner-city churches can make that happen.

3. *Set up an employment agency.* Recognizing that inner-city jobs that are viable for the semiskilled workers who live in poor urban neighborhoods are seldom accessed by those people, churches might get together and set up an employment agency to serve the neighborhood unemployed. This agency should not only locate jobs for community people, but also work to negotiate assurances for employers that the workers sent to them will be "job-ready" and effective. Such an agency might even promise to keep tabs on the employees that they recommend, seeing to it that they are punctual and not guilty of unnecessary absenteeism. If churches could give employers assurances that those whom they recommend would not be more trouble than they are worth, the chances of getting employment for neighborhood people would be greatly enhanced.

4. *Churches can provide "job-readying" programs for the unemployed in their neighborhoods—especially for those who are trying to make the transition from school to work.* Many of those who live in urban ghettos do not know how to apply for employment, handle an interview, or behave when they get jobs. In many cases, the so-called urban underclass unemployed have had little opportunity to observe people who hold down regular jobs or who could be role models to show them how to conduct themselves in order to be desirable employees. Many of these unemployed ghetto dwellers are from second- and even third-generation welfare families and know nothing of the routines that go with holding a job. Somebody has to teach them how to dress, the importance of punctuality, the need to call in when sickness strikes, how to talk to people on the job, and how to become valuable assets to the companies that employ them. In one of our inner-city job creation programs, the four young men who worked with us were constantly coming to work late. The director of the program became exasperated with them, but before he fired them, he decided to have a conference, give them some final warnings, and then one more chance. At one point in the discussion he said to these young men, "I don't understand why you don't get it. I can't figure out why you don't wise up and come to work on time." Then, without realizing the

importance of his question, he asked, "What I want to know is, what do you do when the alarm clock next to your bed goes off in the morning?"

There was dead silence! It was then that he realized the significance of what he had just said and asked, "Do any of you *have* alarm clocks? Not a single hand went up. The program director then went out and bought four cheap alarm clocks for these young men. Thereafter, lateness to work was seldom a problem.[11]

In the subculture where these young men lived, alarm clocks were a rare commodity. By analyzing the cause of their problem with respect to punctuality and helping them to resolve that problem, the program director made these young men more "job ready" for employment opportunities in the future.

Many urban black people have developed mannerisms, ways of dressing, and facial expressions that can prove quite threatening to possible employers.[12] The sometimes angry demeanor, especially of young men, makes them undesirable for most jobs that require them to meet the public. Studies of ghetto dwellers show that projecting an intimidating manner is a survival technique. Not to appear dangerous or as "somebody-you-don't-mess-with" is often to invite being constantly hassled or even beaten up by neighborhood toughs. The problem is that once having adopted this sullen, threatening demeanor, it is usually difficult to cast it aside in other situations where it is counterproductive. Church job-readying programs can teach young men how to improve their presentations of themselves for the workplace and help them to see that the macho behavior that works well in some situations does not work well in others. These programs also can help the urban unemployed learn how to handle interviews.

Most young people anticipating their first attempts to get jobs need to practice filling out application forms. Role-playing in an interview-type situation will also help the inexperienced get a "feel" for what a job interview will be like. Those who are unfamiliar with what goes into securing a job often fail to ask the right questions or even understand what is going on. Working through these things is what job-readying programs are all about. The church job-readying program might even provide the job seeker with emotional support by having someone accompany him or her to the interview.

5. *Churches can organize to establish a kind of mini chamber of commerce for the purpose of bringing some new businesses into their neighborhoods.* For example, in West Philadelphia, some of us have put a great deal of effort into trying to get a food-processing company to relocate

some of its production operations to our neighborhood. The owners of this company have deep Christian commitments and want to do all they can to live out their faith by helping the poor. They have always been willing to financially contribute to the ministries that our organization, EAPE/Kingdomworks, has developed in the city, but now we are asking them for something other than money. We are asking them to provide jobs for some of the unemployed of West Philadelphia. They have an expanding company and are constantly developing new plants to process new food products. We are pleading with them to establish their next plant in our neighborhood, because we know that the employment this would create would do more to keep some young people off drugs and get them into positive lifestyles than any educational program we could invent.

There are many reasons why establishing a production plant in our neighborhood would be an undesirable move for these Christian business executives. But their desire to live out the commissions of the Gospel to help the poor will probably outweigh those concerns. For our part, we have promised the company owners that we will do all we can to help those whom they might employ to become job-ready and to stand beside them to hold these possible employees to a high level of accountability. We are promising to these potential employers a pool of reliable workers from which to hire new employees.

6. *Churches can become incubators for job-creating entrepreneurial ventures.* In a very unique situation in Minneapolis, a visionary pastor, Art Erikson, deliberately established his church in one of the most troubled sections of the city. He wanted his church to be a primary agent for urban renewal, so he planted it in a neighborhood where he knew there were desperate needs to be met. This pastor then made contact with a very creative Christian entrepreneur, and together they developed a plan that would prove highly successful both in establishing an exciting and vital inner-city congregation and in creating a successful job-creating factory.

Erikson, a white pastor, led his predominantly African-American congregation to buy a good-sized warehouse to be their church. Part of the building was set aside as a place for worship and religious education; the rest of the warehouse was designated for the factory. Ed Flaherty, for his part, bought out a small, struggling electronics company located in a suburban industrial park, then proceeded to relocate the operations of the company to the warehouse part of the church building.

Over the next few months the church took it upon itself to prepare some of its own members who were unemployed, as well as some non-church community people, for jobs at this relocated electronics plant. Through a variety of programs, the church trained people how to function effectively in the workplace, raised their consciousness about the values that go with being employed, and helped them to integrate Christian faith and morality with the demands of business life.

The overall impact that this church/factory arrangement has had on the neighborhood has been remarkable. It has enhanced the profile of the church dramatically and given it the credibility to call together a cross-section of community leaders to consider ways to revitalize, reform, and renew the surrounding area. With these community leaders, the church has been able to attract other small businesses to the neighborhood. Through the concerted and cooperative effort of the church and community leaders, drug pushers have been run off the street, and the hookers who once hung out on street corners have disappeared. New stores have opened up in the neighborhood. It would be impossible to review the entire chain reaction of positive consequences that have come from this church related microeconomic development effort, but this story proves that the church can be the lead institution in social change in an urban setting, especially if it is willing to take the kind of daring and innovative action that was taken by Art Erikson's church. Such a challenging role for the church ought to be explored and developed considering the potent possibilities that it has.

A book by the late E. F. Schumacher, published several years ago, titled, *Small Is Beautiful,* had a great influence on the development of my ideas about microeconomics.[13] Deriving values from both Jesus and Buddha, Schumacher proposed a set of guiding principles for economic development. While his proposals were primarily designed for the economies of Third World countries, he made a strong case that, unless highly industrialized nations adopt these principles, there would be severe consequences that could lead to economic disaster. Certainly, as we consider doing economic development in the inner-city, Schumacher's principles must be given serious consideration.

One of the most important proposals of Schumacher is that new businesses and microindustries must be environmentally responsible. This involves avoidance of any kind of harm to the environment through such practices as the dumping of toxic materials and irresponsible consumption of non-renewable resources (for example, fossil fuels). It also requires that resources be developed and utilized in such a way that the natural environment will be sustained for long-term use. As a case in point, in Haiti, the production of charcoal for cooking purposes is widespread. All over the country, the poor find that one way to earn money is to cut down trees, turn the lumber into charcoal, and bag it for sale in the capital city. The cutting down of trees across the hillsides of this Caribbean country has resulted in the deforestation of the steep slopes of Haiti, making them vulnerable to erosion. When the rains come to Haiti, topsoil is regularly washed into the ocean, and the land is rendered unusable for growing food. This devastation is so extensive that 70 percent of the fertile land that was available for food production twenty years ago has been lost.

When our missionaries in Haiti got into job creation by manufacturing wooden toys, we had to raise the question of what they were doing to plant trees to replace those that provided the lumber used in the production of toys. Not planting enough new trees to more than compensate for those being harvested for toymaking, or not allowing enough time for these replacement trees to grow, would be environmentally irresponsible.

In urban America, as well as in the Third World, a sensitivity to environmental concerns is a necessary part of faith-based economic development. I have been very encouraged along these lines by a scheme that has utilized discarded soda cans and worn-out tires to make a variety of attractive toys. Producing these toys does not require sophisticated machinery or highly skilled workers. This business not only earns money, but it recycles trash.

A second principle put forth by Schumacher is that what is produced should make life better for those who buy it. That certainly is true for the creation of toys that contribute to the fun of children. But it certainly could not be said regarding the production of something like cigarettes or crack cocaine.

At the Hutterite community in Ripon, New York, a small faith-based company is making quality equipment to aid in the mobility of physically impaired children. This is a good example of what Schumacher had in mind. This group of radically committed Christians living "in community" manufacture an array of unusual wheelchairs, specialized beds, and complicated machinery that enables these special children to get in and out of bathtubs on their own. Everything these Hutterites produce is sold at very affordable prices, while still providing good incomes for their several hundred community members.

Third, according to Schumacher, the jobs created should provide the workers with emotionally fulfilling work. Work that is so boring that it leaves the workers emotionally dead, according to Schumacher, ought not to be allowed. He contends that even if a job is extremely uninteresting, it still can be carried out in a context of human interaction that will give the workers a sense of joy.

Recently, I was in a plant where apples were being sorted and then boxed for shipment. The work in and of itself was so routine that after several hours it could do damage to a person's soul. But the Christian family that owns and runs this plant has created a work environment in which the employees can talk and joke with each other, even as they work. Time flies for these men and women, and their lives are enriched because of the fellowship they enjoy.

Just on the edge of the city of Lancaster, Pennsylvania, the Mennonite denomination has established a production plant in which elderly church members, most of them widows, are brought together daily to do quilting. I was moved by the fun and fulfillment written on the faces of these women as they sat on the four sides of the quilts they were putting together. They turned work time into a time for visiting. The quilts they produce are works of art which are sold at good prices with the profits going to missionary work. Schumacher would have been pleased with this arrangement.

As I train my students to do economic development among the poor, I have them read Schumacher's book. These principles derived from the scriptures of Christianity and Buddhism have abiding importance for those who want not only to create jobs for the poor, but to do it in ways that enhance their humanity.

Chapter 10

Incubating Churches

The most obvious thing that many inner-city churches have going for them when it comes to starting new businesses is that they have buildings with unused space. The typical inner-city church gets little use from Sunday to Sunday. For six days a week, most of its facilities just sit there, often in the midst of a community that is aching for something to be done for the unemployed. The typical urban church has Sunday school rooms that have no functions other than as places where small groups of children meet for an hour once a week. Why not use these facilities to house new job-creating business enterprises? Why couldn't each of these almost unused Sunday school rooms be a place for a microindustry? Why couldn't the rental costs that often burden new entrepreneurial efforts be eliminated by a church offering some of its seldom-used space for free? Couldn't rooms that were used for microbusinesses during the week still be available for Sunday school classes on Sundays?

Any study of the reasons why new businesses so often fail will reveal clearly that near the top of the list is undercapitalization. The cost for running these businesses usually proves to be higher than anticipated, and the financial resources to cover the costs are not available. One thing that can be done to overcome this problem is to have reserve funds available to cover those unanticipated costs. But another answer is to dramatically cut down on the start-up and overhead costs. There are many ways that a church can help to do this, and offering free space to the new businesses is one of the best. Not only will offering the space help these businesses, but it also will bring the people involved in the ventures into a place where

127

the church can nurture them socially, psychologically, and spiritually. As we will see, such nurturing is crucial to the success of any job-creating program among the underclass.

Housing these new businesses in the church also will strengthen the witness of the church in its community. It becomes a way of saying that the church is not interested just in saving souls for heaven but is also committed to meeting people's everyday needs here on earth. It gives witness to a holistic gospel that not only answers the quest for spiritual salvation, but also demonstrates that the God of the Bible is at work through the church, answering the needs of people for economic opportunities and justice.

The first time an urban congregation is approached with the suggestion that its building be used to house some job-creating businesses, one question—among the many that are bound to be raised—is how such profit-making enterprises will affect the tax-free status of the church. Churches have had an incredible gift handed to them in the way of tax exemptions for their building facilities, and losing those exemptions would create financial burdens for many inner-city churches. The good news is that, if properly done, housing some for-profit enterprises within the church will not threaten the church's status as a nonprofit institution in any way and will not jeopardize the tax exemption that the church enjoys.

According to law, the tax exemption a church enjoys is given for a variety of reasons. One is related to the U.S. Constitution's requirement of separation of church and state. But another reason that the church enjoys its tax-free status is because it is believed that the church does good and renders valuable services to the community. In line with the latter reason, if it can be demonstrated that the businesses that have been established within the church building were created for the good of the community and not to make a profit for the people of the church, then the tax exemption can be held intact.

Careful analysis of how best to handle this ticklish arrangement between church and state has been made by Tom Jones, a special consultant for World Vision and other church-based organizations.[1] Jones also serves as a part-time faculty member at Eastern College, teaching a course that explores all the legal details and complications that go with church-based entrepreneurship. He *strongly* suggests that professional legal help be sought in the earliest stages of planning.

According to Jones, if a church does not receive any income from the businesses, the church's tax-exempt status is not affected. If "housing" the business means leasing or giving space for no charge in the church building, then the income received from the business for the cost of utilities and care is generally considered "passive" income and, as such, is exempt from federal taxation. However, exemption from federal taxes does not guarantee exemption from state taxes. The laws vary from state to state, which is one reason legal counsel is an imperative.

A bit of good news is that if the church organized, financed, staffed, controlled, administered, and sold the goods or services from a business dedicated to helping its own members and their relatives, then the business is considered a "service to the membership" and is usually considered exempt from federal taxation. Again, the arrangements may vary when it comes to state taxes.

Related to the problem of how to use the church building for starting small businesses without causing problems for the church is how the people of the church can maintain some control over what goes on in these businesses. For instance, a church might not want any alcoholic beverages on its premises, and it probably would not want its people to be outraged by one of its businesses getting into something like the production of pornographic videos. Once again there are some directives to follow that will enable a church to have the kind of controls and supervision that will protect its integrity. Also, the people of the church will be concerned about matters of liability. If one of the companies it houses becomes the target for a liability suit, will the church be involved? Might the church find itself in a position where it could be sued out of existence by a party that had a grievance against one of the entrepreneurial enterprises it sponsored? How can a church protect itself against such a thing happening?

If the church owns the businesses and the businesses operate under the direction of the church, there is little problem in the way of exercising control. However, what is more common is having businesses incorporate as separate entities. The purpose of such incorporation is so that the church could escape any liability suits that might be leveled against any of the businesses housed in the church building. Again I must issue a warning that in today's society there is really no way to establish a foolproof arrangement that will protect a church against some aggrieved or disgruntled party, regardless of how unjustified or frivolous the complaints may be. Incorporation of businesses as separate entities might help a church's case in court, but there is just no telling how a judge or jury will decide things, regardless of attempts by the church to establish legal separation from the businesses that it houses. It may be that separate incorporation would diminish the liability of the church, but there is no way to safely eliminate it. It is just that kind of world.[2]

If it is decided to incorporate the business separately from the church, there are two options for doing so. One possibility is to incorporate as a nonprofit corporation with a 501(C)3 standing with the Internal Revenue Service. Another is to incorporate as a for-profit corporation. In the former arrangement, the profits will have to stay with the businesses to be used for the charitable benefits promised in the incorporation papers, but if all that is desired is to create paying jobs for the workers and to render a service to the community, this might be the desired arrangement.

If the latter course is taken and the businesses are established as for-profit corporations, then the profits from the businesses will be taxable, just as any for-profit businesses would be taxed.

If either incorporation route is taken, Jones suggests that the church's sponsorship and relationship to the businesses be well defined so that both those in church membership and those in the community understand why the church is involved and the good that the church is trying to accomplish. It should be clear to everyone why the church is involved in sponsoring these businesses and what it hopes will be the benefits to both the church's congregation and to the community at large. Then, if the businesses should fail or do not live up to the intended expectations, the church can distance itself from the businesses based on the announced purposes that the church had in sponsoring them. Generally, the businesses housed in the church are so dependent on the church for resources, use of the building, and consultant help from church members that informal means for controlling what goes on in these businesses is not too difficult to maintain.

Office Services

New businesses need offices with a lot of equipment. Fax machines, word processors, duplicating equipment, computers, and telephones are all essential for business enterprises. More important, every business needs at least one person to handle correspondence, answer telephones, do bookkeeping, take care of billing, and perform a host of other chores. Establishing a supporting office system for a new business is expensive, and the process can all but obliterate the limited financial resources that a fledgling entrepreneurial enterprise has available. The good news is that once again the church can come to the rescue. The typical urban church already has an established office and usually all the necessary equipment and supplies required to undergird a new business enterprise. Furthermore, in most cases this equipment is underutilized. With careful planning, the same equipment can be used to serve not only the needs of the church, but also the needs of the new business.

Even more important, a church secretary can render some essential services for one or more new entrepreneurial ventures. With multiple phone extensions, a single secretary could handle calls for several new businesses and still be able to answer church calls as well. There simply needs to be a separate extension for each new business on the same telephone system that serves the church. In their early stages, new businesses do not get so many calls that this arrangement would be a heavy burden for the secretary.

Furthermore, the new businesses could be expected to make some financial contributions to the maintenance of the office and the secretary so that a church that had had only a part-time secretary would be able to have a full-time secretary. The cost of the maintenance of a photocopying machine also could be shared between the businesses and the church. All in all, this kind of a setup could be a win-win arrangement for all the parties involved.

With the church office serving new businesses, these enterprises would have the essential but limited services that they need in early stages of development without a lot of high expenses. Cutting office costs in this way could solve the problem of undercapitalization that so often brings down new business ventures.

Consulting Services

Those who have tried to figure out the success secrets of new entrepreneurial enterprises almost always point to the importance of consulting services. McDonald's franchises, for instance, seldom fail because the company has a great team of consultants with a wealth of experience. These consultants usually can keep each new franchise from making unnecessary mistakes or committing the errors of earlier franchises. Good consultants know where to locate a new business, how to position it in the market, and how to handle production at an optimal level. Most business experts marvel at the effectiveness of the McDonald's consultant teams and attribute the success of this fast-food business to the good direction that these teams provide.

While the new businesses within the incubating church probably would not have a team to match one of McDonald's, they still can get some really good consulting services if some of the members of the church are called in to help. In many an inner-city church, there are members who have just the skills and experiences that new businesses require. It is not unusual for an old city church to have a lawyer or two who can volunteer services to handle the legal matters. There is a good chance that there are people in the congregation who have backgrounds in bookkeeping and marketing. There may be technical know-how for developing production skills among church members. It usually is surprising how many people in a relatively small inner-city congregation possess abilities and expertise that can be tapped for service. What makes such experienced consultants even more desirable is that they are usually retired and have the time to give to such church-based business enterprises.

There is little doubt that churches generally have underutilized the laity. The men and women in most congregations are seldom given tasks that challenge them or use their skills. A banker ends up counting pennies from the Sunday school offerings. A corporate executive spends endless hours in trustee meetings discussing what kind of carpet to buy for the narthex. A person skilled in marketing is asked to do little more than to figure out where to buy choir robes. If a church becomes an incubator for some new businesses, people can be called on to use their training and background experiences in optimum fashion for the work of God's kingdom. When a church becomes an incubator for microbusinesses, it can provide some of the members with a sense that their vocational skills have new importance for ministry and give them a new sense of calling.

Marketing Help

Selling goods and services is not always easy, especially for new businesses. Developing good markets can take a great deal of time. Sometimes the marketing process is so slow in getting up to a viable level for supporting a business that the business fails in the interim.

When it comes to marketing, the church has a variety of advantages to offer the businesses that it nurtures. First of all, the people in the church, or those in neighboring churches, can become customers. For instance, a moving business operating out of a church-sponsored incubator might call on any members of the church who plan to move to use its services. A simple notice from time to time in the church bulletin to remind the members that the moving service is available could do much to ensure a flow of business not only from church members but also from friends and associates. Also, other churches in the neighborhood might be willing to advertise the moving company on their bulletin boards and in their church newsletters. People recognizing that the business is a ministry of the church to the unemployed are likely to go out of their way to lend support to the marketing process.

A faith-based print shop in Camden has been created by our missionary organization, EAPE/Kingdomworks. The ten young people who operate this business enterprise print greeting cards, decorate note paper, and offer specialized T-shirts for various organizations and special occasions. In their effort to market their products, they follow me around to the speaking engagements I have at various churches and organizations. I have several speaking engagements in their area each month, and whenever I speak anywhere that is accessible to these young people, I can count on them showing up, setting up their wares and doing all that they can to make my audiences into customers. They expect me to promote their business when I get up to speak—which I usually do—and they capitalize on the relationship that they have with me. I usually tell the people that when they buy from these young folks they are helping to create jobs for the unemployed of Camden. I point out that their purchases are contributing to EAPE/Kingdomworks' effort to provide an alternative for these teenagers, who face a scarcity of jobs. It always works![3] While this method was the primary marketing means in the early stages of their business, these young entrepreneurs have increasingly utilized telemarketing to sell their products and depend on me less and less.

Recently I have been capitalizing on the religious base of some of our business ventures as part of a concerted effort in economic development that has been initiated by the Philadelphia Development Partnership. PDP is an umbrella organization that coordinates the more than 700 Community Development Corporations in the city. Together with EAPE/Kingdomworks, Eastern College, and the Philadelphia Leadership Foundation,[4] PDP has sought to help developing church-based businesses as a means of combating the unemployment in the city. The leaders of PDP gradually have come to realize that churches can provide the resources and human support systems that microenterprises need in their early stages of development. Consequently, they have led the way in forming this coalition of organizations to encourage faith-based entrepreneurial ventures. Together the members of this coalition have come up with a unique form of marketing that we believe is going to ensure the success of a number of our new businesses. This unique marketing program sells services and products to prospective buyers even before they are available. We are going to the purchasing agents of large corporations located in and around

Philadelphia and asking them to enter into contract arrangements with us. We are asking them to buy products and services from our microbusinesses even before these businesses exist. We approach companies like the Einstein Medical Center or Herr Food Corporation, and ask what are the goods and services they presently purchase that could be supplied by the church-based microbusinesses and cottage industries that we are developing. We explain that as charitable institutions endeavoring to help inner-city young people, we could easily be on their doorsteps begging for donations and grant money to support our work. Instead, we tell them, we are asking them to help us help urban young people by joining in an effort to create jobs for them. We emphasize that the best way to help urban young people escape from poverty and embrace a positive lifestyle is to get them gainfully employed. We point out that, since there are few jobs available for people at their skill level, there is a need for us to create jobs for them. Then we go on to say that we have gotten into the job-creation business to provide work opportunities for these young people and that their company could make a major contribution by contracting to buy the services and goods that we will provide. In the case of the Einstein Medical Center, which is located in one of the depressed neighborhoods of the city, we explain that it makes for good community relationships to help us create jobs for those young people who live in their immediate vicinity. The results are usually positive.

With a signed contract from the Einstein Medical Center, we find it easy to tell the young people we are trying to reach that if they want to make a living by owning and running their own company, we have a sure thing for them. We can tell them that if we can just get them organized to produce the goods or to provide the services that the hospital needs, we have a guaranteed buyer that will keep them in business. As a case in point, we are presently putting together a laundry service for the hospital. This ought to provide employment now and in the future for a dozen or more young people.

Providing Help with Short-Term Loans

Most businesses need a line of credit that can be used in times of emergency or when expansion requires investment capital. But getting loans can be exceedingly difficult for new business enterprises, especially if they have no collateral. Once again, if a business is being sponsored by a church, this problem might have some ready solutions.

Some inner-city churches, like my own, have established credit unions and are able to function like banks in making loan money available. Those who do the borrowing are really using funds entrusted to them by the church people, and this establishes a special bond between those in the church and those in the business that needs the loan. The level of accountability is dramatically raised for both the borrowers and the church people who are the lenders.

In some cases, churches may have some financial reserves in their own treasuries that can be available for business loans. If a church has extra money in the bank, then why not help out the businesses it is sponsoring?

Some may suggest that if the loan money comes from the church treasury, no interest should be charged on the loan. This, they say, would be in accord with the biblical doctrine that it is against God's will to charge interest on the poor.

> And if thy brother be waxen poor, and fallen in decay with thee; then thou shalt relieve him: yea, though he be a stranger, or a sojourner; that he may live with thee. Take thou no usury of him, or increase; but fear thy God; that thy brother may live with thee. Thou shalt not give him thy money upon usury, nor lend him thy victuals for increase. (Lev. 25:35–37)

However, a closer examination of what is meant in this biblical text and how it is interpreted in the Talmud will show that charging interest on a loan for a business is quite legitimate. It is one thing, according to scripture, to charge interest to the desperately poor who must borrow in order to meet an urgent need. It is quite another thing to charge interest when the loan is to provide investment capital. If the loan is going to be a means of earning more money for the borrower, then the lending party, according to scripture, has a right to share in the profits.

Finally, those who are looking for needed financial capital may be able to go to a local bank and ask for a loan if the church will back up the borrowers, perhaps using its building as collateral. In such a situation, it is likely that the bank will take the chance and make the funds available. Again, the church can find itself in a position to create high levels of accountability from those borrowers who are involved in the business enterprise it is sponsoring.

When we stop to think about what can come from churches being involved in creating new business, it is surprising that churches all across

America are not stepping forward and getting into job creation. I want to challenge them now to do just that.

Churches can do much more for the unemployed than what we have discussed up to this point. The experts know that in economic development among the poor, the development of the people themselves is even more important than creating new businesses. If the church cannot be the primary instrument for nurturing underclass people into the kinds of people who have the traits and character to be economically productive, then there is little hope for these people.

Chapter 11

Faith-based Programs in Economic Development

O ver the past few years, it has become increasingly clear that faith-based social programs are proving to be more successful than those that are not faith based. The reasons are multiple and the explanations often complicated. But the evidence leaves little doubt that faith-based social programs deliver more bang per dollar invested than do those that are not established under religious auspices. In his book, *The Tragedy of American Compassion*,[1] Marvin Olasky further claims that the optimum levels of cost-effectiveness in social programs are achieved primarily by those that *overtly* make the proclamation of the Christian gospel an omnipresent element of their operations. Olasky goes so far as to suggest that programs lacking a strong evangelical emphasis are not very likely to succeed. Religion, for Olasky, is not enough. It is only evangelical Christianity that yields the desired results. Olasky assumes a political posture on social programs that, to many, seems extreme. He calls for an end to most government social welfare efforts and calls on churches, particularly evangelical churches, to assume the primary burden of helping the poor.

Olasky gains support from another controversial writer referred to in Chapter 3, Charles Murray. However, Murray simply attacks government welfare programs and calls for an end to them cold turkey. Murray's *Losing Ground* traces the consequences of the massive social welfare programs initiated during Lyndon B. Johnson's administration. With extensive use of statistics, he shows that these well-meaning efforts only made things worse for the poor. Olasky, on the other hand, calls for the church to step up and to assume responsibility for helping the poor and organizing social welfare efforts. Olasky believes in the biblical admonition to help the poor and the oppressed, but he contends that this is something that the *church* is commissioned to do, rather than the government. According to Olasky, when the government gets into the act, it only messes things up.

A couple of decades ago, Olasky's assertions might have been easy to dismiss. But in the early 1990s, when his book became popular, there was a growing consensus that government-sponsored welfare programs had indeed failed and that a whole new approach to welfare programs was needed.

The claims that government handouts had created a mentality of dependency, particularly among urban blacks, was a message not only being constantly reiterated among white political conservatives, but also being heard by an increasing number of black leaders. Louis Farakhan, the head of the Black Muslim movement in America (now one of this nation's fastest-growing religions), claimed that the welfare system was designed by whites to enslave black people's minds and souls by making them dependent on the white establishment for survival. Farakhan argued with passion that the U.S. government had behaved demonically through welfare laws to foster laziness and shiftlessness in the black community.

While Olasky, an intensely evangelical Christian himself, would hardly support the Black Muslim religion, he would, nevertheless, probably agree that this black version of Islam could create a better system for helping the poor than any system that a secular government could devise. He would probably find much to praise in the economic development programs that have been initiated by the Black Muslims and the self-help programs for blacks that Farakhan has created through mosques.

More liberal leaders gradually are joining the chorus of praise for Farakhan. In cities like Philadelphia and Chicago, his Black Muslim movement has created employment for African-Americans by starting up black-owned and -operated businesses. Clothes-cleaning establishments, credit unions, restaurants, auto repair shops, food stores, and a host of other businesses crop up with amazing frequency as Black Muslims become a strong presence in an African-American neighborhood. So impressive are the accomplishments of the Black Muslims in urban communities that the Christian black clergy have a difficult time standing up to the encroachment of the Black Muslim movement into the lives of their people, especially their young people. In spite of what many see as its anti-Semitic beliefs, African-American leaders such as Jesse Jackson are well aware of the fact that their political survival depends on staying in the good graces of Farakhan and his followers.

The issue is now beyond debate. John J. DiIulio Jr., working with the Brookings Institution, has done an exhaustive study of faith-based social programs. The results of his study show conclusively that faith-based programs work at a much more efficient level and are dramatically more cost-effective than government programs or other privately sponsored programs of a secular nature.[2]

Faith-based social programs achieve high levels of success primarily because, at their best, they operate under the assumption that the people who need to be helped need more than just some good counseling and some good opportunities. Those who develop the faith-based programs, especially those in the programs sponsored by evangelicals, believe that the people they are targeting have a need to be spiritually converted. Sociologists like Peter Berger who want to express this idea in terms that find greater acceptance in the halls of academia, may refer to it as an "alteration of consciousness," or a "consciousness change."[3] But they are only providing fancy words for that experience so well described almost a century ago by William James in his book, *The Varieties of Religious Experience*.[4]

It is nothing new to those who observe social behavior that religious conversion can take listless, spendthrift people who have hovered on the verge of economic disaster and transform them into hardworking, thrifty, upwardly mobile achievers. Max Weber, in a classical essay long known to social scientists, *The Protestant Ethic and the Spirit of Capitalism*,[5] carefully correlated economic productivity with religious commitment. Weber gave special recognition to the ways in which those who adopt Calvinistic convictions are especially prone to economic productivity and prosperity. But even before Weber, John Wesley, the founder of Methodism, provided a clear account of how religious conversion affects socioeconomic status:

> . . . religion must necessarily produce both industry and frugality, and these cannot but produce riches. . . . We ought not to prevent people from being diligent and frugal; we must exhort all Christians to gain all they can, and to save all they can, that is, in effect, to grow rich.[6]

Both Weber and Wesley observed that conversion to Christ gets people to turn away from many behavior patterns that are destructive to economic well-being and to adopt positive and productive habits. With conversion, drunks give up their drinking; gamblers give up their gambling; spendthrifts start saving money; the carefree unemployed become diligent job seekers; and the lazy become hard workers.

In highly evangelical churches, it is expected that such changes will follow conversion, and there are biblical justifications for such expectations. Romans 13:13 admonishes Christians to abandon drunkenness, and among the more evangelical, Leviticus 10:9 provides grounds for forbidding the drinking of *any kind* of alcoholic beverages. In 1 Cor. 3:16–17, the body is defined as "the temple" of the Lord, and many evangelicals believe that this prescribes that we should take nothing into the body that would "defile" it. This means to them that the convert should give up not only booze but cigarettes as well.

When we stop to consider how much money some people who smoke and drink heavily spend to satisfy such destructive habits, it is easy to see that a spiritual conversion putting an end to smoking and drinking would leave them with much more money in their pockets. Converts who decide to give up gambling are also likely to enjoy some economic benefits. Evangelical Christians using such passages of scripture as 2 Thessalonians 3:10–11 believe that God commands people to work for their living and not try to get something for nothing. Since wealth is more likely to come from hard work than from gambling, the effects of conversion are obvious.

From the famous parable of the talents given by Jesus, many Christians are led to believe not only that they ought to shy away from wasting money, but that they are called to invest money wisely as well. They are led to believe that wealth is entrusted to us by God and that God expects us to use it for capital investments that will generate even more wealth:

> For the kingdom of heaven is as a man traveling into a far country, who called his own servants, and delivered unto them his goods. And unto one he gave five talents, to another two, and to another one; to every man according to his several ability; and straightway took his journey. Then he that had received the five talents went and traded with the same, and made them other five talents. And likewise he that had received two, he also gained other two. But he that had received one went and digged in the earth, and hid his Lord's money. After a long time the lord of those servants cometh, and reckoneth with them. And so he that had received five talents came and brought other five talents, saying, Lord, thou deliveredst unto me five talents: behold, I have

gained beside them five talents more. His lord said unto him, Well done, thou good and faithful servant: thou has been faithful over a few things, I will make thee ruler over many things: enter thou into the joy of thy Lord. He that also had received two talents came and said, Lord, thou deliveredst unto me two talents: behold, I have gained two other talents beside them. His lord said unto him, Well done good and faithful servant: thou has been faithful over a few things, I will make thee ruler over many things: enter thou into the joy of thy lord. Then he which had received the one talent came and said, Lord, I knew thee that thou art an hard man, reaping where thou has not sown and gathering where thou has not strewed: And I was afraid, and went and hid thy talent in the earth; lo, there thou hast that is thine. His lord answered and said unto him, Thou wicked and slothful servant, thou knewest that I reap where I sowed not, and gather where I have not strewed: Thou oughtest therefore to have put my money to the exchangers, and then at my coming I should have received mine own with usury. Take therefore the talent from him, and give it unto him which hath ten talents. For unto every one that hath shall be given and he shall have abundance: but from him that hath not shall be taken away even that which he hath. And cast ye the unprofitable servant into outer darkness; there shall be weeping and gnashing of teeth. (Matt. 25:14–30)

It is easy to see that reading this parable could turn converts into upwardly mobile capitalists.

Of all the important influences that might come from a religious conversion, none is more important than its ability to create within people a diligent work ethic. The Bible says:

Servants, be obedient to them that are your masters according to the flesh, with fear and trembling, in singleness of your heart, as unto Christ; Not with eyeservice, as menpleasers; but as the servants of Christ, doing the will of God from the heart; With good will doing service, as to the Lord, and not to men: (Eph. 6:5–7)

This passage, in most evangelical preaching, calls converts to an awareness that when they go to work, they ought to be faithful to their responsibilities not just when the boss is watching, but also when no earthly observer is around. The born-again Christian is expected to be aware that God is always watching and therefore "whatsoever ye do, do it heartily, as to the Lord, and not unto men" (Colossians 3:23). If zealous

converts spend every hour in the workplace carrying out their employment obligations believing that what they do is being observed by an
ever-watchful God, it is easy to understand how their religious experiences can translate into a profitable work ethic. But it doesn't stop there.
The convert also is led by scripture to believe that diligent labor in the
workplace is part of his or her testimony and evangelistic witness to an
unbelieving world. Converts are taught that their honest and productive
work will make nonbelievers more ready to accept the gospel and
become Christians. This is an easy conclusion to reach from reading
such biblical passages as

> Let your light so shine before men, that they may see your good
> works, and glorify your Father which is in heaven. (Matt. 5:16)

When social scientists analyze the impact of religious conversion on economic behavior, their observations help us to see a variety of latent functions of conversion that might not otherwise be considered. As a case in
point, onetime Harvard scholar Edward C. Banfield believed that there
had to be a necessary change in "time awareness" before lower-class people could become upwardly mobile.[7]

Banfield taught that what made people economically upwardly mobile
was wrapped up with their willingness to sacrifice the pleasures of the
present in exchange for greater benefits in the future. He believed that
this willingness to commit to deferred gratification was highly contingent
on the way people perceive time. Lower-class people, he argued, are so
engaged with the present that it is difficult, if not impossible, for them to
comprehend the future as something that is real to them. The future does
not exist as part of their everyday consciousness or worldview. If the
future is unreal to them, then it is highly unlikely that they will be willing to sacrifice either the limited resources they have or the pleasures of
the present for greater benefits in some future tomorrow. In contrast,
says Banfield, those upwardly mobile members of the bourgeoisie owe
their economic successes to the fact that the future is *very* real to them.
As a matter of fact, he points out, there are some middle-class people for
whom the future is so real that they seem incapable of smelling any of
the roses in the here and now. There are middle-class citizens who are so
geared to what they hope to enjoy in the distant future that when we try
to relate to them, they seem to be absent even when they are present.
But whatever criticism we might have of these future-oriented middle-
class types who lack the spontaneity and impulsiveness that make for

being fun-loving in the present, we have to admit that they do possess the willingness to make the sacrifices of time and resources that go with successful entrepreneurship.

It is easy to figure out why lower-class people are so predisposed to being present oriented. Often their lives are so hard that getting through the day is about all they can handle. If they started thinking about what might be waiting for them in the future, they just might become suicidal. As poor people, they find it easy to take the admonition of Jesus in the Sermon on the Mount when he said:

> . . . Take no thought for your life, what ye shall eat, or what ye shall drink; nor yet for your body, what ye shall put on. Is not the life more than meat, and the body than raiment? (Matt. 6:25)

It can be argued that the simplicity of lifestyle and the carefree disposition toward life that goes with being oriented to the present go with the kind of life that Jesus prescribes. Certainly his most faithful follower since the first century, St. Francis of Assisi, would concur with such a conclusion. But those who want to escape poverty would do well to realize that such perspectives on the present and the future hinder their aspirations for success.

Milton Yinger of Oberlin College picked up Banfield's observations about the relationship between perspectives on time and upward class mobility and adds to them his own observations of how religious beliefs play into all of this. Yinger suggested that if economic success requires that those in the underclass escape their preoccupation with the present, then religious conversion can be a primary means to bring about such a change in consciousness.[8] When the present-oriented individual is overtaken by the redefinitions of reality that usually accompany religious conversion, an alteration of the ways in which he or she relates to time is a common side effect. For the new convert, eternal life in heaven becomes a primary concern. That in itself creates a powerful motivation to be future oriented.

Personally, I can say that Yinger's theory has certainly had verification in my own experience. I remember as a young Christian singing with great fondness an old gospel chorus that went like this:

> With eternity's values in view, Lord,
> With eternity's values in view,
> I will live each day for Jesus
> With eternity's values in view.

With ideas such as this rushing through my mind, I quickly began evaluating what I did and how I lived. With eternity's values in view, I developed an eye to the future consequences of everything I did. You can't get any more future oriented than that. I increasingly judged all that I did not only in terms of how things would impact my future in this life, but also in terms of how they would impact the life to come.

It is easy to see from all of this how religious conversion can create the disposition toward time that, according to Banfield, is required for entrepreneurship. The entrepreneur has to be willing to sacrifice present pleasures and take great risks with his or her resources in any given economic venture. If via religious conversion the future becomes very real and it becomes possible to vividly imagine the benefits that will probably come from such sacrifices, then the willingness to make those sacrifices is greatly enhanced.

In Third World countries, all of this has constant verification. New converts regularly leave their carefree lives of living in the now to become responsible family members looking for ways in which they can provide for the future well-being of their kin. An easy correlation between upward mobility and evangelical conversions has been established by many observers, especially in Latin America.

Some years ago I was deeply involved in a variety of development programs that were designed to help the poor of Santo Domingo, Dominican Republic, and saw firsthand how religious conversion can play itself out in delivering people from poverty. Our missionary organization, EAPE/Kingdomworks, made its earliest efforts in the area of public health. Joining with the work of a truly inspiring and charismatic young doctor, Elias Santana, we helped initiate a clinic in a barrio slum that lay along the riverfront of the city. It was one of those horrendous hell holes that often emerge on the edges of Third World cities, literally built on the sewer refuse that flowed out of the city. The shacks were home to more than 20,000 people, and the diseases and illnesses that pervaded the place made the need for a public health program desperate.

Elias Santana was not content to heal only the body; he was just as committed to healing people's souls. Whenever he gave medical care, he also gave the gospel. People were converted to Christ because of his efforts, and the economic effects of these conversions were soon evident in their lives. New Christians became good family members and, in some instances, couples who had been living together without benefit of clergy got married. Young people made commitments not to have sexual intercourse prior to marriage, delivering many of them from the disastrous effects of premarital pregnancies. But of special interest to me was the way the new religiosity of people influenced their economic activities.

Together with this young doctor, we began discussing with the neighborhood priest, Tomas Marrero, the idea of starting some cottage industries in this slum. We hoped to provide some means for employment for the young people who lived there. Father Marrero had created a youth club in the slum, and many of Dr. Santana's converts were members of it. It did not take long for us to conclude that this club was ideally suited to become involved in a microindustry that we had in mind. At this point I will not critique all the things we did wrong in this project, but in spite of the flaws, the project succeeded.

The microindustry that we created was a sandal factory. With very limited skills and very few tools, the young men in the club could make sandals out of old automobile tires. It did not take much skill to cut up the tires into the shapes of sandal soles, attach some leather thongs, and have marketable items to sell on the street corners of Santo Domingo. We paid children in the community 50 cents apiece for worn-out discarded tires, which they collected off dumps and vacant lots throughout the city. It wasn't long before we had every old tire in Santo Domingo in our hands. Then we started to get a lot of *new* tires! (I guess it has to be said that the effects of salvation do not immediately touch all areas of life.) We quickly found other sources for raw materials, and the project continued to grow. Soon it provided solid employment for a half dozen young men.

What was of particular interest to me was the way in which their Christian commitments influenced the economic lives of these young men. Whereas in times past they had resorted to whatever means seemed viable to satisfy their immediate needs (which often included robbery, selling drugs, and conning people), religious conversion made them into people willing to work for a living. Heeding the words of scripture, they became good and faithful laborers:

> Let him that stole steal no more; but rather let him labor, working with his hands the thing which is good, that he may have to give to him that needeth. (Eph. 4:28)

More specifically, these young men talked endlessly about how they were going to expand their business so as to provide for their families. They even talked about seeing to it that their younger brothers and sisters had the opportunity to get a university education. They had, through a religious conversion, adopted an orientation to the future that made them into entrepreneurial dreamers and diligent workers.

Contrast the results of this economic development project in the Dominican Republic with a Heifer Project in Haiti, at the other end of the island. The Heifer Project is a program in which heifers are given to poor people who live in rural areas of Third World countries. The idea is to teach the people how to raise these heifers so that in the future they might have a variety of dairy products. A major part of the program is to show people that if they patiently breed their cattle they will soon have a growing herd on their hands and be well on their way out of poverty. However, the Haitians involved in this program were so oriented to the present and the meeting of their immediate needs that waiting for such a payoff in the future was beyond their ability. Instead of following through with the desired plan, they soon killed the heifers and ate them. Sacrificing immediate gratification for greater benefits for themselves and their families in the future was not a part of their way of thinking. I cannot help believing that religious conversions might have made the Heifer Project as successful as the sandal factory.

Our sandal factory was in a Third World country, but there is no reason to think that similar changes in consciousness could not take place under the influence of religious conversion among urban youth in North America. It seems to me that, regardless of the cultural context, conversion to Christianity could lead people into a new time orientation, making them into future-oriented persons, a necessary condition for entrepreneurial daring.

Chapter 12

Old Things Pass Away,
All Things Become New

While Edward Banfield and Milton Yinger give us insight into the consciousness of the underclass, and the ways in which religious experience can alter that consciousness, the most famous (and the most controversial) social scientist to deal with the mind-set of the underclass is Oscar Lewis. In his studies of the Mexican, Puerto Rican, and North American poor, Lewis developed the concept that he labeled *The Culture of Poverty*.[1] He claimed that in capitalistic societies there often emerges a subculture among certain poor people who find themselves alienated from the dominant society and have little hope of ever achieving its goals or embracing its aspirations. Those in the culture of poverty have lost close connections with kin and find themselves part of a "lonely crowd" of similarly isolated neighbors. Often living in sections of the city cut off by a highway, a river or other natural barrier, these people have little to do with anyone outside of their nuclear family.[2] This group of underclass people can develop a distinct subculture with traits and values that are counterproductive when it comes to achieving success in the larger dominant society.

Lewis was convinced that those who attempt to improve the economic conditions of people socialized into this culture of poverty will be frustrated if they think that all that is necessary is to provide better job opportunities or eliminate such barriers to success as racial prejudice. The culture of poverty, he argues, renders people unable to take advantage of any new opportunities for education and employment which might become available in the dominant society. Their under-standing of themselves and their abilities leaves them without the kind of confidence that is required to succeed. Their values and lifestyle are such that these people prove incapable of developing the work habits or meeting the behavioral expectations that go with being functionally fit for the typical workplace. To make it in the dominant society, those who have been socialized into the culture of poverty must be resocial-ized to think and act with a work ethic usually associated with the mid-dle class in America.

A summary of the causes and characteristics of the culture of poverty as defined by Lewis are as follows:

1. The culture of poverty exists in the context of a society wherein the dominant class has a set of values that explains low economic status as the result of personal inadequacy or inferiority. Such definition has oppressive consequences for those who live in this subculture.

2. The culture of poverty is marked by illiteracy. In a literate society, illiteracy creates a self-concept of inadequacy and generates anger among the illiterate toward those who have information power over them. Lack of literacy closes many people out of a job market that usually requires that appli-cants know how to read and write.

3. The culture of poverty tends to perpetuate itself from gen-eration to generation. Once socialized into it, children are not psychologically prepared to take advantage of changing conditions or increased opportunities that may occur in their lifetime.

4. Victims of the culture of poverty are alienated from the dominant culture. Those people who are socialized into it have lost any sense of their former tribal identities. They are not integrated into the institutions of the dominant society and have little sense of "belonging." They are not members of political parties, labor unions, churches, or other commu-nity organizations, and make very little use of museums, banks, or department stores.

5. Welfare creates a sense of hopelessness in those inculcated with the culture of poverty. That hopelessness contributes to those in this culture living only in the now and being only interested in having the wherewithal to meet immediate

needs and to gratify immediate wants. Consequently, with poverty comes a high incidence of pawning personal goods, borrowing from local money lenders, and buying small quantities of food many times a day as need arises. Consequently, the amount spent on food is much higher than it ought to be.

6. Those who are socialized into the culture of poverty have a critical attitude toward some of the basic institutions of the dominant class. They mistrust government, hate the police, and *are cynical about the church.* They are locally orientated and have no concerns beyond their own neighborhoods.

7. Those who are imbued with the culture of poverty are aware of middle-class values, and even claim some of them as their own, but on the whole do not live by them. It is, therefore, important to distinguish between what they say and what they do. For instance, most believe in marriage by law and by the church, but many do not marry.

8. Men without steady jobs want to avoid the expense and difficulties of marriage. Women often turn down marriage offers because they see men as immature, punishing, and generally unreliable. Without marriage, women have a better legal claim to children and find it easier to own their own property. Consequently, there is minimal organization of both the nuclear and extended family.

9. There is an absence of childhood. There is early initiation into sex, a high incidence of abandonment of wives and children, a tendency toward mother-centered families, a strong disposition to authoritarianism in family life, and a lack of personal privacy in the home. There is a lot of talk about family solidarity, but it is rarely achieved because competition for limited goods and maternal affection creates high levels of sibling rivalry. There are high incidences of maternal deprivation, widespread belief in male superiority, and high tolerance for psychological pathologies of all sorts.

10. There is a lack of impulse control, strong present-time orientation, little ability to defer gratification, little ability to plan for the future, and a widespread sense of resignation and fatalism.

No one of these traits taken individually is distinctive of the culture of poverty. It is in their conjunction that the culture of poverty is defined.

Within a given neighborhood, there will be gradations of the culture of poverty. When a class consciousness arises or when people start joining voluntary organizations, they are no longer part of the culture of poverty. *Organization of any kind destroys the psychology of the culture of poverty.*

Karl Marx and Frederick Engels called those in the culture of poverty the *lumpenproletariat* and wrote them off as hopeless.[3] Frantz Fanon, with his experience in the Algerian struggle against the French, saw that the *lumpenproletariat* could be drawn in as a potential revolutionary force that could be organized.[4] About 20 percent of those who live below the poverty level in America are in the culture of poverty.

Those who work among the poor soon come to realize that it is easier to eliminate poverty than it is to eliminate the culture of poverty. The latter requires the creation of a whole new *Weltenschaung* (worldview). Eliminating the culture of poverty requires a consciousness change so profound that some would claim that making this happen would require something akin to a miracle. But such a miracle is exactly what many of us believe is possible through religious conversion and spiritual nurture.

Charles Cooley once said, "A person's self-concept is determined by what he thinks the most significant person in his life thinks of him."[5] From this it can be concluded that if an individual thinks the significant other in that person's life considers him or her to be capable, intelligent, and destined to succeed, then such an individual will embrace this self-definition as true. Furthermore, there tends to be a self-fulfilling prophecy so that those so defined live out the definitions of self provided by the significant other. If those in the underclass are ever going to succeed, each of them needs such a significant other to provide this kind of self-concept.

Religious conversion can meet this need. I believe that with God's help, it is possible to overcome the feelings of personal inadequacy and inferiority characteristic of those who have been socialized into the culture of poverty. Through personal conversion, a person can come to affirm God as the most important significant other in his or her life. Such an individual is likely to develop a positive self-image. In conversion, the person can embrace a whole new definition of self by coming to believe the good things he or she thinks that God thinks of him or her. A classic definition of this process was provided a century ago by the classic psychologist of religion, William James, who wrote:

> To be converted, to be regenerated, to receive grace, to experience religion, to gain an assurance, are so many phrases which denote the process, gradual or sudden, by which a self hitherto divided, and

consciously wrong, inferior and unhappy, becomes unified and consciously right, superior and happy, in consequence of its firmer hold upon religious realities.[6]

This change in self-definition is essential for socioeconomic success. As Henry Ford once said, "Whether you think you can, or you think you can't—either way you're right!" The mindset of those in the culture of poverty is such that they believe they are failures because they are inferior people incapable of succeeding. This, it is easy to surmise, dooms them to failure and renders them unwilling to even try to succeed. But religious conversion can change all of this. So radical is the change, in some cases, that new converts can become obnoxious to be around. Far from presenting themselves as inadequately inferior types, these new converts often cast themselves as superior people whom God has elected for some glorious destiny. They believe that they are "special" before the God who has become their ultimate significant other. Even when the effects of conversion are not so extreme, the redefinitions of self often gained by new Christians is such that those definitions given by others in society are rendered irrelevant.

I believe it is fair to conclude that, when someone comes into a relationship with God whereby a new and positive self-concept is gained, such an individual will experience enhanced possibilities for success in all areas of life. The convert consequently will become psychologically prepared for successful ventures in his or her economic endeavors. For instance, conversion can be an important factor in generating the desire and confidence necessary to become literate.

To those who are illiterate, reading seems like an awesome ability that is beyond them. Overcoming the sense that they lack the intelligence that reading requires can be a side effect of conversion. Being related to Christ through faith is one of the best confidence-builders imaginable. Converts are convinced that "with God, all things are possible!" (Matthew 19:26). By becoming part of a church, they gain a fellowship with other Christians who can be there to encourage them and even to help them along in their lessons.

While in Haiti visiting one of the literacy centers sponsored by our missionary society, EAPE/Kingdomworks, I watched a middle-aged man demonstrate his newly acquired skills of reading and writing. We all sat in nervous stillness as the man picked up the chalk, walked to the blackboard, and laboriously wrote out his name followed by the words ". . . loves Jesus."

When he finished, the class broke into wild applause. The man, with a smile that was too big and expressive to describe, said, "Now I feel like I am a human being! I never felt like that before I could read."

What he had found in Christ and through his fellow Christians had helped him to gain his literacy.

Knowing the sense of empowerment that comes from literacy, it is not surprising that most ghetto churches that want to help people rise above the demoralizing influences surrounding them start tutoring programs aimed at developing reading skills. The ministry of such churches contributes greatly to helping those acculturated into the underclass to overcome the fatalistic despair that the culture of poverty generally nurtures. Learning to read and write ends the anger that the illiterate have toward those who have "information power" over them. Becoming literate is so much more to people than those who take for granted their capacity to read and write can possibly imagine.

New converts have a strong desire to study scripture and are readily convinced that their spiritual growth depends on the daily reading of God's word. Around the world and through the years, the passion to read scripture has created strong motivation for learning how to read. In our own literacy centers in Haiti, we have found that people plead for an opportunity to learn to read once they have been converted to evangelical Christianity.

Recently, some Haitian people who had been through one of our literacy programs presented me with a Bible that was chained and locked so that it could not be opened. When I asked what the gift meant, I was told, "This book, the Bible, was under lock and key for us until you made it possible for us to read. We want you to keep this gift where you can see it daily. We do not want you to forget that there are hundreds of thousands of other Haitians for whom this book is still under lock and key because they are still illiterate."

When all things are considered, I am convinced that it will be clear that no single factor has influenced the spread of literacy as much as people coming into a deeply evangelical conversion. Wherever people have been touched with the gospel story and have had their lives transformed by the power of the Holy Spirit, the desire for literacy has been highly intensified. In those places, you will find a church that is hard at work making sure that new converts are able to read the book that tells them of God's revelation in history and provides them with the inspiration that will strengthen them for the challenges of everyday life.

A New Community

One of the most important effects of Christian conversion is that, ideally, it brings people into meaningful relationships with others who have a like-minded faith. Christianity is, by definition, a fellowship of people who have a common commitment to Christ and to other members of that body of believers called the church. Nowhere is this powerful sense of spiritual community more evident than it is among new converts. That newfound relationship with Christ, which the Book of Revelation poetically refers to as a "first love" (Revelation 2:4), is an ecstasy that converts feel driven to share with one another. So powerful are the emotional commitments that come out of conversion experiences that they can be stronger than the ties to the kin of one's nuclear family. Like Jesus, new converts are prone to ask:

> While he yet talked to the people, behold, his mother and his brethren stood without, desiring to speak with him. Then one said unto him, Behold, thy mother and thy brethren stand without, desiring to speak with thee. But he answered and said unto him that told him, Who is my mother? and who are my brethren? And he stretched forth his hand toward his disciples, and said, Behold my mother and my brethren! For whosoever shall do the will of my Father which is in heaven, the same is my brother, and sister, and mother. (Matt. 12:46–50)

Entering into such a loving fellowship represents a significant transformation for converts coming out of the culture of poverty. Whereas they were once people who shied away from voluntary associations of any kind, new converts generally find in their fellow Christians joyful and fulfilling relationships which, in turn, have a dramatic effect on who they are and what they do. They find that being together with their sisters and brothers in Christ is something so gratifying that they develop a hunger for it.

It was not unusual for those who were converted to Christ from the hippie way of life during the sixties to go to church every night of the week. These converts, often referred to as Jesus Freaks or Jesus People, thrilled at joining together to sing worship hymns and to devour the Bible studies. Their desire for Christian fellowship with their new family in Christ was very intense. Calvary Chapel, in Costa Mesa, California, the birthplace of these kinds of gatherings, still maintains such high-energy nightly get-togethers. The Vineyard movement (a spin-off of the Calvary Chapel movement) recently spun off a group known as the Toronto Airport Fellowship. The independently created Assembly of God church in Brownsville, Florida, with its even more intensive nightly worship, provides the latest dramatic expressions of this spiritual community.[7]

In such highly emotional fellowships, converts find deliverance from that sense of personal isolation so common to those within the underclass. Whereas others in the culture of poverty, cut off from any kind of communal ties or institutional affiliations, experience an emotionally debilitating sense of alienation, those converts who have entered into the fellowships of their new communities of faith gain a deep sense of belongingness.[8] Milton Yinger points out that their integration into the church provides these individuals with an introduction into a social organization that, in turn, prepares them for integration into the institutions of the dominant society.[9] Their participation in church establishes a very necessary transition for them in their escape from the imprisoning effects of the culture of poverty.

Overcoming alienation from the institutions of the dominant society is crucial to achieving social success for the underclass. The culture of poverty imbues them with a self-defeating cynicism about all social institutions, including the church. This cynicism sets them up for continued estrangement from middle-class success. They have to overcome their mistrust of government if they are ever going to learn how to make government work for them to improve the conditions of their social environment. There must be an abating of their hatred for the police if they are going to succeed in creating a safe community in which to live, work, and worship. If their children are going to be free from fear and assured of a healthy environment in which to play, then cooperation with the police becomes a necessary arrangement. The church cannot continue to be regarded as a rip-off organization. Those in the culture of poverty must not view the church as being made up of holier-than-thou types who have transformed what might have been a good thing created by Jesus into a status-giving social club. While the church is far from what it should be, it is hardly deserving of the often bitter judgments that are passed on it by the underclass. In spite of all its shortcomings, the church can still be an instrument of help, hope, and upward mobility for those in the culture of poverty.

Christian conversion changes the way a person looks at things. Heeding the Apostle Paul's teaching, government and the police are no longer seen in negative ways but as instruments of God designed for the good of people.

> Let every soul be subject unto the higher powers. For there is no power but of God: the powers that be are ordained of God. Whosoever therefore resisteth the power, resisteth the ordinance of God: and they that resist shall receive to themselves damnation. For rulers are not a terror to good works, but to the evil. Wilt thou then not be afraid of the power? do that which is good, and thou shalt have praise of the same; For he is the minister of God to thee for good. But if thou do that which is evil, be afraid; for he beareth not the sword in vain: for he is the minister of God, a revenger to execute wrath upon him that doeth evil. Wherefore ye must needs be subject, not only for wrath, but also for conscience' sake. (Rom. 13:1–5)

Members of the underclass, under the influence of their newfound faith as born-again Christians, sometimes will become politically active, working hard to get others to register to vote. Some will even run for public office themselves.

In the city of Philadelphia, there is at least one U.S. Congressman, Chaka Fattah, who, under the influence of his faith experiences, moved from life on the street corner to being a key legislator in government. This particular congressman has been instrumental in bringing needed funding for education and economic development into his district. He has been a key figure in bringing new businesses into his old neighborhood and has led major efforts in urban renewal. Because of his efforts, several centers to serve the elderly and a variety of health services are now available for the poor. He is a brilliant example of how a faith commitment can change attitudes toward the governing institutions of a society and make these institutions into the kind of "principalities and powers" that are in the service of God for the good of the people.[10]

A right relationship with God affects the way people look at each other. Faith not only gets people to believe in God, but also to believe in each other. Those who become new persons in Christ have a hope in people that the rest of the underclass in its cynicism might find laughable. But without such faith and hope, there is little likelihood that the corporate trust that makes government work will ever exist in those places where it most needs to work.

Of utmost importance, as far as I am concerned, is the changed attitude toward the church that usually accompanies religious conversion. If the socially and economically disinherited give the church a chance, they will find among its people those who are most willing to lend a helping hand.

As has been suggested, church people can often provide the networking systems to help the unemployed find jobs. They also can help by communicating to new converts those traits and values that are essential for effective living within the dominant society. Church people can even provide the kinds of support groups that those who are struggling to escape such self-destructive habits as alcoholism and drug addiction desperately need.

Conversion changes people's attitudes toward the church and enables those raised in the culture of poverty to view working-class and middle-class church members as brothers and sisters in Christ. They discover the miracle that

> There is neither Jew nor Greek, there is neither bond nor free, there is neither male nor female; for ye are all one in Christ Jesus. (Gal. 3:28)

Conversion generates a oneness with people who would otherwise be strangers and connects those who have been victimized by the isolation and estrangement so typical of the underclass to new friends who can help them on their way to socioeconomic achievements.

The Impact of Conversion on Family Life

Perhaps the most noticeable changes coming from the new lifestyle generated by Christian conversion are in the area of the family. To start with, the new life in Christ is marked by living under the guidance and power of the Holy Spirit rather than living "according to the flesh" (Romans 8:4–12). What this means in simple language is that converts are committed to having their behavior determined by what they believe is God's will rather than being governed by their sexual appetites. The sexual promiscuity that too often characterizes those who live within the culture of poverty is countered by Christian commitment. Hence, there will be less likelihood of out-of-wedlock births among the converted and a greater likelihood that sex will be within the context of marriage. The inclination to adultery and divorce will decrease.

Those in the underclass generally give lip service to beliefs in traditional family values and claim to believe in marital fidelity, but in reality, they tend to live with high levels of disregard for these beliefs. Conversion, followed by spiritual nurturing from church friends, changes all that. The new familial lifestyle of converts is such that in the urban ghetto they will tend to stand out as "special" people. Women find that with converted husbands, marriage can be secure and fears about the future of their children can subside. Men who become religiously committed take on a new maturity that encourages sexual and fiscal responsibility to their families. Conversion changes people's character and those changes are delineated by the Apostle Paul.

> Now the works of the flesh are manifest, which are these; Adultery, fortification, uncleanness, lasciviousness, Idolatry, witchcraft, hatred, variance, emulations, wrath, strife, seditions, heresies, Envyings, murders, drunkenness, revelings, and such like: of the which I tell you before, as I have also told you in time past, that they which do such things shall not inherit the kingdom of God. But the fruit of the Spirit is love, joy, peace, long-suffering, gentleness, goodness, faith, Meekness, temperance: against such there is no law. And they that are Christ's have crucified the flesh with the affections and lusts. (Gal. 5:19–24)

What changes the parents obviously affects the ways in which children are reared. Children come to be understood as gifts from God who are deserving of loving sacrifice, rather than as by-products (often unwelcomed by underclass fathers) of sexual gratification. The children of born-again believers are raised to see themselves as loved by a God who has a good and wonderful plan for their lives, and they are encouraged to think about what they will do with their lives. The kind of parental neglect that creates insecurity is dramatically diminished, and children are allowed to *be* children, instead of having to grow up fast.

All of these changes in familial attitudes and behavior put an end to the cycle of underclass people re-creating themselves in their children. Boys and girls are delivered from the probability that they will be nurtured into the culture of poverty that once marked the lives of their parents. The hopelessness, cynicism, listlessness, and absence of purpose that so characterizes the underclass tends to evaporate under the pervasive influence of newfound spirituality. Even the power structure of the family changes under the impact of Christian conversion. Whereas the familial system within the culture of poverty tends to be matriarchal (especially in light of the fact that most of the families within this culture are devoid of responsible fathers), the families created under the influence of a vital Christian faith tend to be of a biparental nature. Actually, the Christian family is likely to exhibit the traits that sociologists usually find in middle-class families. The authoritarianism that typically marks underclass families gives way to more egalitarian relationships. Violence and abuse within the family are no longer readily accepted. Instead, discussion and persuasion become the characteristics of interaction and discipline.

Needless to say, all these changes foster an upwardly mobile lifestyle. The alterations in family lifestyle so reorient and redefine the converts as persons; that they are delivered from the culture of poverty. What is important to note is that without the effects of religious conversion, it is difficult to figure out how these necessary "alterations in consciousness" can be facilitated.

Since the focus of our study is on the socioeconomic consciousness of the urban underclass, it behooves us to consider just how converts alter their behavior in this area of their lives.

Obviously, conversion brings an end to immoral and illegal ways of getting money. The selling of drugs and stealing are out of the question for committed Christians. But even within what is legal, the changes in economic lifestyle fostered by conversion are significant. Being nurtured into Christian living almost always involves assuming a new rationality about economic planning in life.

Impulsive buying, so characteristic of the underclass, is no longer seen as acceptable behavior. It is viewed as poor stewardship of the financial resources that God has placed in our hands.

Impulsive buying is usually a psychological sickness that affects people who have a need to shore up their low self-images by owning certain consumer goods. Products are sold through advertisements that aim at convincing spiritually and psychologically needy buyers that these goods will enhance their status, make them sexually attractive, provide some sense of emotional well-being, and satisfy their souls. Any survey of what is being sold and how it is being sold on TV, especially on The Shopping Channel, will give all the evidence necessary to support this claim. Recognizing that impulsive buying is a problem of the soul, several Christian leaders have created entire ministries to help people out of this economically disastrous spending pattern. There is a growing awareness in the Christian community that impulsive buying is often addictive behavior and as such must be treated as a spiritual problem.

Some other ways in which the economic lifestyles of converts are altered can be found in their declining involvement in pawning and borrowing. The rational budgeting that generally is adopted by maturing Christians makes this typical and costly means of meeting the constant emergency needs for cash less necessary. The culture of poverty generates tendencies for people to be in and out of pawnshops, often resulting in the loss of everything from home furnishings to precious family possessions.

The underclass lives in constant fiscal crisis. Failure to pay credit card bills results in high finance charges and often leads to the loss of credit. Finding themselves in such straits, people have few options and are easy targets for loan sharks. Borrowing at exorbitantly high interest rates out of desperation, they give little thought as to how these debts will be repaid.

After Christian conversion, this kind of destructive behavior tends to wane. The work ethic and the rational budgeting that are promoted by their new Christian lifestyle makes such poor home economics both unnecessary and unacceptable. The religious community frowns on fiscal irresponsibility, and converts quickly pick up that message.

New converts are likely to go off public assistance. I believe that studies will show that religious persons involved in the life of a worshiping community are less likely to be on welfare.[11] In some cases, the message of churches is that being on welfare, unless one is disabled, does not go with living the Christian life. One of the largest churches in my city of Philadelphia puts a great deal of effort into programs designed to get its members off public assistance. This particular church does everything from serving as an employment agency to providing extensive counseling for any of its people who find themselves on public assistance.

The Black Muslim movement views welfare as an instrument of spiritual oppression of African-American people by the white establishment. The leaders of the Black Muslims preach that welfare was created to encourage dependency and a loss of personal dignity among blacks. They claim that African-Americans must learn to be self-sufficient and gain control over their own destinies. There are many outside the Black Muslim movement who share this same appraisal of what welfare does to people.

The major religions of America all promote a work ethic that makes working for a living a virtue. But increasingly, religious leaders recognize the futility of calling people to honest work when few job opportunities are available. In response to urban joblessness, churches across America are becoming involved in economic development efforts. Inner-city pastors know that without jobs their people will be left with the guilt feelings that come from unemployment. They are aware that joblessness quickly moves from being an economic problem to being a spiritual curse.

Fortunately or unfortunately, depending on one's political-economic philosophy, welfare, as we have known it, is coming to an end. Large numbers of underclass people who are presently on welfare will soon be driven off the rolls. The new system, passed into law in 1996, allows healthy, able bodied persons a maximum of two years on welfare in any one period of unemployment. Furthermore, no person who is able to work will be granted more than a total of five years of welfare benefits in his or her lifetime. These changes are going to dramatically impact the poor, and especially the underclass. Conservative estimates suggest that as many as an additional one million children under the age of twelve will be driven below the poverty line. While Marx saw little probability that the *lumpenproletariat* would ever develop a group consciousness and organize for revolution, others, such as Franz Fanon, are not convinced.[12]

Most of those in the underclass are unaware of what the repeal of welfare as they have known it is going to mean to them. They only concern themselves with the everyday affairs of life in their immediate neighborhoods and cannot imagine what awaits them in the not-too-distant future. The impact of the welfare changes will blindside them. But there is still time for churches to make a difference!

The effects that religious conversion can have on the consciousness of the underclass have already been demonstrated. This makes evangelism part of the answer. But something more than just a consciousness change challenging the values of the culture of poverty is needed. Churches must also, as has been suggested, get into job creation. They must step forward to do it because, given the existential situation, they are the only institutions left that have the resources to do what needs to be done.

It will take imagination, heroic restructuring of ministries, new ways of connecting with people, a great deal of networking with private business, new ways of interacting with government, and an incredible amount of commitment from church members. But it can be done! It must be done! And in the next chapter, some direction will be given as to *how* it should be done.

Chapter 13

Job Creation
through Koinonia

In the task of job creation, the church can do things that no other institution can do. Among them is selecting and grouping together those who are ideally suited for owning and running church-based microbusinesses and cottage industries. The church can bring together people from the underclass and mold them into support groups. These groups, in turn, can undergird the long-term unemployed during their difficult transition into the lifestyle of reliable workers. The church can be the catalyst for the formation of small groups able to impart to those who come out of the culture of poverty the confidence and values that make for dependability and effectiveness in the workplace. For the sake of reference, let us call these special groups created under the auspices of the church *koinonia* Bible study groups.

The term *koinonia* has had wide usage in the life of the church. It refers to the unique kind of fellowship which Christians can have based on their shared spiritual experiences and their common commitment to establish caring relationships with one another. It is best described in scripture:

> And all that believed were together, and had all things common; And sold their possessions and goods, and parted them to all men, as every man had need. And they, continuing daily with one accord in the temple, and breaking bread from house to house, did eat their meat with gladness and singleness of heart, Praising God, and having favor with all the people. And the Lord added to the church daily such as should be saved. (Acts 2:44–47)

While measuring up to such a high standard of spiritual intimacy and friendship is unlikely in the normative realities of today's urban society, small groups established by inner-city churches for the underclass unemployed can do much to bring some semblance of this *koinonia* into play. Church leaders can bring people together and help them develop into Christian friends who will help one another to become accountable workers. *Koinonia* Bible study groups make it possible for conversion and faith commitments to positively impact the economic productivity of the group.

Those selected for each group need to be carefully chosen. They should be persons who have demonstrated signs of Christian commitment, show a willingness to be discipled, and appear to be inspired to adopt a responsible family lifestyle. Ideally, they should be Christians who, in their new spiritual commitments, have a strong desire to find out what the Bible says and how its teachings can be applied to their lives.

From the beginning, group members should know that the primary purpose of this Bible study group is to put together a "team" of fellow Christians who will own and run their own business or microindustry. Participants should be aware that creating a sense of spiritual camaraderie is deemed essential for the success of any cooperative entrepreneurial venture, and that the fellowship they can experience in the Bible study group may be the best way of achieving this camaraderie. If the group is to achieve the desired results, there are some guidelines that should be followed.

First of all, when the group meets, the facilitator of the Bible study must make a special effort not to dominate the discussion. When the members come together, it is of crucial importance that they feel free to express themselves. Each person should be encouraged to express the insights that he or she may have gleaned from the scripture under consideration. The facilitator should do nothing more than ask questions. If the facilitator comes across as an expert or some kind of biblical scholar, it will stymie discussion and cause others in the group to become withdrawn. It would be very helpful for the facilitator of the Bible study to receive training in small group process or at least read up on the subject. An excellent guide for developing these *koinonia* groups has been written by Roberta Hestenes. Her book, *Using the Bible in Groups,* is considered one of the very best in the field.[1] It cannot be emphasized enough that the primary purpose of the *koinonia* Bible study is not so much to expand technical knowledge of biblical texts as it is to build a faith community of individuals who will care for and support one another in economic ventures. In this particular Bible study, "the medium is the message." It is what happens to the people involved, and what happens between them, that is of primary importance.

When conducting the discussions at these *koinonia* Bible studies, it would be useful to secure a copy of *The Serendipity Bible,* developed by Lyman Coleman and his associates.[2] This particular study Bible provides a variety of good questions for group discussion. The questions are listed in the margins of each page of the Bible and thus are readily available for consideration while the group is in session. The questions are designed to stimulate the kind of exchanges of thought that build group solidarity—questions that elicit thoughtful consideration from the participants and lead them to reflect on how the scripture applies to their lives.

When it comes to choosing which passages of scripture to study, there are a variety of good options. Personally, I think it is good to start with the gospel of Luke. This is the gospel that I believe best presents Jesus as a helper of the poor and a champion of the oppressed. Luke seems especially suited to making the message of Jesus' "good news for the poor." Group participants will find it easy to identify with the characters in the stories and parables of this book.

In studying the scriptures, it is not essential that every single chapter be covered in order. Genealogies, for instance, are not particularly edifying for group discussion! Furthermore, it is not necessary to move immediately on to a new passage after a particularly meaningful passage has been examined. As long as there are questions to be asked, insights to be explored, and good discussion to be had, stay with a given passage for as many sessions as that passage will carry the group.

The book of Acts is a good place to gain an understanding of what went on in the way of community building in the life of the early church. Comparisons between the kind of camaraderie first-century Christians developed among themselves and what is going on in their *koinonia* group would be meaningful to *koinonia* group members.

The book of James should be studied because this particular epistle addresses the ways Christians should talk about and treat one another. It also has a great deal to say about the role of money in the lives of Christians.

The kind of intensive commitment that can develop among group members through Bible study is exemplified in what happened in a microindustry developed out of a church in Mexico. The men in the group developed a small remanufacturing plant in which they fixed and reconditioned household appliances. They rebuilt and sold everything from toasters to washing machines. What was especially significant was the way in which their reading of 1 Corinthians 12 had led these men into a unique system of ensuring that each showed up at work and fulfilled his responsibilities as a member of their business co-op:

> For as the body is one, and hath many members, and all the members of that one body, being many, are one body: so also is Christ. For by one Spirit are all baptized into one body, whether we be Jews or Gentiles, whether we be bond or free; and have been all made to drink into one Spirit. For the body is not one member, but many. If the foot shall say, Because I am not the hand, I am not of the body; is it therefore not of the body? And if the ear shall say, Because I am not the eye, I am not of the body; is it therefore not of the body? If the whole body were an eye, where were the hearing? If the whole were hearing, where were the smelling? But now hath God set the members every one of them in the body, as it hath pleased him. And if they were all one member, where were the body? But now are they many members, yet but one body. And the eye cannot say unto the hand, I have no need of thee: nor again the head to the feet, I have no need of you. Nay, much more those members of the body, which seem to be more feeble, are necessary: And those members of the body, which we think to be less honorable, upon these we bestow more abundant honor; and our uncomely parts have more abundant comeliness. For our comely parts have no need: but God hath tempered the body together, having given more abundant honor to that part which lacked: That there should be no schism in the body; but that the members should have the same care one for another. And whether one member suffer, all the members suffer with it; or one member be honored, all the members rejoice with it. Now ye are the body of Christ, and members in particular. (1 Cor. 12:12–27)

If a member did not show up on a Monday morning and no word had been received explaining why he failed to show, some radical action was taken. The others closed down the factory and went out looking for him. If they found out that he hadn't showed up for work because of a hangover, you can imagine their reaction. Undoubtedly, they had some tough talk for their wayward brother, but he could not conclude that they were unconcerned about him or that what happened to him was unimportant to them. In a very literal sense, they made sure that they fulfilled the scripture that says that if one member suffers, then all the members suffer. Their rule was that they would keep on looking for the worker who did not show up for work until they found him, because that was what Jesus the Good Shepherd would do.

> What man of you, having a hundred sheep, if he lose one of them, doth not leave the ninety and nine in the wilderness, and go after that which is lost, until he find it? And when he hath found it, he layeth it on this shoulders, rejoicing. And when he cometh home, he calleth together his friends and neighbors, saying unto them, Rejoice with me; for I have found my sheep which was lost. (Luke 15:4–6)

This particular practice of bringing a wayward brother back to work can build a sense of responsibility to others so that he cannot say, "It's none of your business what I do!" What is further notable in this example from Mexico is that the others, while stern, were still prone to be forgiving. They had not only gained some guidance from 1 Corinthians 12, but were also aware of what the Apostle Paul had written:

> Brethren, if a man be overtaken in a fault, ye which are spiritual, restore such a one in the spirit of meekness; considering thyself, lest thou also be tempted. (Gal. 6:1)

Each member was hindered from haughtiness by the message gleaned from this passage that there might be a time in the future when he might need support and restoration from the very person who was then in trouble.

The system developed by these men encouraged them to be responsible coworkers, not because of the threat that they could be fired but because of a sense of obligation to their friends. They realized from their Bible study that not only were they called to be forgiving and to restore any of their group who failed, but that in order to be good partners in the co-op each had to be willing to heed verse 5 of Galatians 6 where Paul writes, "For every man shall bear his own burden." This verse made them aware that individual responsibility was a requisite for discipleship.

The Bible is full of passages that can be applied to the activities of those involved in cottage industries and microbusinesses. For example, there is the passage in Luke where Jesus warns of the danger of not considering the cost of production and ending up as the laughingstock of those cynical bystanders who are always waiting around to ridicule the first sign of failure.

> For which of you, intending to build a tower, sitteth not down first, and counteth the cost, whether he have sufficient to finish it? Lest haply, after he hath laid the foundation, and is not able to finish it, all that behold it begin to mock him, Saying, This man began to build, and was not able to finish. (Luke 14:28–30)

The kind of theological understanding that can evolve in a *koinonia* Bible study group has the ability to transform those who have been socialized into the culture of poverty into risk-taking entrepreneurs with the "stick-to-it-iveness" that makes for success. As a case in point, if the group initiates a business enterprise believing that God has directed them to do so they will be significantly more inclined to make daring decisions. Even if they suffer from those self-defeating feelings of inferiority that usually deter risking limited financial resources in a business venture, they will be willing to "step out in faith" if they believe that God is in their efforts. It is easy to imagine them quoting Romans 8:31 and saying "If God be for us, who can be against us?" or saying to themselves, "I can do all things through Christ which strengtheneth me" (Philippians 4:13). To timid souls who would never dare to do anything as challenging and risky as starting a new business, the words of Jesus, "With God, all things are possible" (Matthew 19:26), can be just the inspiration needed to prod them to try.

If I were able to prescribe the kind of Christianity that would be most advantageous for underclass persons engaged in entrepreneurial ventures to embrace, I suppose I would choose a version that was somewhat Pentecostal or charismatic. The intensive awareness of the presence of the Holy Spirit that is so evident in the talk of those in the Pentecostal tradition seems to be just what those coming out of the culture of poverty need to endure the pressures and trials that go with entrepreneurial activities. Pentecostals have a strong propensity to give a "God spin" to everything that happens. They, of all Christians, are most prone to tell you that they have had a special word from God instructing them to do what they are doing. Furthermore, their charismatic Christianity has an enthusiasm about it that easily translates into energetic efforts.

Just as important as it is in getting a business started is the way in which a *koinonia* Bible study can keep group members *committed* to their venture in the face of adversity. In business, as in most spheres of life, things seldom go as smoothly as planned. Murphy's Law is all too often validated: "If anything can go wrong, it probably will." As a matter of fact, in most business ventures it is easy to conclude that Murphy was an optimist! It is far too easy when the going gets tough for those who have recently been recruited from the underclass to give up. They probably lack the experience that would help to keep them going in the face of major setbacks. But acceptance of defeat becomes less likely if they can give a Pentecostal spin to what is happening. If those in the group believe that it was God who led them to initiate their business, then it will be easy for them to conclude that the things that are happening to frustrate their success are the work of the devil. Giving up or giving in can readily be defined as "letting Satan win a victory over the people of God." It doesn't take much imagination to recognize that this kind of thinking will probably keep the group members going through hard times. The difficulties that they face will be defined as spiritual warfare, and their Pentecostal Christianity will encourage them to struggle against the "demonic forces" that would hinder their efforts. We can almost hear them saying in the midst of adversity:

> What shall we then say to these things? If God be for us, who can be against us? He that spared not his own Son, but delivered him up for us all, how shall he not with him also freely give us all things? (Rom. 8:31–32)

Every true entrepreneur knows that the one secret of success is the capacity to endure failures, bounce back, and keep on trying. The fragile character of those socialized in the culture of poverty lacks this resiliency. Defeat, for them, usually proves to be devastating, and in the face of major setbacks in business ventures, they are very likely to give up. This propensity to quit in the face of failure is something that can be overcome by having a religious perspective of the situation. If members of the group are led to believe that their business troubles originate with Satan and that with God's help, Satan and all he tries to do can be overcome, then their willingness to press on in the midst of adversity will be greatly strengthened.

One of the very important functions of a *koinonia* Bible study group engaged in economic development is the help that it can provide as members try to figure out what to do with money once their entrepreneurial venture starts turning a profit. Those who have lived within the culture of poverty are inclined to impulsive buying, and money earned can quickly disappear. Members of the underclass who suddenly come into money can run through it very quickly and soon be left with nothing. What is even worse is that men and women who have never had anything often use newly acquired wealth in ways that are self-destructive.

It is not uncommon for those who suddenly find themselves with cash in their hands to blow it on things like drugs and alcohol. The *koinonia* Bible study group can help keep such things from happening. The members can help one another to understand money as a trust from God and challenge one another to use it responsibly. Attention should be given during group discussions to issues such as how to make up a family budget and how to employ the profits of production in ways that fit in with a Christian lifestyle. Above all else, those in the group should come to recognize the need for giving. It is very easy for those who were once oppressed to forget where they came from and to get caught up in the consumerism that commonly plagues the middle class. It is all too easy for them to leave behind their needy former neighbors and act as though they have a right to use their hard-earned money selfishly. The belief that prosperity is a responsibility must be grasped. Those who succeed should be led by Christian concern to lend a helping hand to those less fortunate.

A primary responsibility of a *koinonia* Bible study group should be to explore the values of the kingdom of God, especially as those values challenge the egotistic materialism that pervades our society. This limited description of how a *koinonia* Bible study group could impact the lives of its members, significantly improving their probability for economic success, is highly idealized. It might be described as a hypothetical construct that does not yet exist but, like all ideal types, it could exist. However, there *are* many church-based economic development ventures across America in which Bible study and times for prayer are very much a part of the programming. In case after case there is evidence that the effects of group devotions play a crucial role in the success of these business enterprises and significantly contribute to helping the long-term unemployed gain the habits and consciousness that will ensure their reliability as workers.

In Philadelphia, a large Pentecostal church established a store called Second Mile House. The store sells secondhand clothing, household appliances and bric-a-brac—all of which are donated by people from other churches. This entrepreneurial venture not only has created decent-paying jobs for a couple of dozen people but also has become a spiritually nurturing community. Each morning the entire staff gathers for an hour of prayer, worship, and Bible study. It is inspiring to observe the effects of this time of spiritual togetherness. Workers develop deep affection for one another and create a sense of mutual accountability. This translates into responsible behavior as they encourage and counsel one another through difficult times. Their morning devotional hour is highly informal, giving each member an opportunity to share with the others what is in his or her mind and heart. This enables the members to pray for one another and to bear "one another's burdens" (Galatians 6:1–2). In socioeconomic terms, this daily spiritual renewal and Bible study has created a loyalty to the store so that absenteeism and tardiness are rare and employee turnover is almost negligible.

Cross-culturally there is even greater evidence of how small Bible study groups can alter the consciousness of those in the culture of poverty and reorient them into values that make for economic success. This is especially evident in the fallout of recent missionary efforts of the Roman Catholic Church in Latin America.

During the 1930s, the Pope—alarmed by the inroads being made by Protestantism in Central and South America—called on the vital and wealthy churches of North America to send at least 10,000 missionaries to Latin America to reevangelize and strengthen the Catholic ministries there. His challenge was met with a very positive response, especially among the missionary order known as the Maryknolls. However, the area that these missionaries were asked to cover was so vast that they soon found themselves far too spread out to come anywhere near reaching optimum effectiveness. In the face of this dilemma they came up with the strategy of starting what they called "base communities." These base communities were simply gatherings of poor peasants with lay leadership who came together for Bible study and reflection. The theologically trained missionaries would visit these groups from time to time to check up on things and sometimes to perform mass for the members. But for the most part, these lay-led base communities were left on their own to read scriptures and to interpret the meaning of the Bible for their everyday lives.

It wasn't long before the hierarchy of the church learned that it can be a dangerous thing to leave the Bible in the hands of a laity with none but the Holy Spirit to guide their interpretations of its words. The professional clergy quickly realized that these simple untrained peasants were expressing radical theological ideas and perspectives that were disturbing on the one hand, but exciting and inspiring on the other.

Perhaps the most revolutionary belief that emerged from the base communities was that Jesus was on the side of the poor. The downtrodden peasants and the poor who lived in the slum barrios of the Latin American cities always had been led to believe that God was allied with the rich and the powerful. The archbishops were always conspicuously at the sides of the ruling dictators and kings. The church had generally suggested that these rulers, whatever their faults, were ordained to their roles by God and that those who resisted these rulers were setting themselves against God's will. Using Romans 13:1–7, religious leaders had easily legitimated their claims that those who did not submit, even to the injustices of the ruling establishment, were the enemies of God. However, when the poor read the scripture on their own, they soon found a different understanding of God and came up with another interpretation of how God regards the rich and the powerful.

They discovered that, in the historical struggle of the rich and powerful against the poor and oppressed, the God of the scriptures always sided with the poor and oppressed. In the book of Exodus they read how, out of all the peoples of the earth, God chose to identify with an oppressed enslaved people in Egypt. And when these chosen people sought freedom from their oppressive rulers, the God of the Bible fought for them, delivered them, and eventually led them into the Promised Land. They read how, when Israel became an established nation and unjust social arrangements emerged, the biblical God sent prophets to rail against those who lived in luxury at the expense of the exploited poor. They read the prophets like Amos, who wrote:

> . . . I will not turn away the punishment thereof; because they sold the righteous for silver, and the poor for a pair of shoes; That pant after the dust of the earth on the head of the poor, and turn aside the way of the meek . . . (Amos 2:6b–7a)

And they read from the prophet Isaiah, who preached:

> Woe unto them that decree unrighteous decrees, and that write grievousness which they have prescribed. To turn aside the needy from judgment, and to take away the right from the poor of my people, that widows may be their prey, and that they may rob the fatherless! And what will ye do in the day of visitation, and in the desolation which shall come from far? to whom will ye flee for help? and where will ye leave your glory? (Isa. 10:1–3)

Within the New Testament they also found a liberating message. They read how Mary, the mother of Jesus, responded to the Annunciation that she would give birth to the Messiah with the declaration that he would be the deliverer of those who suffered in poverty and powerlessness.

For he that is mighty hath done to me great things; and holy is his name. And his mercy is on them that fear him from generation to generation. He hath showed strength with his arm; he hath scattered the proud in the imagination of their hearts. He hath put down the mighty from their seats, and exalted them of low degree. He hath filled the hungry with good things; and the rich he hath sent empty away. (Luke 1:49–53)

They also discovered that when Mary's baby initiated his ministry, he declared good news for the poor by declaring a "jubilee." The jubilee was the "acceptable year of our Lord" described in Leviticus 25:1–17, wherein the oppressed were promised deliverance and the poor were promised that their needs would be met.[3]

The Spirit of the Lord is upon me, because he hath anointed me to preach the gospel to the poor; he hath sent me to heal the brokenhearted, to preach deliverance to the captives, and recovering of sight to the blind, to set at liberty them that are bruised, To preach the acceptable year of the Lord. (Luke 4:18–19)

As they read the book of Revelation, those in these base communities recognized that the political economic system that had frustrated their aspirations for dignity and well-being was designated in this book as that evil empire called Babylon. Furthermore, they came to believe that God was at work in them creating a new society called "The New Jerusalem," where the values of the Kingdom of God would be realized.[4]

These readings of scripture gave the underclass members of the base communities new definitions of who they were and what their place was in the world. Through their reflections on the Bible, these poor people gained a sense of calling to resist the social forces that had frustrated their aspirations for a life wherein their basic needs and the needs of their families would be met.

Kenneth Sharpe, in his book, *Peasant Politics,* gives a comprehensive account of how a base community in the Dominican Republic became the means for freeing some poor coffee growers from economic exploitation.[5] Coming together in prayerful fellowship, these peasant farmers found in their mutuality the spiritual fortitude to break away from the middleman coffee buyers who were paying them unjustly. Together they formed a co-op that got their coffee beans to market in the port city and sold them at a fair price. This co-op also established its own store, which enabled the coffee growers to buy the hardware, food, and clothing they needed at reasonable rates. Previously, they had had to pay inflated prices at the only store in town, owned by the town "godfather." The co-op also established a kind of credit union so that members could get short-term loans without having to pay loan-shark interest rates to this "godfather."

This case study traces the ways in which their base community enabled those peasant farmers to pursue economic justice as a Christian obligation. Through their discussions of biblical truths (for example, Isaiah 65), they came to realize that it was a divine calling to create a village where workers got to enjoy the fruit of their labors, everyone had decent housing, and everyone was fed.

> For, behold, I create new heavens and a new earth: and the former shall not be remembered, nor come into mind. But be ye glad and rejoice for ever in that which I create: for, behold, I create Jerusalem a rejoicing, and her people a joy. And I will rejoice in Jerusalem, and joy in my people; and the voice of weeping shall be no more heard in her, nor the voice of crying. There shall be no more thence an infant of days, nor an old man that hath not filled his days; for the child shall die a hundred years old; but the sinner being a hundred years old shall be accursed. And they shall build houses, and inhabit them; and they shall plant vineyards, and eat the fruit of them. They shall not build, and another inhabit; they shall not plant, and another eat: for as the days of a tree are the days of my people, and mine elect shall long enjoy the work of their hands. They shall not labor in vain, nor bring forth for trouble; for they are the seed of the blessed of the Lord, and their offspring with them. And it shall come to pass, that before they call, I will answer; and while they are yet speaking, I will hear. The wolf and the lamb shall feed together, and the lion shall eat straw like the bullock: and dust shall be the serpent's meat. They shall not hurt nor destroy in all my holy mountain, saith the Lord. (Isa. 65:17–25)

Sharpe also chronicles how the interactions of those in this base community encouraged members to develop as persons. Those who previously had been afraid to speak before a group gained the courage to do so. Peasant farmers who had never thought their opinions were worth anything came to recognize that what they had to say did have worth. It can be said that through the sharing of their ideas and convictions in the base community, they gained some of the dignity and sense of self-determination that fosters being human.

The missionaries who had encouraged the creation of the base communities were soon humbled by what they were hearing from underclass people. They were amazed at the new insights and implications for social life that these theologically untrained men and women were gaining from the scriptures. The missionaries looked on as people, many of them illiterate, gathered around lanterns in wooden huts and heard the Bible read to them. They listened as these onetime listless creatures of the culture of poverty talked in depth about what the scriptures meant to them. Gradually the missionaries learned anew what the Apostle Paul had tried to teach the church:

> Because the foolishness of God is wiser than men; and the weakness of God is stronger than men. For ye see your calling, brethren, how that not many wise men after the flesh, not many mighty, not many noble, are called: But God hath chosen the foolish things of the world to confound the wise; and God hath chosen the weak things of the world to confound the things which are mighty; (1 Cor. 1:25–27)

What the missionaries realized as they listened to those in the base communities gradually led to a new way of doing theology. In the past, they had tended to look to scholars for interpretations of scripture. They had assumed that those who knew Hebrew and Greek and could read the scriptures in their original languages had the best handle on the truth. They had taken it for granted that theologians were the authorities when trying to figure out what to believe. But what happened in the base communities challenged all of that. The missionaries began to ask questions:

- "Can it be that God's truth does not come down to us from those scribes and scholars whom the world calls wise and that, instead, comes up to us from those lowly people whom the world calls foolish?"
- "Can it be that God has chosen to make wise those whom the world calls 'nothing' while reducing to irrelevancy the knowledge of the world's *intelligentsia?*"
- "Can it be that the words of Paul are to be taken literally in 1 Corinthians 1, and that only those who are humble enough to learn from the poor and oppressed can know the things of God?"

If the answer to each question is "Yes!" then we are all going to have to do a great deal of readjusting. What the Maryknoll missionaries had to do when confronted with what was coming out of base communities in Latin America is what we all are going to have to learn how to do. It is what any of us who want to do economic development with the under-class in North America are going to have to do.

We, who are used to leading, must learn to become humbly still when we are part of a *koinonia* Bible study group. We are going to have to learn to listen to what God is trying to say to us through these brothers and sisters whom we have all too often considered socially and intellectually beneath us. Our know-it-all attitudes have to be abandoned, and our desire to be in control will have to be set aside. Our earned degrees will not make us authorities in this new arrangement, and the prestige of our past experiences will count for nothing. We, the onetime masters, will have to learn to be servants, while those whom we once considered to be servants become our masters (Matthew 19:30).

In the kingdom of God, that's the way things are, and given what we want to see happen in the way of urban economic development among the underclass, it is time for us all to learn how to be kingdom people. Only by adopting this biblically prescribed posture for ourselves will we be able to treat those from the culture of poverty with respect and recognize in them the dignity that they deserve.

In the end, we may find that these *koinonia* Bible study groups change not only the consciousness of those we thought we were trying to help, but our own consciousness as well. We may find, to our surprise, that the fellowship of believers that we thought was going to be the salvation of those unfortunate underclass types proves to be *our* salvation as well. Maybe we will discover that, in the end, those *koinonia* Bible study groups that we hoped would transform brothers and sisters from the culture of poverty into reliable workers with a work ethic will transform *us* into true Christians. It just may be that in trying to meet the needs of the underclass poor, our own need for the truth of God will be met.

Chapter 14

The Churches
and Urban Education

The church has got to do something about education. All across
America schools are failing, but the city schools are failing most of
all. In high schools located in urban ghettos, it is not uncommon for more
than 50 percent of the students to drop out, and many of those who do
graduate do so as functional illiterates. In many instances, the schools do
not even pretend to educate their students. They simply pass them from
one grade to the next whether or not they have mastered what should
have been learned.

It is appalling to prospective employers to find out how many high
school graduates applying for jobs lack basic literacy skills and how many
of them would be hard put to compose a legible letter. Everybody from
the U.S. President to concerned parents knows that something has to be
done, but mustering the collective will to effectively address the problem
is easier said than done.

The neglect of urban education is permitted mostly because of the
negative attitudes toward public schools that pervade our society, and
those negative attitudes are generated by a variety of groups that support
the status quo for their own reasons. One group that has increasingly
turned its back on the educational needs of our society, and especially on
the educational needs of the poor, are the elderly. When confronted with
referendums for increasing the financing of schools, senior citizens tend
to vote against them. When evaluating candidates for office, they invari-
ably want to know if potential office-holders support using more tax dollars for education or for programs that will reap benefits for them. Having

already raised *their* children, older people too often feel as though they have no vested interest in voting for increased expenditures for education. It is not unfair to say that a streak of selfishness evidences itself in their voting patterns. They are not anxious to see their often fixed incomes nibbled away by the ever higher taxes that the would-be reformers of urban education demand.

Part of the negativism older people have toward requests for increased spending on education lies simply in their failure to understand that the world has changed in ways that make increased spending for education necessary. Having grown up before the advent of computers, it is easy to see why senior citizens often fail to understand why it is essential for children to have the expensive technology required to make them computer literate and to connect them to the information highway. In many instances they point out that kids, especially in urban schools, can't even read, write, or do basic arithmetic. "Why," they ask, "should we be spending so much money on all this hardware and software when the children being targeted for these computer skills are functionally illiterate?" Nor do older people understand why so much money has to be spent on hiring additional teachers in order to have small classes and provide more individualized attention for students. When *they* went to school, most classes were composed of thirty-five to forty students, and these relatively large classes did not seem to have any negative influence on the learning ability of the students.

There is some truth in these judgments made by the elderly. Studies have indicated that even when more money is spent on education, there is nowhere near the kind of improvement in learning that is promised by those who demand increased funding. Throwing money at education has not generated the kind of results that those who requested more spending have expected and promised.

One of the most common gripes of senior citizens is that the additional tax dollars spent for schools do not really go toward educating kids anyway. Instead, they claim, it is being swallowed up in bloated school administrative bureaucracies. Who can deny that there *is* an increasing and disproportionate number of special consultants, vice principals, educational specialists, and school counselors who have been brought on board in most public school systems? Checking out how school budgets have changed over the past few decades will readily prove that administrative costs *are* taking an ever increasing piece of the financial pie while the portion of those budgets being spent on actual instruction is diminishing.

On the other hand, the existential situations facing educators today are vastly different than they were fifty years ago. More than half of all schoolchildren have mothers who are employed outside the home, and school officials and teachers find themselves without the kind of home support system that was formerly available. Many of the children who come from families where there is no stay-at-home parent have difficulties that those from the older generation find hard to grasp. Add to this the fact that 30 to 40 percent of children in America today are being reared in single-parent homes. In many urban schools, that figure is as high as 95 percent. When schools have to handle kids who come to them emotionally scarred because parents are separated or divorced, the problems are legion.

Sometimes the parents of underclass urban kids give only lip service to education and really don't care about whether or not their children go to school. These children feel no strong encouragement to attend school and often are not all that convinced that working hard at school will do them much good. The net result is a nonchalance about school attendance. One school day, while driving through one of the government housing projects where EAPE/Kingdomworks has some of its ministries, I spotted a youngster who was in one of our programs. I yelled after him, "Yo! Why aren't you in school?"

He answered, " Hey man! I went to school yesterday!"

The idea that one ought to go to school regularly was foreign to him as it is to all too many children and teenagers who live in disadvantaged urban neighborhoods. In one of the most rundown high schools in Philadelphia, more than a third of all the students enrolled do not even show up on a given day. The principal of the school told me that if they did all come on the same day, there would not be enough desks to hold them. The school had at least two hundred fewer desks than it had pupils! Such helter-skelter attendance makes a good education nearly impossible.

Senior citizens are often unsympathetic to pleas for extra help for underclass city children because they blame the victims of parental neglect for what is not their fault. Sometimes the elderly simply contend that they can't be expected to put up their hard-earned dollars to compensate for what parents have failed to provide.

Television is a dramatically negative influence on schoolchildren that the older generation finds difficult to comprehend. With some studies pointing out that children are watching television from four to six hours a day and showing that in certain urban neighborhoods that figure can go as high as eight hours a day, there is little question that television is wreaking havoc on the educational process. Few of us have even begun to understand how the *content* of these shows, so filled with violence and illicit sex, is impacting the lives of schoolkids. But even if the content of television shows were not warping the minds of the young, it is more than clear that the sheer amount of time devoted to watching television makes getting homework done very difficult. Furthermore, Neil Postman, in his book, *Amusing Ourselves to Death,* clearly demonstrates that the intensity and style of television shows make it difficult for teachers in classrooms to seem interesting by comparison.[1] How can a teacher come across as entertaining after kids have been nurtured by the fun and excitement of *Sesame Street*? An alphabet written on a blackboard is not in the same league as letters that sing and dance under the direction of Big Bird, Bert, Elmo, and Ernie.

There are those who argue that teachers are just going to have to adapt to television and use it as an aid to teaching, rather than trying to compete with it. But the truth is that those would-be educational shows usually make teachers look dull in contrast because they avoid the boring parts of learning. Whether anybody wants to admit it or not, some things like multiplication tables or square roots of numbers are boring to learn but nevertheless, are necessary to memorize. Television makes all of learning seem like a blast and a half, leaving the hardest part of education to struggling teachers. If you don't think that this is problematic, think again.

As old-fashioned as this might sound, the only way that kids are going to do better in school is for them to watch less television. And when it comes to kids in poor urban settings, this isn't likely to happen. Even spending the extra money that can provide some help for teachers who have to compete with TV probably will not resolve this problem.

Some senior citizens sternly say, "Parents just ought to turn off those television sets!" But it is not as easy as that in a youth culture where ignorance about what is on television can have horrendous social consequences for youngsters. Furthermore, look who's talking! The studies on the elderly point out that they are even more hooked on television than the kids are.

One more thing that ought to be considered when the elderly think about the high cost of educating children in the inner-city is that schools, especially urban schools in bad neighborhoods, have become dangerous places to teach. Once teachers listed such things as talking in class, failing to stand in a straight line, and chewing gum as the most serious problems that they had with children. Nowadays, urban teachers are concerned about their students carrying weapons to school and fear things like bodily assault and rape. Extra pay is required to get teachers to work in such hostile environments.

To give you an idea of how bad things can get, consider a letter that was sent to the pastor of my home church from some students at neighboring Sayre Junior High School:

> *Dear Pastor Campbell,*
>   *Things are bad here at Sayre. There are metal detectors at all the doors and police patrolling the halls. But that does not keep students from bringing weapons to school. There are so many fights in the lunchroom that a lot of students do not even want to go to lunch. People so misbehave in class that nobody can learn. Most of the good teachers have left because they do not want to be here anymore. Can you and your church help us?*
>
> *Sincerely yours,*
> *Concerned Students*

Racism

Racism is also a factor impacting what happens in America's schools. White suburbanites give evidence that they are not convinced that African-American children have the intellectual capacities to learn, regardless of how much money is spent on their education. They gain support for this prejudice from books such as *The Bell Curve* by Richard J. Herrstein and Charles Murray.[2] This is not the place to critique this book, nor is it the place to try to explain what the book was really all about. Murray claims that he in no way wanted to make the case that African-Americans are inferior intellectually, but his claim is not really important in light of the impact of his book. I believe that most of those who purchased this long and statistically laden tome probably never really read it anyway, but what people *thought* it said has been painfully disastrous with respect to public opinion about African-American students. The popular interpretation of what these authors have said is that our social problems, and especially our school problems, are caused by people who are low in intelligence, and that IQ tests show that African-Americans are disproportionately represented among those with low intelligence. Prejudiced people who are already convinced that African-Americans have less brain power than other races can now readily cite *The Bell Curve* to support their claims. People who think this way conclude that spending a great deal of money on trying to educate urban African-Americans is a waste. In my mind, there is little doubt that this kind of thinking heavily influences people as they consider whether or not society should invest more money in city schools.

The emerging African-American youth subculture hasn't helped to counter such prejudicial thinking. In urban schools across the country, African-American young people have fostered the opinion that studying and getting good grades is a "white thing." Often, when African-American kids work hard and get good grades, they feel they must conceal their accomplishments from their peers lest they be called Oreos and be accused of acting white. A very bright young man in one of our EAPE ministries told me that he actually had his teacher issue a phony report card each marking period so that he could maintain acceptance with other African-American teenagers in his neighborhood, while the teacher recorded the outstanding grades he had actually earned on his official records.

Adding to the myth of their intellectual inferiority is the role that sports has played in the African-American community. While subconsciously yielding intellectual superiority to whites, African-American young people make sports their thing. In almost any black neighborhood, you will find young men playing hoops morning, noon, and night. Given all the time that they spend playing the game, it is not surprising that African-Americans dominate both college and pro basketball. I recall former Philadelphia 76ers player Julius Erving once saying that it's hard to figure out if African Americans do so well in the sport because they have some innate superiority when it comes to playing basketball, or if it is because they practice at the game so much.

Now there is government funding to put lights on their asphalt inner-city courts so that inner-city kids can play hoops all night long.

White racists have always been willing to grant physical superiority to African-Americans as long as the flip side of that designation was that intellectual superiority would be ascribed to them. What goes on in the African-American subculture, both in school and in play, subtly lends credence to that arrangement. Given this kind of thinking about African-Americans, it is easy to figure out that huge expenditures for the schools in their communities are considered a waste by racists.

The Liberal Menace to City Schools

The liberal establishment has provided fuel for the fire. Through groups like the ACLU, restraints have been placed on teachers and administrators that have made it difficult for them to maintain a learning environment in their schools. It has become almost impossible to expel students, regardless of how unruly or disruptive they become. Students' rights have been defined in a way that makes it hard for teachers to maintain discipline. In many urban schools, teachers simply have given up trying.

The ACLU's almost fanatical crusade against allowing any expression of religion in the public school system has all but crippled the ability of educators to communicate moral values to their students, in spite of the fact that society in general is expecting the schools to solve an increasing number of moral problems. Schools are being asked to provide sex education that will reverse the rising trends of premarital sexual intercourse and pregnancies. Yet they are expected to do this without any reference to religiously legitimated concepts of right and wrong. Educators are being asked to mold the consciousness of the young so that they will become honest citizens who are respectful of the dignity of others. And they are supposed to do this without any reference to a God who establishes the infinite value of persons and requires truthfulness in all of our dealings.

In place of moral education, the liberal establishment has promoted a curriculum called "values clarification." With values-clarification techniques, teachers are supposed to help students articulate their own personal perspectives on right and wrong, without any suggestion that those perspectives might be in error. Moral relativism reigns supreme in the process, and a neo-religion of secular humanism increasingly has become the undergirding ideology for public education.

Supporting this moral relativism is the emphasis on multiculturalism, that has become a dominant buzzword among contemporary urban educators. There are many loud voices in the liberal community that suggest that to have all ethnic groups conform to and learn in a single language and culture is tyranny. It seldom occurs to those liberal minds that their emphasis on multiculturalism, with its assumption that we give equal respect to the values of every ethnic society, runs counter to their own beliefs about human equality. How can they call for children to highly respect some Muslim cultures that define women in ways that are oppressive and still hold to their own feminist convictions? And how can children be taught to believe that we ought never to judge negatively the values of another culture when certain cultures support the idea that people of other races are inferior? Nevertheless, our educators are expected to give credence to such apparent contradictions in the name of "openness."[3]

I remember with amazement conservative journalist William F. Buckley being interviewed on Mike Douglas's show and asked why he couldn't respect the opinions of those who didn't agree with his religious beliefs. Buckley answered that he was quite willing and even felt obligated to respect the *personhood* of others, but firmly stated that he could find no basis for respecting those opinions that his own religious convictions led him to believe were wrong. Mike Douglas, ever the embodiment of the popular mind, did not seem to be able to figure out the obvious reasonableness of Buckley's position.

According to Yale legal scholar Stephen Carter, the moral morass in which our public schools now find themselves is due in part to a mistaken interpretation of the Bill of Rights.[4] According to Carter, the courts have tended to confuse freedom *of* religion with freedom *from* religion. He contends that the framers of the Constitution never intended for religion to be excluded from the public domain but rather intended only that no *one* religion be legitimated officially in public institutions.

If our schools are to be saved, and if they are going to serve as a means for creating the kinds of citizens who can live together in a just and moral society, we must find ways to educate children to the core values of our society that come out of the Judeo-Christian tradition. We must figure out how to do this without violating the principle of separation of church and state. There must be room for God in our public schools. In the words of the Russian novelist Fyodor Dostoevsky, "If there is no God, then anything is permissible." And not just *any* God will do when it comes to creating the kind of society that most Americans deem desirable.

The Conservative Menace

Having attacked the liberal establishment, let me equally offend the conservative political establishment, especially as it is represented in my own evangelical community. This sector of the American society has done more than its share of harm to public education in general, and to urban schools in particular. For example, in the most ludicrous stance of all, politically right leaning Christians have either remained silent or lent support to the National Rifle Association, even when the NRA has opposed President Clinton's efforts to ban guns from public schools. If any group has misconstrued the constitutional right to bear arms, it has to be the NRA with its idea that the federal government should not be allowed to restrain the carrying of weapons to school. But conservative groups like the Christian Coalition have lent little support to the president's efforts to disarm schoolchildren and have become cozy, uncritical supporters of the NRA's agenda.

The most troubling action that politically conservative Evangelicals have taken has been to remove their children from the public school system. And the impact of this has been felt most severely in urban schools. Many Christian parents, for good reason, have removed their children from public schools in the city because they see them both as threatening to the well-being of their children and as failing to provide quality education. All across America, sectarian parochial schools are being created as alternatives to the public school system. In addition to that, there are many Evangelicals who are opting to homeschool their children instead of letting them remain in public schools.

Most Evangelicals who are pulling their children out of public schools are aware that they are disengaging those very children who might provide a leavening Christian influence in those schools. These parents are aware also that, as they seek alternatives to public education, they themselves tend to be cut off from involvement in what goes on in those schools where most American children receive significant nurturing and socialization. But these parents justifiably point out that, until the public schools can be straightened out, they should not be expected to sacrifice the well-being and the future of their own children for the sake of the public good. Furthermore, they believe that public schools are not as neutral about religion as they claim to be. In many instances, these parents claim that the public schools are actually anti-Christian. They make the case that some of what goes on in sex education classes does not seem to denote neutrality. When Planned Parenthood enables schools to make condoms available to students, these parents are outraged.

To many Evangelicals, the refusal of public educators even to consider creationism as an alternative to biological evolution seems an unjustifiable secular humanist bias. And, in the face of not being able to have their own faith mentioned, the willingness of the public schools to teach about other religions, such as the beliefs of Native Americans, seems to them to be highly unfair. Christian radio talk show hosts add to this discontent by constantly bombarding their listeners with the idea that public school teachers are secular humanists, in spite of the reality that most of these teachers are regular churchgoers and many even consider themselves born-again Christians. Consequently, many Evangelical parents declare that until public schools abandon their prejudice against Christian convictions, they will not risk their children in public classrooms.

On top of all of their criticisms of public education, or perhaps because of them, conservatives regularly call for what many consider to be severe limitations on spending for public schools. The usual rhetoric against taxes that is so characteristic of conservative spokespersons seems especially threatening to those who are struggling to make the public schools work. This is particularly upsetting at a time when the number of students in American public schools is increasing in dramatic fashion. Richard Riley, the secretary of education, points out that, unless we immediately invest more for education, our classrooms will be overcrowded beyond the limits that *any* teachers can be expected to handle. Add to this the fact that the physical plants of most urban schools are falling apart and will require significant repairs if they are going to be useable in years to come.

Not only is there a reluctance on the part of conservatives to invest more money in public education, but there is also a strong commitment on their part to promote school vouchers. If vouchers for public education become legal, critics of vouchers say there would be even less money available to run our public schools. Compounding this problem is the fear that the use of vouchers would lead to the public schools having a disproportionately large share of society's problem students. This could prove to be especially difficult for city schools. The private schools would have the right of selection and rejection, and it is unlikely that they would keep incorrigible students enrolled. If such problem students were to be shut out of the private schools, they would, in all likelihood, be dumped into the public schools, which by law would be forced to take them. With such increased burdens and with disproportionately fewer tax dollars to spend, the voucher system championed by conservatives would, in the view of its critics, lead to a crisis in urban public schools.

What Is to Be Done
About All of This?

The crisis in urban education provides a crucial opportunity for the church to step forward and assume its calling for servant ministry. There are so many things that can be done by churches that it is hard to know just where to begin. First, and perhaps most obviously, the church is in a good position to provide tutoring help for city kids. And the good news is that, when it comes to tutoring urban children, the response of the church has been encouraging. In many urban churches, after-school programs have already been created, and they are reaching large numbers of children with fairly good results. Children who get these tutoring services usually show marked improvement in their grades, probably more the result of the caring attention they receive rather than because of the quality of the tutoring. These tutoring programs are providing good opportunities for lay people in the churches to use their gifts in this vital ministry. Retired people, especially, are finding that they are wanted and needed in tutoring programs. Elderly suburbanites, who used to drive into the city only to attend Sunday morning worship, are now finding that after-school tutoring programs are giving them a meaningful way to reach out through their churches to people in the immediate neighborhood.

What makes tutoring programs so user-friendly for churches is that no special training is needed to prepare most church members for the task. Their life experiences, coupled with their basic educational background, makes them adept at tutoring. However, I am aware that this may change as the use of computers in education becomes more prevalent. It may be that in the future tutors will have to have some kind of computer knowledge to tutor city children.

How to Set Up a Tutoring Program

There are a variety of models that can be employed in developing an after-school tutoring program. In the work of EAPE/Kingdomworks, we have tried most of them, and we know the strengths and weaknesses of each. Here are our suggestions for implementing several differently structured tutoring programs:

1. Set up your tutoring program to meet once a week. Choose an afternoon for younger children. For those in their teen years, an evening is usually better. Tutors should commit themselves to being there faithfully each week at the appointed time. Each week, time should be spent going over with each student what happened in school during the past week, finding out how the student fared in tests and assignments, and just talking with each student to see if he or she has any special problems. Then, help should be given with future assignments and, when necessary, to prepare the students for upcoming tests. A given tutor cannot handle more than three students at the time. This model is the easiest kind

of program to staff because most potential volunteers do not think it is unreasonable to give a few hours one day a week to help needy urban kids.

2. Using the same model as above but having the sessions twice a week is even better, for obvious reasons. The effectiveness of the tutoring and the level of accomplishment of the students are greatly enhanced by having sessions more than once a week. The problem with this model is that it is much more difficult to get volunteers for more than one day a week for tutoring. Getting one volunteer for one day and another volunteer for the other day won't work because it is the student's personal attachment to the tutor that encourages him or her to work hard. It is most important to have only one "significant other" playing the role of tutor.

3. Hold the sessions four or five days a week. This is great if it can be done, but the time required of tutors is more than most volunteers can be expected to give. A paid staff is almost a necessity for such a program.

4. Use a combination of the above. It is possible to have a team of the same people keep a daily program going for all the children being tutored and at the same time have volunteers who come in and help out once a week by giving individual attention to especially needy children. On a designated day, a given child leaves the group session conducted by the staff people who are involved on a daily basis and is tutored in a personal manner by a volunteer who works only with that child.

EAPE/Kingdomworks has been able to implement the fourth option cited above because we have many college-aged young people who commit a year of their lives for urban missionary work. We have made involvement in after-school tutoring programs part of their service responsibility. As the Mission Year program which we are now promoting picks up momentum, more and more urban churches will have teams of workers who can provide a *daily* program of this kind.

Recruiting volunteers and keeping them faithful to their responsibilities requires a good bit of work. Here are some important guidelines: First of all, ask them to volunteer only for one school year. A common problem that surfaces when churches recruit volunteers is that the would-be recruits are seldom given the exact length of the tenure of their service. People often are afraid to volunteer because they get the sense that once they take the job, they will be expected to stay with it until their health fails, they move away, or die. What happens in most churches is that volunteers end up with a permanent assignment, be it serving as sponsors of youth groups or teaching Sunday School classes, until they burn out. And burning out is what many of them do. Then these beaten-up servants of God slink away from their ministries feeling a sense of failure and defeat. When a specific and relatively short tenure is prescribed, everything changes. If a volunteer sees a specific end date in sight, he or she is much more willing to stick it out through the hard times (and there will be hard times).

When the term of service is ended, there ought to be a recognition dinner given to send volunteers off with their flags flying. If they want to volunteer again, that's fine, but the important thing is to make sure that the volunteer does not fear that he or she will be permanently trapped in a job.

Second, there must be a very careful job description that outlines some reasonable and specific goals. If the volunteer does not know exactly what is expected and which achievements mark success, he or she will be unable to evaluate what is accomplished by the end of the term of service. It is important that the goals be realistic. Few things prove more discouraging than living under the weight of expectations so high that even spectacular achievements seem like failures.

Constantly check with volunteers, weekly if possible, to see to it that they have everything they need to do their work. Make sure that proper teaching materials and supplies are available. Check to see if any volunteers are finding their children especially difficult to handle. Some of the boys and girls who enter these programs come out of very dysfunctional families and from very troubled backgrounds. It is not unusual for a particular child to be in need of psychological help that a typical lay worker cannot provide. Those who supervise volunteers must be ready to rescue them from those situations that prove impossible for them to handle.

Encourage the volunteers to get to know the families of the children they tutor. If possible, house calls should be made. It is important if volunteers go to visit the home of a student that they take at least one other person along, not only because it's biblical (Matthew 10), but because it is a good way to prevent trouble and to ensure safety.

Both during home visits and as a part of the tutoring process, volunteers should make it a habit to regularly share their faith and to call both children and parents to make commitments to Christ. If volunteers don't use the relationships being established through the tutoring program for evangelistic purposes, they are missing out on a golden opportunity to win people to Christ.

Tutoring should be done in the church building because it is important that a link between the program and the church be established. Eventually, efforts need to be made to get both the children and their families into the life of the church, where they can be nurtured in the faith.

Above all, make sure that the volunteers understand the importance of being faithful for their tutoring sessions. I have seen children cry with disappointment because their tutors did not show up on the appointed day. For many of these children, the volunteer tutor may be the source of the only tender concern they receive all week. The children get attached to their tutors, and any failure of the volunteers to keep their promised appointments can have painful consequences for the children.

Some comments must be made about using college students as volunteers for tutoring programs. As part of his program on volunteerism, President Clinton has provided financial incentives for colleges to involve their students in after-school tutoring programs. In addition, there will probably be legislation passed that will provide the collegians with some remuneration for tutoring. I have a concern about all of this, because if funds are forthcoming from the government, it is likely that programs may have religious content removed and evangelism excluded. What is also likely is that the tutors assigned to work in churches may not themselves be Christians. Given these realities, I think that churches ought to be leery about such arrangements with college and university students. Evangelism must be at the core of all that churches do in carrying out their mission in the world. Working for spiritual change in the lives of the children and the families involved in the tutoring program is too important for the church to readily abandon this part of its ministry.

On the other hand, it is better to have a secularized tutoring program for the children of a neighborhood than no program at all. If churches cannot get their own people to volunteer, then accepting help through the president's program may be the only way left. If such is the case, we are faced with a sad necessity that speaks volumes about our inability to motivate people with a sense of mission.

It should be noted that many Christian colleges and universities have long been involved in tutoring programs without any help or encouragement from the government. These Christian schools of higher education have deployed their students as tutors out of a sense of biblically prescribed obligation to the less privileged. Their willingness to send college students into the cities also comes from a knowledge that this kind of involvement with urban boys and girls can be an important learning experience for many ivory tower students. My own college has been a pioneer in this sort of ministry. Thirty years ago we had students from Eastern College going into both Philadelphia and Trenton to help inner-city kids improve their reading skills. These tutoring programs at Eastern proved to be a model that other colleges have replicated. It can properly be said that Eastern College students set the example that started the whole movement to get collegians involved in tutorial service.

A recent development in some urban church tutoring programs using college students concerns me greatly. Over the past few years, certain Christian colleges and universities have begun giving academic credit for community service, and the students who tutor often do so as part of their course requirement. At Eastern College, all students have to be involved in community service during their first semester at school.

I believe that required tutoring or a reward system for tutoring has a very negative impact on the tutors. Whether the reward for service is financial remuneration, as with President Clinton's plan, or grades, as with the service programs at schools such as Eastern, the negative effect is the same. Service that was once rendered out of a sense of caring and for the joy that comes from helping others is transformed into something that is done in order to get some kind of a payoff. When the volunteers served out of altruistic motives, it seemed as though no sacrifice was too great to ask of them. They went over and above the call of duty, often visiting the youngsters they tutored on weekends and even, in many cases, having them come out to stay overnight in the college dormitories. But now things are quite different. Too often, college students who come to tutor will ask how many hours of tutoring they have to put in to meet course requirements or how many times they can miss and still get credit for the course. Sometimes they even grumble about why the time they spend getting to and from the work is not counted toward their community service requirement. The children being tutored deserve better than that.

I used to have to work hard to get recruits for tutoring by appealing to my students' sense of Christian obligation. Now students simply come to the task of tutoring because it is part of the curriculum leading to graduation.

Another concern I have is that Christian colleges like Eastern not exploit children in their efforts to "broaden" their students through involvement in urban ministry. Children in the city ought not to be used to enhance the educational experiences of collegians, who then abandon these children when assigned hours for academic credit requirements are fulfilled. So far as I am concerned, I would as soon these collegians not tutor at all as to have them come with such negative attitudes. I still invite students from Eastern to tutor in EAPE's urban ministry programs, but now I will take only those who have already completed their community service requirements and volunteer out of concern for the children they will tutor.

Of all the sources for tutors, there is one that proves vastly superior to all others: the parents of the boys and girls we are trying to help! These parents often are deeply concerned over the academic progress, or lack of it, of their children and are more than willing to do what they can to help. If the church recruits such caring parents, the results can be spectacular. Studies indicate that volunteers who tutor students help the students improve their grades more because of the interest and commitment that they show than because they are skilled teachers. However, other studies show that, as significant as the improvement that comes from the concern of volunteers may be, there is even greater improvement when the tutors are the parents of the children involved in the program. Getting parents to serve in a church-based tutoring program can result in dramatic academic improvement, and it is also a brilliant way for the church to become involved in the lives of the parents.

Even when parents have only limited education and are themselves in need of tutoring, they still can be outstanding tutors for their children. Studies show that as parents learn right along with their children, there is a bonding effect between them and that the children learn faster and with more enjoyment. Another side effect is that having a parent teach his or her own child along with some other children from the neighborhood enhances the stature of that parent in the child's eyes and builds respect for the parent. Furthermore, it is easy to see how relationships developed in the training sessions for tutors can get these parents involved in the full life of the church.

Chapter 15

The Church in a Servant
Ministry to Public Schools

It is very common for Christians to allude to the command of Christ for us to assume the role of servants. If we are to follow Jesus, it is good for us to remember his words.

> But so shall it not be among you: but whosoever will be great among you, shall be your minister: And whosoever of you will be the chiefest, shall be servant of all. For even the Son of man came not to be ministered unto, but to minister, and to give his life a ransom for many. (Mark 10:43–45)

Now it is time for the church to live out this biblical directive in relationship with the public school system. It is time for us to ask about ways that we in the church can help those in charge of the schools to get their job done.

In Philadelphia, John White Sr., a deacon in my home church, Mt. Carmel Baptist, is working out of the mayor's office to develop a unique program that holds much promise as a way for the church to help public schools. It is called the Adopt-a-School program. He is asking that churches in the city each adopt a specific school. These churches commit themselves to being in touch with the principals of their respective adopted schools and to explore ways that their people can be of help. Some of the churches are providing their schools with supplies, such as drawing paper, crayons, and in a few cases, computers. With recent cutbacks in government spending, some schools had been without many of these basic supplies, but now the churches are making them available.

191

Several churches are supplying volunteers to serve as teacher's aids. Teaching in urban school can be so exhausting that the teachers not only enjoy having help in their classrooms but absolutely require some relief help in order to survive.

Perhaps the most significant thing that is being done by the churches in this Adopt-a-School program is their effort to help build up the Parent-Teacher Associations in the schools. Making telephone calls to promote attendance, providing transportation for parents who have no means of getting to PTA meetings safely, and working with the leaders of the PTA groups to help develop good meetings have given these associations new life. Once again, it is being discovered that the surest way to improve urban schools is to get the parents involved, and these churches are working hard to make that happen through building up the PTA programs in these schools.

There is no way that I can overemphasize the importance of developing strong participation by parents in PTA activities. If any church in the city wants to know what it can do to improve the schools in its neighborhood, this is the place to start. By cooperating with school officials to promote and support the school's PTA program, a church will make its most significant contribution. And among all the benefits that are likely to be forthcoming from this effort, one thing is certain: The church will be sending a loud and clear message that it is a church committed to the welfare of the children in the neighborhood.

Churches cannot give up on public education. In a multiethnic, religiously pluralistic society, it is essential for different kinds of people to come together and learn to live peacefully with one another. Neighbors must learn to understand one another and to respect one another's cultural traditions. One of the best ways to help this happen is for children from various backgrounds to come together and interact in the classroom. It was this hope of creating a society of people who have unity in spite of their diversities that was the prime motivating factor in giving birth to public education in the first place. Now more than ever, the public schools need to be viewed as one of the best instruments available to foster the kind of mutual understanding between peoples that is so basic to the survival of our cities. For the sake of unity, the churches must commit themselves to saving public schools. Their calling to a servant ministry in their neighborhoods requires no less of them.

In the midst of all the good things that they can provide for public schools, church people must not neglect being involved in the politics of education. Churches should be organized to participate in school board meetings and to give serious attention to those who are being elected to serve on school boards. They need to sponsor "candidate nights" to make sure that those who will determine school policies are grilled on issues that are of crucial significance.

The Church and Sex Education

Basic education for neighborhood children should be a primary concern of church people. But too often all that educators and politicians ever hear from church people, and especially from Evangelicals, is an array of concerns about sex education. So frequently do we initiate hot discussions over sex education that school board members groan when they see us coming. When we come to their meetings, they see trouble. This is not to suggest that the issue of sex education should not be of great concern to parents. But, in a pluralistic society, Christians should not expect the public school system to teach their religiously based values and approved sexual lifestyles. Instead, we need to be looking for ways to do sex education that will satisfy most people and relieve the school system of a burden that it often finds extremely heavy to carry.

One way to do this is for churches to become involved in sex education through such efforts as "released-time" programs. It is both legal and proper for the religious institutions in a community to petition the school system to set aside a particular afternoon for sex education purposes. On that designated day, the children can be dismissed from school early and bused to their respective churches to receive instruction on this emotionally tense and religiously laden subject. With each church doing its own education on sexual matters or with several churches of similar values and theologies about sex working together to sponsor a unified program, it is possible to see to it that sex is interpreted for children in ways that are harmonious with the religious traditions of their parents.

Synagogues and mosques can set up similar arrangements for their children. Secular humanists can have their own programs, and some may choose to just let their children stay in a school-run program that teaches sex without overlaying the subject with sectarian values. Such a variety of options would allow parents to see to it that children learn about sex in a manner that is in accord with their own personal convictions. Furthermore, school officials probably would give a sigh of relief to be delivered from the responsibility and the difficulties of trying to come up with a sex education program that is acceptable to all the special interest groups in the community.

Setting up an effective released-time program for sex education will take a great deal of time and effort on the part of church leaders, but it will probably be time and effort well invested. If the churches in a given urban neighborhood are going to do anything to try to curtail the increasing rate of premarital pregnancies among schoolkids, then getting involved in sex education is a good place to start. I believe that the biblical requisites for sexual behavior *must* be communicated to students. Young people *must* be given a God-ordained sense of what is right and wrong. And just as important, they *must* understand how sex is related to love and commitment. These matters can be addressed properly only within a religious value system, and we cannot expect public schools to present that system for us. Premarital sex among teenagers has become one of the major problems of our times, and it is certainly one of the most serious problems of inner-city schools. The churches cannot remain out of the picture when it comes to this urgent concern. With children begetting children, something has to be done to help youngsters to understand what God intended sex to be all about. Only a spiritually prescribed understanding of sexual morality has any chance of keeping future generations of young people from wandering into a sexual wilderness that threatens personal destruction. It is time for churches to accept this challenge, and I believe that through released-time programs we have one of the best ways to do it.

If we resolve the sex education controversy, it will be easier for church people to get together with the rest of the community and to deal with other politically charged concerns. The school board should be able to look to the churches for support when the need for additional funding is discussed. Those who are responsible for public education ought to know that churches are with them when they have to deal with incidents of racial prejudice in the schools. If public schools are to be saved and if the needs of the young are going to be met, then public educators must be able to count on church people to be their partners.

In the midst of the many positive things that churches can do, they need to encourage their people to stop putting down public school teachers. Recently, public school teachers have been lumped together by some of our most famous preachers as "secular humanists." Too often those on "Christian" radio describe public school teachers as close to being agents of the demonic, and this is simply not true.

Most public school teachers find themselves struggling against almost insurmountable odds to help urban kids into a decent life, and the last thing they need is condemnation from Christians. We should be praying for them and supporting them in every way possible. As a matter of fact, it would be a good thing for every inner-city church to give a recognition banquet once a year to show appreciation to the teachers in their local schools for their sacrificial service. Furthermore, churches should be encouraging their young people to view teaching in difficult urban schools as a missionary opportunity.

While there are laws that prevent the overt communication of the Christian faith in the context of the public educational system, there is ample evidence that Christian teachers can have a great impact on urban schools just by living out the love of Jesus. St. Francis of Assisi once said, "We should always declare the gospel—and sometimes we should use words."

There may be constraints on the words that teachers can use in public schools, but there are certainly no constraints on loving and caring for emotionally needy students in the love of Christ. There are laws that require separation of church and state, but there is nothing that can separate students from the love of Christ coming through spiritually committed teachers. The love of Christ can be communicated even within classrooms that are defined as part of the secular domain.

To those who accept a calling to teach in the public schools of America's cities, there is something more that must be said. The government doesn't tell you what to do on your own time. After school hours when you are not on the public payroll, you are very free to talk to students, visit in their homes, and even invite them to church. Instead of complaining about what you can't do as public school teachers, you should be taking advantage of what you can do—especially after school hours are over. Loving care for students during class time can earn teachers a lot of positive emotional capital, which can be drawn on when the school day is over. Yet even as I encourage this, I am concerned that the law, as it is now written, may prevent what some would consider to be the unfair exploitation of the goodwill and stature teachers have with their students.

Once I was conducting evangelistic services in a small city in Kentucky. The meetings, which we held at a high school football stadium, were well attended, especially by the young people of the city. One night during this series of meetings a teacher showed up with about twenty of his students. When I gave the invitation to accept Christ, more than half of his students came forward to the altar for prayer. Afterwards I talked with that teacher and asked him how he had been able to invite his students to attend evangelistic meetings, given the limitations placed on him by the constitutional requirements prescribed by the doctrine of the separation of church and state. The teacher exclaimed, "Oh! I didn't invite these young men to attend these meetings during school hours. I called all of them on the phone last night and invited them. I'm their football coach and we've become good friends over the past few years so they accepted my invitation as a favor to me. I would never have invited them during school hours. That would be against the law!"

What that football coach did may have been legal, but it does raise some serious questions:

- Did a player who really did not want to hear the gospel find himself in a situation where he felt that not showing up for the evangelistic services would diminish his chances for being in the starting lineup?
- What if a player belonged to another religion or came from an agnostic background? Was he unfairly influenced to give Christianity a chance?
- Because some players would do anything for a coach they loved, was it unfair for that coach to use his influence to get them to go to the meeting?

There are a lot of existential questions that must be raised, because none of us wants to see unfair coercion or influence exerted on children and teenagers.

Teachers in the public schools *can* be "the leaven" that Jesus called us to be (Luke 13:20–21). They can make a gigantic difference in the lives of countless inner-city kids if they are willing to go beyond the call of duty. We should be encouraging urban school teachers to put in the extra time and effort that reaching kids for Christ "after hours" requires, but we must also ask them to be guided by a sense of fairness in addition to obeying the law.

Requiring Good Teaching

Even as we support public school teachers, we must hold them accountable to ensure that they do a good job of teaching. There are too many incompetent teachers in our urban school systems. Often they are there because school officials have a difficult time recruiting good teachers and in the rush to fill every vacancy, they may settle for inferior candidates. Administrators who are doing the hiring may have to work extra hard to secure effective teachers, but we must not let them settle for anything less.

Another reason why there are incompetent teachers in the public school system is because the teacher's unions protect them and will not let those in school administration remove them from the classrooms. Even when there is ample evidence that some teachers are obvious detriments to the well-being of their students, too often unions seem to feel obligated to keep these incompetents employed. There was an instance at my alma mater, West Philadelphia High School, that exemplifies how a teacher's union can prove irresponsible when it comes to protecting the jobs of its members. A white teacher in this almost completely African-American school not only did a horrendous job at teaching history, but regularly offended his students by making racial slurs. Sometimes he interpreted history in such a way as to champion the racial superiority of whites. Parents complained and demanded that this teacher be fired, but the teacher's union stood behind him, even though there was ample evidence proving his incompetence.

Marches and demonstrations organized by church leaders finally caused action to be taken. The city school board eventually transferred this teacher to another high school in a predominantly white neighborhood. This helped the students at West Philadelphia High and it also defused what had become a volatile situation, but it can be argued that this teacher should not have been transferred to another school. He should have been fired! Furthermore, the students in that predominantly white school did not need a racist teacher to lend support to some of their own latent racism. This man's career as a teacher should have ended, but the teacher's union wouldn't let that happen.

Churches must find ways to stand up to any teacher's union that does something like that. They need to express their concerns and to demand justice for the children in their neighborhoods. They must see to it that every effort is made to ensure a quality education for all of those in the public school system.

A major step toward ensuring quality education in the public sector can be taken by requiring competency tests. Nobody should be allowed to teach who lacks the basic skills and knowledge required in the classroom. Once again, the teacher's unions prove to be a major obstacle to what is just and necessary. These unions have, over the years, opposed competency tests, and for good reason. When testing has been tried, the results have been embarrassing for many teachers.

A few years ago in one urban school district, a trial testing system was employed. But no sooner was it initiated than the teacher's union stepped in and threatened a strike if the testing continued. The reason for doing so was that so many teachers were showing an inability to read on a tenth-grade level and to do math on a sixth-grade level. The teacher's union did not want word about this to get out. This is the kind of situation where the churches of that city should have organized and stood up to the teacher's union and demanded that the testing be continued.

Recently, the National Education Association has realized that the American public is not going to put up with incompetence in teachers and that some kind of testing system for teachers must be implemented. Knowing that there is no avoiding it, the NEA at its 1997 convention discussed establishing its own testing system, thus keeping the whole evaluation process in house. It remains to be seen what will come out of all this, but some standardized nationwide testing system must be put in place if we are to have decent city schools.

Testing Students

One other concern that demands our immediate attention is the matter of creating a standardized testing system for students. The Department of Education in Washington is pressing for an arrangement whereby at the end of each school year every student will be tested to see whether the learning requirements for that student's grade level have been met. In too many instances, students in our urban schools are promoted with decent grades when they have not mastered the academic material that those grades suggest. It is not enough to get urban kids to stay in school. We must make sure that they are making progress in their studies. Only a standard national testing system can ensure that this happens. Furthermore, there must be special federal funding available to provide remedial help when testing shows it is needed to improve the test scores of students in poor school systems.

Achieving such goals for schools will be extremely difficult, not only because the people in Washington are in a budget-slashing mode, but also because education is a political minefield. Both Democrats and Republicans are so anxious that the other party not get the credit for improving the schools, that each party can be counted on to block the progressive legislation of the other.

Church people cannot tolerate political gridlock on this matter. The urgency of the situation requires that something be done. I believe that churches should lead a grass-roots movement to bring about the necessary changes in urban education. Putting pressure on local school boards, speaking out at PTA meetings, and holding forums on education all can be used to exert pressure on elected officials to establish a national testing system.

National testing has become a political football that is kicked around by those in Congress. Conservatives argue that more controls from the federal government are to be avoided. They want local school boards, and not the federal government, to establish testing standards. On the other hand, liberals who believe that a national testing standard should be established say that only through a national testing system can there be any assurance that high school graduates are uniformly prepared for life.

I appreciate the views of conservatives and share their concerns about increased bureaucracy in education. However, the unevenness in the educational experiences of children across the nation leaves little doubt in my mind that unified expectations and standards that are binding for all students in all schools need to be established.

The Church and Alternative Education

When it comes to churches starting their own schools, those in public education get nervous, and rightly so. Public educators not only are afraid of losing some of their best students and most supportive parents to alternative education, but also fear losing much of their funding. The situation has become especially serious for them with the advent of faith-based crusades to secure government-funded vouchers. If vouchers are legalized, and they probably will be, public educators fear a mass exodus of the children of many of the most concerned parents from the public school system. With many parents viewing city schools not only as ineffective but, in many instances, as unsafe, it would not be surprising if this does happen.

At the same time, there is growing support for vouchers in the African-American community. Whereas urban African-American parents once saw vouchers only as a means for others to take money away from their urban schools, they increasingly see them as a viable solution to the problems of education. A recent survey shows that more than half of the urban black community now favors vouchers. More and more African-Americans are beginning to see vouchers as a means to exercise greater choice for their children.

For vouchers to really make private education available for poor and working-class families in the city, they would have to be worth at least $3,000 per child. That may not seem like much when compared to the

$8,000 per year that it takes to educate a child in the public school system, but private schools require less money to educate a child than do public schools, primarily because teachers' salaries generally are lower and administrative costs are significantly less. Also, public schools have more costly sports programs and bear the high expenses of special education programs. At $3,000 a year per child, vouchers would provide the kind of funding that parochial schools need to adequately function, and there is no doubt that vouchers in this amount would prove to be an incentive to start a host of new church-sponsored schools.

One argument made by many who favor vouchers is that they would create competition between private and public schools, which would force the public schools to shape up and make necessary improvements and corrections that they presently seem reluctant to make. That may be a valid argument, but I am still worried that vouchers might significantly damage the public school system rather than help it and that the victims of the damage will be the poor kids in urban ghettos.

Schools for Those Who Are Falling Between the Cracks

There is one kind of private school that public education might welcome as a partner. This is the kind of school that our own missionary organization, EAPE/Kingdomworks, has initiated in West Philadelphia. About a decade ago, we came up with the idea of starting a school that would target "at-risk" children who come from truly disadvantaged backgrounds. Through our extensive ministries in the government housing projects of the city, we had become aware that there were many children in those housing units who were falling between the cracks. The public school system did not seem to be able to meet their needs. These children required more than just training in the basic three R's—they needed special attention. These were children whose home life lacked the kind of moral training and character building that is necessary to function in an orderly social situation. We believed that the kind of socialization and alteration of personality that these children needed could best be gained in the context of a school that promoted biblical values and a spiritually inspired change of character.

It was in response to such needs that EAPE/Kingdomworks created Cornerstone Christian Academy, a school especially designed for those children from the projects who, for the most part, came from single-parent families on welfare. Many of these children were proving too difficult for the public schools to handle. Given the kind of children we were trying to reach, public school administrators in the neighborhood of Southwest Philadelphia, where Cornerstone Christian Academy is located, welcomed our efforts.

Today, Cornerstone Christian Academy serves more than 350 children in kindergarten through eighth grade. No longer are all our students "at risk" children, but the effects of a *Christian* education on each child is obvious.

In addition to a quality faculty composed of mostly African-American teachers recruited from the Philadelphia area, a dozen missionary interns work at the school. These interns are young people recruited from across the country who have committed a year of their lives to working with inner-city children. They serve as teacher's aids and do visitation evangelism with the families of the children in addition to running after-school tutoring programs for children in the neighborhood who are not enrolled in Cornerstone Christian Academy. These interns play an essential role in the overall success of the program. They are sacrificial young people who serve without pay and raise the funding for their room, board, and health insurance from friends, relatives, and supporters in their home churches.

A primary source for raising the money to maintain our school consists of church people outside the neighborhood who see this urban Christian school as a missionary opportunity. We have been able to recruit hundreds of people from across the country to make monthly contributions of $25 per month to support CCA. Most of these supporters have been challenged to give through messages I have preached in their churches. In my sermons I often work in stories of the needs of children who live in government housing projects, and I call on those in the congregations to commit themselves to giving so that we might be able to reach out to those children. The response has been generous.

I am well aware that this method of raising financial support cannot be ongoing. CCA will not always have a spokesperson who has access to various pulpits where pleas for help can be made. Right now, we are making plans to get the teachers involved in fund-raising, tapping into their church friends and relatives for support. We also are working hard to secure funding from foundations interested in alternative education. Another important step has been to secure Valerie Black as Head of School. She is an effective speaker and has been able to promote CCA by preaching in local churches and making presentations at service clubs.

There is little doubt that coming up with the funding for a school like Cornerstone Christian Academy is a major challenge. We want to keep tuition at a very low level in order to make the school available to poor families, and we also have to maintain a significant scholarship fund for children whose families have no means at all to pay tuition. Ironically, if the vouchers I fear will harm the public school system become legalized and available in the state of Pennsylvania, the funding problems of CCA will be largely solved.

The Camden Forward Academy

A unique approach to faith-based alternative urban education has been initiated by Urban Promise, the ministry that EAPE/Kingdomworks started in Camden. We recognized that most teenagers enrolled at Camden High School were failing to get the kind of education that would prepare them for life. A significant majority of these students were dropping out before graduation, and many of those who stayed in school did so in such a half-hearted fashion that they often missed classes. These young people learned so little that even those who managed to graduate were lacking in basic skills.

During the 1997–98 school year, Urban Promise took the bold step of pulling ten students out of Camden High to become part of what we named "Forward Academy." During the previous school year, these young people had missed school more than half of the scheduled days and were, for the most part, earning "D" and "F" grades. They seemed doomed to failure, not only in academics, but in life.

We divided these students into two groups of five and assigned each group to a person who homeschooled them at our ministry center. Utilizing homeschooling materials that have been used by hundreds of thousands of parents who wanted to keep their children out of public schools, our two relatively inexperienced teachers provided personalized education.

The curriculum we employed, developed by Christian Liberty Academy in Illinois, is so easy to use that untrained teachers who follow instructions can do an excellent job in directing the learning process. Christian values and doctrine are integrated into the prescribed lessons, so that the students not only cover the required subject matter but also are taught what is at the core of the Gospel. This homeschooling program provides testing and an outside independent grading system so that we know whether or not our students are measuring up to the levels of expectation required by the state board of education.

Since the students were in small groups, it was easy to transport them to various cultural events and museums in both Camden and Philadelphia. Regular day trips broadened the educational experiences of these teenagers beyond anything that they would have had at Camden High School.

After one year, the test results gave evidence of success. Students who had been absent from school more days than they were present in previous years now had almost perfect attendance for both semesters. Actually, *only one student missed even one day of school!* When I asked these young people why they attended so faithfully, one of them replied, "They notice if I'm absent and call my home to see why I'm not in school. They really care about me being here."

The academic achievements of these young people have been even more amazing. There were students who had started the year reading on a fifth-grade level and ended the year reading on a tenth-grade level. Improvements in math test scores were just as remarkable.

There is no doubt that these teenagers are getting the kind of education that every youngster needs. The size of our programs has tripled. As word has gotten around Camden, parents have lined up to get their children enrolled in Forward Academy, so there is now an extensive waiting list. Many caring parents have found hope after long despairing that their children would ever have a decent future.

I very much appreciate the simplicity of this Camden program. There is no need to develop a new curriculum. The way we are operating, ordinary people without any special training can be the teachers, and the cost is only about $600 per student per year. It seems to me that programs like Forward Academy could be instituted in urban communities across the country. Retired persons could be volunteer teachers. Suburbanites who have the time and desire to do something about the crisis in urban education could become involved.

There is ample evidence that we are on to something here that could revolutionize the way in which church people address the crisis in urban education.

Urban Promise has established this program for students in *secondary* education because we know that it is in secondary education that specialized Christian education is most needed. Studies show that children from schools in relatively affluent suburbs and those from schools in much poorer urban communities perform at just about the same level up until about sixth grade. Their capabilities in basic learning skills are quite comparable. It is during the last half of their years of schooling that the differences between kids in suburban schools and those in urban schools become pronounced. After the sixth grade, the learning rate of urban youngsters goes into sharp decline. This is why our Urban Promise program concentrates on teenagers at the junior high and senior high levels. We want to help them just at that point where they are most prone to lose interest in school and give up on the whole academic process.

I am sure that there are other innovative ways by which the church can significantly contribute to rescuing urban education. As a case in point, there are even now attempts by churches to start up charter schools. These are small *secular* schools created by community people as alternatives to regular public schools. Charter schools are fully funded by the state, but those who create them are responsible for management and staffing. One of the advantages of charter schools is that they can offer small congenial classes to students who find the huge urban schools too difficult to handle. Also, in charter schools, it is more possible to keep the quality of education high and to see that disruptive students are not ignored.

Because charter schools are state funded, those who teach in them cannot make religious content part of their instruction of children. But there is evidence that charter schools are providing good education. Churches that are not able to get into the hassle and expense of parochial education ought to consider participating in the organization of charter schools by offering their buildings as places where classes can be held.

Regardless of whether or not urban churches start their own programs, one thing is certain: Urban churches cannot act as though the schooling of children and teenagers is not their concern. Responsible ministry requires that churches see to it that those in the next generation get the necessary education not only to become viable and employable citizens in tomorrow's cities, but also to have every opportunity to become the fully realized human beings that God wills for them to be.

Chapter 16

What the Church
Can Do about Crime

It is obvious to anyone studying American cities that crime is an over-arching problem. The streets of our cities can be dangerous places to be—even in the daytime. Carjacking has become common, and druggies burglarizing homes have terrorized people in places like Camden into putting bars on their windows.

As commonplace as crime has become, the *perception* of what is happening in urban America is even worse than the reality. *Fear of crime* exceeds what is actually warranted. Television shows as well as the evening news programs make it seem as though muggings and murders take place more frequently than they actually do. The evening newscasters exacerbate things by making crime stories the main substance of their broadcasts. Rumor mills in urban neighborhoods spread exaggerations and lies about what is going on. Consequently, interviews with city dwellers reveal that they believe their streets are becoming more dangerous daily, even though statistics indicate that between 1992 and 1998 there has been a dramatic decline in urban crime. For instance, New York City registered a lower level of violent crime in 1997 than in 1977, and there is substantial reason to believe that there will be an even further decline in the incidence of violent crimes during the next few years.

But the statistics declaring the cities as increasingly safe do not cut it with most people, because as W. I. Thomas, the famous University of Chicago sociologist, once declared, "If things are real in the imagination, they are real in their consequences." In spite of statistics that confirm how much safer city streets are today than they were a couple of decades

205

ago, people are more afraid than ever of being assaulted when they venture out at night.

What is especially disturbing is that the number of African-American males who are arrested and put in jail for urban crimes is disproportionately higher than the number of African-American males in the general population. I use the qualifying phrase *arrested and put in jail* because there is a great deal of white-collar criminality that does not show up in crime statistics.[1] For instance, white-collar criminals, who are usually Caucasian corporate executives, are not punished in the same ways as are blue-collar criminals. The executives of cigarette companies are not likely to be designated as felons by the judicial system even though they cause more damage to the public good than do the peddlers of marijuana on city street corners. The latter rather than the former are the ones who most often end up behind bars. Those in the ruling elite of the corporate community are able to see to it that the sorts of criminal acts that they are likely to commit are not labeled as crimes. Thus, the white corporate executives of the tobacco industry are not labeled by lawmakers as drug pushers—even though that is what they are. We criminalize those who commit crimes in "low-class" fashion. Those who are regarded as "common" criminals are those who commit crimes using methods employed by the lower class (for example, using a gun to rob a gas station is low class, while embezzling money at a bank is upper class). Since blacks are disproportionately represented among the poor, it is therefore not surprising to find that they are disproportionately represented among those who end up behind bars or are under the surveillance of the courts. What is surprising, however, is just how disproportionately they are represented. At present, close to 35 percent of all black males between the ages of 15 and 25 are either in prison or on probation because there is no room for them in America's overcrowded jails. According to studies done by criminologists at Princeton University, we can expect the proportion of African-American males convicted of major crimes to increase to 50 percent by the year 2010.[2] Since African-Americans are more and more concentrated in our cities, their criminality has come to be seen as an urban problem.

The reasons for this unusually high incidence of crime among America's inner-city African-American males is more than just the result of class biases in reporting crime. There are other factors to be considered. Cornel West, one of the foremost sociologists studying African-American young people, believes that a major factor is the nihilistic cultural mindset that now pervades the thinking of African-American teenagers.[3] West believes this nihilism arises because these young people live in a society that has deceived them into believing that consumer goods will give them ultimate fulfillment in life. They lack legitimate ways to secure these things, yet they are constantly bombarded by the media with everything from cars to stereos and told that they *must* possess these material things to be fully actualized human beings with positive self-identities. African-American teenagers, who watch television more hours per day than does any other cohort in our society, learn that to be "real" men or "real" women, they must be able to buy certain carefully designated items. They are told that they must drive certain kinds of cars, wear the correct commercially prescribed clothes, and possess a whole array of other advertised accessories. Our consumeristic society has convinced these young people that, in order to be worthy of respect or perceived as sexually attractive, they must go out and buy what they are told to buy. Since these teenagers lack the financial means to do that—and are well aware that they also lack the skills and opportunities that could make earning that kind of money possible—they frequently just give up on the idea of using socially legitimate means to acquire what the system has made them believe they must have. It should not surprise us, says West, that when legal means to secure what they have been duped into believing they have to have are denied them, such frustrated teenagers resort to illegal means as a way to get what they want. The boys who kill another kid just to steal his hundred-dollar Nike basketball shoes are understandable if we can realize how the ads on television have convinced them that possessing such shoes is of ultimate importance in the grand scheme of their lives. There *are* reasons why these teenagers don't care if they live or die in the pursuit of things they view as necessities.

West is only reiterating in the concrete existential world of African-American teenagers what Robert Merton, one of America's foremost social theorists, stated decades ago in his famous essay, *Social Structure and Anomie.* Merton's belief is that when a society imbues its people with strongly prescribed goals but denies some of its people any socially legitimate means for reaching these goals, then those thus denied will often resort to *illegitimate* means to do what they believe they must do.[4] According to West, the poor male African-American teenagers caught up in our consumeristic society are prime examples of Merton's theory. African-American youth believe that they have no worth as human beings unless they possess those things advertised by the media. They are, therefore, willing to risk their own lives and show little regard for the lives of others in their seemingly irrational pursuit of getting those things in criminal ways.

Conservatives, who are reluctant to see anything wrong with capitalism and the consumer culture that it spawns, generally cite other causes for the rising incidence of crime in urban America. They blame the public school system and the secular humanism that they believe to be rampant in today's public educational philosophy.

Since the 1950s, we have asked the public school system to do more and more in the way of teaching our children morals and values. This used to be the job of the family, but we have turned to the schools as many of the families of America have disintegrated to the point where they are unable or unwilling to fulfill this responsibility. Social conservatives point out that at the same time that the schools were being called on to teach morals and values, the courts were pressuring them into removing any references to God or religion from their curriculum. It doesn't take a rocket scientist to figure out the extreme difficulty of teaching concepts of right and wrong without any religious means for legitimating the standards for moral behavior. When kids ask why something is right or wrong, it is difficult to make the case for morality without being able to say, "Thus saith the Lord!"

Today, there is little room for religion in America's schools. In place of religion, educators have turned to humanistic psychology as a means of providing legitimating values without having to make reference to God or violating court directives regarding the separation of church and state.[5] Utilizing the insights of such proponents of humanistic psychology as Abraham Maslow,[6] these educators have defined self-actualized human beings as persons who have all the virtues of the Christian personality but no connection at all to the Christ who defines these virtues for us and who creates them within us.

A primary means for fostering humanistic values and helping schoolkids to become "good" human beings is to help each child gain a positive self-concept. Educators believe that if schoolchildren can be convinced that they are bright, capable, and good, such thinking can prove to be a self-fulfilling prophecy. Those with positive self-concepts will *become* good because those children will be convinced that they *are* good. They will become successful human beings because they believe in themselves and are convinced that they can be anything they want to be.

All of this sounds good, but the pragmatic evidence is that it isn't working too well. While such a philosophy provides excellent material for motivational talks, the reality is quite different. Those without the talent needed for the kind of achievements that society honors will fail and grow angry at society in the face of their own failure. Such anger among disappointed teenagers can easily translate into destructive behavior.

It is all good and well for some enthusiastic motivational speaker to shout out to flagging students, "You can be anything you want to be if you want it bad enough." But the reality is that there are many kids who just don't have what it takes to achieve the socially prescribed prestigious positions that most socially disinherited inner-city kids have been taught they have a right to hold. What is worse is that those who promote this philosophy and its simplistic formula for success encourage high school kids to settle for nothing less than the realization of their highest dreams and visions.

The results of all this are obvious. Teenagers who fail in their academic studies are sometimes ready to beat up their teachers. In their minds these teachers have put them down by giving them poor grades. The students have been brainwashed into believing that anybody who tells them in any way that they are less than terrific is evil and must be dealt with. Teachers who give them bad grades (regardless of the fact that those grades may be well deserved) must not be tolerated. Consequently, it should come as no surprise that schools have become places where the lives of teachers are in danger and where police officers have to patrol the halls. A school system that is too much into affirming every student's self-concept regardless of his or her achievements should expect violent reactions to occur whenever a student has to be dealt with in a way that might be perceived as self-depreciating.

Another consequence of this emphasis on self-pride—which is so much a part of the ideology being fed to urban youth—is that young people are unwilling to settle for anything that might be considered menial employment. McDonald's offers good opportunities for those who are willing to take entry-level jobs. However, by the time the proponents of humanistic psychology with their messages of self-aggrandizement finish with inner-city kids, many of them view such entry-level jobs as being beneath them. They pass them up in the expectation of getting the more prestigious positions that they believe they deserve. The Bible says that no one should think more highly of himself or herself than he or she ought to think (Romans 12:3). But such sound advice is thrown to the winds by the proponents of that particular brand of humanistic philosophy, which teaches that everybody is special and deserving of the very best that society has to offer, regardless of talent or the amount of effort spent in preparation. It should come as no surprise that disappointed and frustrated urban youth who have been sold this bill of goods, but have never had the education to be all that they could be, should turn out to be a dangerous lot.

Let us not, however, overdo the criticism of what is going on in city schools. Perhaps the greatest cause of criminality in urban America is the judicial/penal system. That may sound strange, but most criminologists are convinced that it is true. Jails have become schools for crime, and if delinquent teenagers are not hardened criminals when they go into prison, there are strong expectations that they will be hardened criminals by the time they come out. This is made blatantly clear in Irving Goffman's book, *Asylums.*[7]

Goffman claims that prisons are "total institutions." These are institutions that strip individuals of any previous identities that they might have possessed and resocialize them into new personalities that "belong" in their new institutional settings. In the case of prisons, those who go through the penal system are resocialized into persons who define and understand themselves as criminals and who learn to act in accord with their new socially prescribed roles. The result, says Goffman, is that the overwhelming proportion of those who are released from prison are soon back behind bars. He contends that in prison these people are socialized into defining themselves as criminals and therefore it is not surprising that they behave accordingly almost immediately upon being let out of jail.

There is general agreement among most sociologists that the penal system just is not working and that we have to find a better way of dealing with those who break the law. I concur! But what my academic colleagues sometimes fail to accept is that we can find an effective alternative to this system in the Bible. I believe that the scriptures do provide us with a truly effective rehabilitative system for those who are guilty of crimes. What is suggested as the biblical prescription for rehabilitating those who commit crimes is not an unrealistic proposal that would work only in some ancient Middle-Eastern societal system. Quite to the contrary—I believe that the biblical directives for dealing with criminals may offer the best and only means we can find to alleviate the pressures of crime in urban America.

The primary error in our present system of dealing with criminals is the fact that so often we demand retribution. America wants criminals to pay for what they do. We want the courts to exact an "eye for an eye and a tooth for a tooth." The Bible tells us that vengeance belongs to the Lord (Romans 12:19), but when those we love are hurt by crime, especially if the perpetrator takes the life of someone we hold dear, we want to exact vengeance.

Coupled with our desire for retribution is our hope that severe punishment will act as a deterrent to committing future crimes either by the one deemed guilty or by others who witness what happens to those who violate the law. What many of us fail to recognize about this approach to dealing with criminals is that it generally fails to deliver what we hope it will. Punishment just does not provide as much of a deterrent to crime as we want to believe that it does. Sociological studies verify this; as does history.[8]

In pre-modern London there was rash of pickpocketing, so the authorities decided to hang anyone found guilty of this crime. They fully believed that hangings would be a deterrent to pickpocketing.

To say that this failed is an understatement. Not only did pickpocketing continue, but the pickpockets found that they could do their best work at the hangings of other pickpockets. With spectators transfixed on the criminal dropping through the trap door, they were not likely to feel their wallets being lifted!

Capital punishment is unlikely to deliver the emotional satisfaction craved by those who have lost a loved one in a capital crime. Vengeance is never as sweet as people suppose it will be. In a way, it actually cheapens the lives of those who have been murder victims to suggest that things can be evened up by taking the life of the murderer. It becomes painfully obvious that the worth of the lost loved one cannot be equated to the death of the one being punished.

Capital punishment is also questionable in the minds of many Christians because it appears to be contrary to the way that Jesus would have us react to crime. Without going any further than the Beatitudes, I have to believe that only those who are willing to show some mercy are deserving of mercy (Matthew 5:7).

It is not just capital punishment that does not work. Our present penal system doesn't seem to deter any kind of crime or rehabilitate any kind of criminal. When we look at the statistics on repeat offenders, we quickly learn that putting criminals in jail does just about nothing to deter them from future criminal activity. As any student of our present prison system will tell you, the overwhelming proportion of those incarcerated end up back behind bars shortly after being released. Retribution just doesn't work in bringing about the desired result of decreasing crime.

The Bible offers us another system of dealing with criminals that I am convinced provides us with some hope of solving the urban crime problem. The four things sought in the biblical model for dealing with crime are:

1. Restitution
2. Repentance

3. Reconciliation

4. Restoration

In Bible times, the first thing required of a guilty party was that restitution be made to compensate the victim of the crime. Most Sunday School kids know the story of Jesus and Zaccheus (Luke 19). In that story, when Zaccheus, in response to Jesus' love, repents of cheating people, he immediately wants to make restitution to those from whom he has stolen. He not only wants to pay back what he has taken from them, he also wants to pay them back fourfold. At first, we may feel that Zaccheus is a bit carried away in his desire to set things right with those he has wronged. But when we understand the biblically prescribed laws of the ancient Jews, we realize that paying back the victims of robbery fourfold was exactly what was required.

Stop and think how things might change in our contemporary society if those who stole from others were, when apprehended, put to work to earn enough money to pay back their victims fourfold.

I have talked to young thieves who have no idea how hard it is to earn money. In case after case they shrug their shoulders and say, "Look! They're rich! And besides, their insurance company will cover their losses." Of course these young culprits generally fail to consider that the insurance companies simply get the money from other hard-working policyholders by raising premiums to cover their losses from robberies.

A friend of mine who lives in the city had his house burglarized and vandalized. When they caught the twenty-year-old man who was responsible and put him on trial, my friend made the unusual request of having the young man released in his custody. He did so with the express purpose of having this burglar work to repair the damage he had done. The judge granted the request and when the young burglar was given this option or prison, he accepted the offer.

My friend had the young man come to live with him in his house and over the next three months put him to work repairing the damage he had done. During that time, the vandal got a good idea, not only of the extent of the damage he had caused, but also of the loss that my friend had suffered. What was even more important was that there was real repentance and reconciliation. My friend and this young man became close friends in the process and remain so, even to this day. Furthermore, the young man is now gainfully employed and has left his old life of crime behind him.

I am not suggesting that what my friend did should be normative. In many cases, that just wouldn't be practical. Most individuals are not in a position to do for a young criminal what my friend did. But an entire church might undertake such a mission. A whole congregation could take on the responsibility of watching over such a person and guiding him through the process of rehabilitation and making restitution.

Regardless of how it is done or who should be presiding over the process, making restitution should be made a part of our dealing with criminals. To simply put them in jail until they have paid their debt to society leaves much to be desired. Those who have been robbed are apt to ask, "Where do they get off saying he is paying his debt to *society*? He didn't rob *society*—he robbed *me*! I didn't get paid anything!" A system of restitution such as the one outlined in scripture would address such concerns.

Reconciliation is another element of the biblical formula for dealing with those who commit crimes against others. A ministry of reconciliation is part of the calling of those who would follow Jesus (2 Corinthians 5:18–19). However, reconciliation cannot occur between persons without confrontation, and confrontation seldom happens within our present judicial/penal system. The victims of crime rarely get the chance to have face-to-face meetings with those who have violated their lives. They are not often offered the opportunity to unburden themselves and tell those who have victimized them just what they are suffering. Rape is an obvious example of this.

Rapists generally delude themselves into thinking that they really didn't do much harm. Actually, some rapists think that if their victims were honest they might even admit that they enjoyed it![9] Nothing could be further from the truth. Rape victims are usually so traumatized that it often requires intensive therapy to restabilize their lives. Many victims of rape have their marriages destroyed, and some never fully recover emotionally and psychologically.

Those who try to counsel rape victims are just about unified in their belief that essential to the recovery of the victims is being able to tell off the one who caused them such pain. But this rarely happens, and being denied the opportunity of a face-to-face encounter during which they can tell their attacker the horror that they have endured and how being raped has ruined their lives is to deny the victims an essential part of the healing process.

Such confrontation is needed as part of the effort to bring the rapists to repentance. It is more difficult for rapists to feel remorse and be repulsed by their crime if they are not made aware of the damage they have done and the hurt they have inflicted. Furthermore, this is true not only for rapists, but for all kinds of criminals.

Laws must be changed to give victims the right to confront those who are guilty of the crimes committed against them. Depersonalizing victims is part of what allows criminals to escape feeling guilty for what they have done. Being forced to confront their victims puts faces on their crimes and improves considerably the possibility that perpetrators of crimes will begin to sense the enormity of what they have done and feel some guilt about it. Until there is guilt, there can be no repentance, and without repentance there can be no restoration or rehabilitation. The ultimate hope that is offered through the biblically prescribed way of dealing with criminals is that the victims and the victimizers can be brought together into a relationship that is redemptive for both.

The "Christian" Prison

An idea whose time has come is the idea of the "Christian" prison, even though the very coupling of the words "Christian" and "prison" seems like an oxymoron. The good news about the kingdom of God as declared by Jesus in his inaugural sermon is that prisoners will be freed.

> The spirit of the Lord is upon me, because he hath anointed me to preach the gospel to the poor; he hath sent me to heal the broken-hearted, to preach deliverance to the captives, and recovering of sight to the blind, to set at liberty them that are bruised, to preach the acceptable year of the Lord. (Luke 4:18–19)

The reality, however, is that we are a long way from the realization of that year of jubilee that Jesus promised. Presently in America more than a million men and women are behind bars, and there is little doubt that the number will increase during the next few years. As has already been said, urban men are disproportionately represented in this number. Since prisons have become schools for criminals, we can expect that as inmates are released in larger and larger numbers, they will provide more problems for our cities.

Prisons across the country are overcrowded. Because of this, the courts, which have the authority and responsibility of seeing that prison conditions are humane, often force cities like Philadelphia and Camden to release convicts after they have served little, if any, time and show no signs of rehabilitation. State and city governments, often lacking the financial means to build more prisons and usually unable to build them fast enough to keep up with the demand, are increasingly calling for the creation of private prisons. With the promise of handsome payments per prisoner, and the prospect of large profits, the idea has gained the attention of many investors and entrepreneurs. In some states, such as Texas, the establishment of such private prisons has already become big business.

Given the encouragement of government to establish private prisons, it is easy to speculate about the possibilities of creating overtly "Christian" prisons. Why not have concerned Christians get together, incorporate, and go into the prison business? The start-up costs would be significant, but once they were up and running such prisons would receive significant financial help in the form of government grants.

Incredible possibilities are inherent in this proposal that would give Christians the opportunity to provide convicts with the kind of care and rehabilitation programs that really could help them into better lives. Imagine a staff of professionally trained guards, social workers, and wardens who viewed their responsibilities as Christian callings. Consider what could happen if the care of each prisoner was undergirded with prayer and if Christian nurturing were part of the rehabilitation and restoration of each incarcerated man or woman.

A program like this has already been initiated in Colombia, and the results have been astounding. Something that would have to be called a revival has broken out in this "Christian" prison and the changes in the lives of the inmates have been dramatic.[10]

A couple of years ago, I came close to being actively engaged in such a venture in my own city of Philadelphia. A prominent building contractor in the city, who is a committed Christian, proposed to the city council that he take over a huge building that once housed the presses of a major newspaper. The building was in good condition and was located right on the edge of the city's downtown section. The central location of the proposed prison was of particular significance because, when prisons are located in out-of-the-way settings, they are often inaccessible to those friends and relatives of inmates who want to visit them. Too many prisons cannot be reached by public transportation, and inmates there find themselves cut off from everyone who matters to them. This isolation has disastrous effects on the emotional well-being of the prisoners.

In light of the fact that the prison being proposed by my builder friend would be located near the heart of the city and easily accessible by public buses and subway trains, I became very enthusiastic about it. But what really got my juices going was that the builder, who was ready to financially invest in the project, asked me to put together the rehabilitation program, giving me free rein, and the financial means to develop it.

I went to work, speculating and dreaming. I contacted Christian business leaders in the city and discussed a released-time program wherein inmates who had been convicted of nonviolent crimes could be engaged in gainful employment. This would have enabled them both to earn money to be sent home to their families and to get training in business for themselves.

We got our proposal as far as having a hearing before the city council, but then the whole project got bogged down in politics. The building that we had in mind has now been sold and is no longer available for the project. But we haven't given up. Some scaled-down plans are still on the drawing board to establish a Christian prison in some other location.

One proposal that excites us is the possibility of establishing a juvenile correction center in one of the large government housing developments in Philadelphia, a project of fifty buildings with twenty apartment units in each building. Several of these units have fallen into disrepair and are now completely closed down and boarded up. The plan being considered is to take over one building, rehab it, and make it into a Christian juvenile correction center.

The proposed center would focus on caring primarily for youngsters who come from the housing project itself. There are more than enough juvenile offenders who come from this neighborhood to fill up such a unit. The residents of this facility would be tutored by volunteers we would recruit from local churches. A mentoring program would be put into place to provide the kind of one-on-one guidance that juvenile offenders need if they are to be saved. Being incarcerated right in the neighborhood where their families live would make these youngsters readily accessible for the kind of visits that would maintain their family connections and keep them from feeling abandoned.

Christian prisons could actually become places where "captives could be set free," even as Jesus envisioned in his Jubilee sermon (Luke 4:18–19). Within such prisons, there could be the kind of loving care and job training that would release inmates from their captivity to the destructive lifestyles that have marked their past lives.

The Church as the Lead Institution

Church people are already making significant contributions to the rehabilitation of prisons through an impressive array of volunteer programs. Many churches, Christian colleges, and a variety of parachurch organizations have established ministries to inmates. Every week, there are tens of thousands of volunteers who regularly visit prisons and jails where they conduct chapel services, educational programs, and a variety of other ministries.

In recent years, former white House attorney Charles Colson has put together an outreach program to inmates with impressive results. His organization, Prison Fellowship, has recruited huge numbers of volunteers and hired scores of full-time professional workers. These people are revolutionizing prison ministry. Through Prison Fellowship, inmates are evangelized, nurtured, and rehabilitated while they are still behind bars. And, just as important, these people are cared for when they are released.

In many instances, prisoners are released into the custody of Prison Fellowship volunteers and "adopted" by local churches. There are a host of wonderful stories about former prisoners who have been looked after by churches as part of the Prison Fellowship program. Sometimes the churches find jobs for these men and women. Securing jobs for those released from prison is often the most difficult part of the process of integrating former convicts into the mainstream of civilian life, but it is easier to accomplish when a church is willing to stand behind the one who needs the job. In some instances, these former prisoners become active members of the churches that are helping them, often finding in their churches the kind of support communities that are so necessary if they are to go straight.

There is no need to reinvent the wheel. Prison Fellowship has become the major instrument of the church in the rehabilitation of prisoners. Churches can take a major step in solving urban crime problems by linking up with Prison Fellowship and becoming part of the outreach to inmates of this highly effective organization. With volunteers from the churches and the professional staff of Prison Fellowship working together, an impact can be made on the crime problems now facing urban America.

A few years ago, I was asked to address a national convention of wardens and other prison workers. As reports were given by the various delegates to the convention, it became obvious that there was despair in the ranks. I did not hear many success stories. Most of those who were involved in prison work offered little hope that anything could be done to keep their inmates from becoming repeat offenders. It seemed as though all of them had bad news to report *except* for the delegates from Prison Fellowship. Not only did they have success stories, but they also had statistical evidence to prove that prisoners in their programs had a high level of success when it came to being able to leave prison for good and become upright and contributing citizens. Everyone was impressed—and well they should have been. Through Prison Fellowship, the church is showing the rest of the world that, given a chance, it *can* get the job done—and that faith-based programs are the best.

Chapter 17

How the Church Can
Help Business Development

While we've spent much time considering how a "bottom-up" revolution can work, we have to face the fact that if a city is going to be truly rescued and have its poor lifted up in a way that is extensive enough to make a massive difference, we need something more. Microbusinesses developed in faith-based incubators can do a lot of good for a lot of people, but, to do the pervasive job that must be done for the kingdom of God to be realized in the city, we have to deal with the major economic power blocks of urban centers. As a case in point, we have to deal with the fiscal institutions of the city. Even a quick trip into the rundown sections of Philadelphia or the beat-up parts of Camden will make it obvious that the savings and loan companies and banks have moved out. People who want to buy houses have nowhere to go to get the mortgages they need, and small loans are not readily available. In these neighborhoods, banks no longer stand on the corners waiting to provide the fiscal services that middle-class folks in the suburbs take for granted.

This is not to say that there are *no* financial services available for the inner-city poor. In the derelict neighborhoods of cities, there are always check-cashing outlets that are eager to help solve the financial problems of poor people at exorbitant rates. A recent study made by the Harvard Business School shows that cashing a check in one of these establishments can cost 2 to 9 percent of the face value of the check, whereas the same service is provided free to those who are able to deal with the regular banks that dot the landscape in wealthier suburban communities. It's easy to get credit at these check-cashing outlets. Almost anyone can take

219

out a small loan to cover a short-term need—if he or she is willing to pay 15 percent interest on a two-week payday loan. A payday loan is made with the expectation that full repayment will be made from the borrower's next paycheck. A 15 percent interest rate on a $400 loan means that $60 in interest will have to be paid by the borrower out of a single paycheck two weeks later. If such a high-interest loan is stretched out over a year, the interest rate can reach close to 400 percent.

When it comes to getting mortgages to buy homes in the worn-out sections of a city, a poor family has little chance. Usually, such a family has no fiscal credibility or track record to prove that it is an acceptable credit risk for a bank. This situation works against efforts to upgrade neighborhoods because having people become homeowners is a primary way to ensure that housing will undergo improvements. It is no secret that people fix up and maintain houses most faithfully when they are homeowners rather than renters. Making home loans conveniently available is an essential part of any plan for urban renewal.

Perhaps one of the most pressing fiscal problems of the urban poor is the need for fairly priced insurance coverage. Many city dwellers do not have automobiles simply because they cannot afford car insurance. And without cars, people often lack access to jobs. Those who study unemployment problems have been aware for a long while that many jobless people would gladly work if they just had the means to get to where the jobs are. These scholars also know that the advent of suburban industrial parks rendered many jobs accessible only to those who have automobiles. For many, not being able to afford car insurance means not having a car and, hence, unemployment.

The good news is that some churches are providing new hope in the midst of all these problems. Pastors of many inner-city congregations have figured out how to make the members of their congregations into collective bargaining units and have begun to gain some of the good fiscal deals that middle-class suburbanites have long enjoyed. For instance, a church leader representing a large pool of individuals can go to a bank and bargain collectively for them in order to secure decent mortgage rates and fair and affordable check-cashing privileges for them. Bankers are not necessarily hard-hearted people, but their responsibility to their investors requires that they lend money to honest borrowers who can be trusted to keep up their payments. When a church with a large membership stands behind each borrower and the pastor gives detailed information about the person's reliability, bankers become more ready to take on the risks that go with making loans.

There are many poor people who are solid risks but have no paper record of their dependability.

My own Italian immigrant family was reluctant to buy anything on credit, paid its bills in cash, and put very little money in any bank. Hence, its credit standing was just about nonexistent. How wonderful it would have been if our pastor, who had learned a lot about our family over the years, could have vouched for us when we wanted to take out a loan to buy a car. Even better would have been a scenario in which our pastor could have used the power of having a whole congregation full of potential investors and depositors to negotiate a low-interest loan for a family like ours. This is what is happening through the efforts of many urban pastors on behalf of their congregations in today's urban settings.

Banks are realizing that churches can be good fiscal partners because they are finding that doing business with urban congregations can be profitable. For instance, many bankers are recognizing that it is possible for a church pastor to teach and encourage church members to establish savings accounts in their bank. They also are learning that if a church member gets a loan through the negotiations of the pastor and with the fiscal power of the congregation, that church member is under tremendous pressure from his or her peers to pay back the loan. A member who defaults brings the credibility of the entire church and its leaders into question, and the church, therefore, will do all it can to keep any member from falling short of a bank's expectations.

A church also can do brilliantly when negotiating various kinds of insurance policies for its members. The pastor can propose a fair but low cost for car insurance policies to an agent and then simply say, "Take it or I'll take these five hundred possible policy sales to another agency."

Poor people are usually poor investors. At best, they put their money into savings accounts and settle for relatively low interest rates. But church leaders are wising up even in this area of fiscal activity. By getting church people to pool their money, they can help them to do what single small investors could never do. One person with a couple of hundred dollars finds it difficult to invest in mutual funds because investing agencies are not eager to do all the necessary paperwork for such a small amount of money. But if a church gets its people to pool their money, then it becomes very possible for low-income people to make high-yield investments in mutual funds. What if several churches got together and pooled the resources of thousands of small investors? Wouldn't a fund management company or a bank be more than ready to work out good-paying investment schemes? Wouldn't financial institutions, under such arrangements, be persuaded to figure out ways to make high-yield investments, like equities, for low-income people?

Churches can be especially helpful in helping people deal with credit card arrangements. A church—or better still, a group of churches—could negotiate a good interest rate and payment arrangement for congregational members. More important, churches could provide seminars to teach people how to use credit cards to their advantage and not fall into the traps that those who market the cards seldom warn them about. For instance, a person who buys a faulty radio using a credit card needs to learn that withholding the payment due to the credit card company with no explanation is not the way to handle the situation. Also, the consumer needs to be made aware of the ballooning interest payments that credit card companies often levy on late payments.

Nonprofit Intermediaries

In helping low-income city dwellers to handle their fiscal problems, establishing nonprofit intermediaries between churches and banks is a good way to go. Often pastors of churches become aware that dealing with investments, negotiating with insurance companies, and doing collective bargaining with banks requires skills beyond their level of expertise. In some cities, nonprofit organizations have been created that can help pastors and their people to do all of this, and more.

Such organizations have professionals who have been trained to handle negotiations, legal matters, and the often confusing paperwork that these kinds of business deals require. Nehemiah Homes is one such organization. Operating in several cities across the country, it has dues-paying member churches whose individual members get the kind of guidance they need to become homeowners and enjoy the kind of clout necessary to secure affordable mortgages from banks. More than five thousand new homes have been built and sold to low-income families nationwide through Nehemiah Homes, and its methods are being replicated by other groups committed to helping the urban poor. It wouldn't take much imagination to figure out that those who want to do ministry in the city could create organizations employing this model.[1]

Nurturing the Big Employers

Everybody knows that cities die without a certain number of industries that can provide jobs by the thousands. When such industries are flourishing, the cities flourish, along with the small businesses that provide services to them. And all of those thus employed enjoy economic health. Similarly, when the key industries of a city collapse, everything and everybody in town gets dragged down with them. In most instances, when faced with major industries closing down, church leaders simply wring their hands and bow their heads in prayer. Too often, they assume that there is nothing that can be done to rescue their cities from the consequences of what appears to be inevitable economic death. While such woes may seem to be beyond church congregations to address, it should be noted that there have been some church leaders who have been ready to take bold action to save their cities when faced with industrial shutdowns.

In Youngstown, Ohio, when the steel mills of that city closed down, the ministers of the churches came up with a heroic plan that might have worked. They put together the financial resources of their churches, got commitments from other people of the city, and asked the workers at the mills to join them in taking over the mills. The ministers did their best to lead the community into owning and running the mills in a heroic effort to save their city from economic ruin.

Sadly, the whole plan fell apart for a variety of reasons. But those reasons should be studied because the mistakes could have been avoided and the city could have been saved. Regardless of the outcome, we all must take off our hats to those church leaders who did their best to create hope and economic well-being for a troubled community.

Philadelphia, as we've already noted, has suffered job losses over the last thirty years that have had devastating effects on the lives of its people. But at least one family has taken up the challenge of developing a major industry in what some have labeled a high-risk location for industrial development. The northeast section of the city had been abandoned by hundreds of major corporations, including Budd Company and Stetson Hats. The shells of buildings that once had been thriving production plants are everywhere visible to those who ride the Amtrak trains from New York to Philadelphia. The array of stripped and burned-out buildings with their broken windows could lead an unknowing railroad passenger to believe that these buildings had been the targets of World War II bombing raids. Yet, it is in this very setting that the Cardone family has established its factories to remanufacture automobile parts. If you recently had a rebuilt engine, transmission, or gearbox installed in your car, there is a good possibility that it came from Cardone Industries.

Michael Cardone, the president of this family business, has been instrumental in leading the company to its place as one of the major remanufacturers of automobile parts in the world. The company is now the major for-profit employer in the city, and it has created over five thousand jobs for the people of Philadelphia. Going against the conventional wisdom that prescribes that factories be established in suburban industrial parks, Cardone Industries has taken over abandoned factories and warehouses once owned by such commercial giants as Sears and made them into efficiently functioning facilities. Contradicting the assumption held by many in the business world that inner-city populations cannot provide a skilled and dependable workforce, Michael Cardone has proven just the opposite. He contends that his work force is as loyal, efficient, and hard-working as any employer could desire. Over the last couple of decades, Cardone Industries has gone out of its way to hire employees from those ethnic groups whose members often have great difficulty securing jobs. Some of these ethnic peoples, such as Cambodians and now Albanians, have trouble finding work because they have difficulty with the English language. Michael Cardone has responded to this situation by hiring chaplains who know the languages of these ethnic groups and who can serve as translators as well as counselors to help them work through not only adjustment problems on the job, but also family difficulties and personal troubles.

At Cardone Industries, the day begins with a voluntary chapel service held before working hours begin. Although only a small percentage of the workers show up, there are enough to form an enthusiastic group of worshipers. As the workday gets under way, the employees gather into small support groups where they not only go over what they plan to accomplish that day but also have an opportunity to share any special personal concerns they might have. If someone's wife is in the hospital or if someone's child is having problems, there is a time for sharing these concerns and enlisting the sympathy and prayers of fellow workers. The camaraderie established in this way has generated a togetherness that encourages employees to feel that their fellow workers are an extended family. It is not surprising that some of the workers have chosen to be married in the company's chapel, and on a few occasions, when workers have died, their families have chosen to have the funerals conducted there. The chaplains at Cardone Industries have built such a sense of spiritual togetherness among the workers of the various ethnic groups that several of these groups have established churches in the surrounding neighborhoods. All these churches are now thriving congregations that incorporate many people outside the Cardone Industries employment family.

Michael Cardone claims that corporate managers are making a mistake if they think that inner cities are not viable locations for industries. He claims that the city government has bent over backward to help and encourage his company's development and says that the supply of good, reliable workers in the city is great. Evidence of this latter fact is that, when a 36-inch snowfall dropped on Philadelphia, the entire business and corporate network of the city closed down—except for Cardone Industries. Somehow most of the thousand employees made their way to work on the day of the blizzard. Loyalty like that says it all.

What must not be ignored is what lies behind all the good things that are happening at Cardone Industries. The Cardone family members are deeply committed Christians who recognize that their calling is not simply to make money by remanufacturing automobile parts, but primarily to create jobs for God's people in the city.[2]

Bringing about top-down economic change in a city is not an easy thing. The examples just given provide some idea of what can be done when church leaders pool their resources, or when "big thinking" entrepreneurs are inspired with visions of how they can be job creators for the poor. The specifics of what can be done or should be done to bring about top-down economic renewal will vary from city to city. Church leaders ought to be in touch with the business and economics departments of local universities to see what research has been done to examine the needs of their respective cities, and to determine if there are any joint efforts that might be made for improving the conditions of the poor and jobless. Certainly churches should be part of their local chambers of commerce to keep abreast of business developments in their cities, and learn how to be a part of efforts to foster the economic well-being of their neighborhoods. Religious leaders are just beginning to understand that not only the fate of their cities, but the fate of their congregations as well, are at stake. When a city declines economically, people move out and churches die.

Chapter 18

Networking for the Kingdom

J ust across the river from Camden is Philadelphia, a city that is in need of prayer—and much more. There are those who say that only a miracle can save this city. The loss of jobs, the dilapidated schools, the tense racial situation, the declining tax base, and other social realities have made Philadelphia a prime candidate for death.

Yet, in this same city there are some very hopeful signs of renewal. Visionaries in business and government dream of a revitalized city. Many churches are attempting to establish microbusinesses and cottage industries along the lines that have been described in this book. There are a variety of faith-based agencies that are committed to working for the kinds of institutional structural change that will bring about increasing justice and social well-being. It seems that all that is needed to turn Philadelphia around is leadership with a unified strategic plan to bring these committed persons, churches, and agencies together.

Now such leadership exists. In 1997, Dr. David Black assumed the presidency of Eastern College, located in St. Davids, Pennsylvania. Eastern has had a long history as an *avant garde* institution in terms of faith-based social action programs, but now, under Dr. Black's leadership, steps are being taken toward some bold new initiatives.

Perhaps the most innovative project of this dynamic young president is the establishment of the Eastern College Institute for Urban Studies (ECIUS). A satellite campus of Eastern College, ECIUS is being established in a transitional zone that separates the downtown business district from the economically depressed neighborhoods housing working-class Hispanic and African-American peoples.[1]

The mission of the institute is to create faith-based neighborhood development programs throughout the city. Those directing the institute will be implementing many of the proposals outlined in this book. They will be doing what needs to be done to test whether the church is able to be the lead institution in bringing about the kinds of social change that can save a city.

Eastern College is already deeply involved in social ministries in both Philadelphia and Camden. Since the mid-1960s, when most academic institutions were maintaining an ivory tower philosophy of higher education, the college has been involving its students in a variety of inner-city social programs. Eastern pioneered the idea of having college students tutor disadvantaged children in government housing projects and challenged its faculty to be involved in training programs for urban church leaders.

Eastern invested great effort in a graduate studies program in urban economic development, which was aimed at job creation in depressed neighborhoods. Graduates from this program are serving in faith-based community development corporations across the nation as well as providing leadership in a variety of development agencies in Third World countries.

As an expression of the college's commitment to urban education, Eastern has "adopted" an inner-city school to which scores of students commute daily to do tutoring and to provide a variety of cultural enrichment programs. Eastern instituted one of the earliest programs in undergraduate social work education, training and the deployment of case workers and community organizers in urban social service agencies in America. All of these past efforts now posture the college for its newest venture—the initiation of the new Eastern College Institute for Urban Studies. The mission of ECIUS is to empower urban churches and to be a change agent for urban renewal. ECIUS will do this in a variety of ways.

One important program emphasis will be the development and expansion of youth ministries programs in the churches of Philadelphia. Already in place is Making Urban Disciples, Inc. (MUD), funded by the Pew Charitable Trust. MUD has, to date, targeted thirty ethnic churches in the city that have shown potential for developing strong youth ministries in their respective neighborhoods. With an experienced staff of urban ministry consultants, MUD provides extensive and individualized support and guidance to the lay leaderships of the targeted churches. Its goal is to make these churches into effective agencies for reaching young people with both the gospel message and the kinds of social programs that will guide them into productive citizenship. MUD leaders also provide a variety of programs beyond those which individual church youth groups could do on their own. For instance, the most promising young people from urban churches are brought together by MUD for weekend conferences and camp retreats. MUD also holds special training seminars for adult sponsors of youth programs and makes it possible for them to borrow the latest youth resource materials such as videotapes and "idea books," which small churches usually would not be able to afford to purchase.

The most recent initiative by MUD has been the creation of college-level youth ministry courses for those who want to learn the theology, philosophy, and techniques necessary for effective youth ministry. Linked to the youth ministry major of Eastern College, these courses are held at the downtown campus of ECIUS and are scheduled at convenient times for lay church leaders. With the completion of the prescribed curriculum, students are certified as graduates of the institute, having earned academic credits that can be used toward a bachelors degree at the main campus of Eastern College.

The Urban Resource Center (URC) is another ministry housed at the Philadelphia Institute for Urban Studies. Headed by Del Deets, a long-standing leader of church development in Philadelphia, the URC provides a variety of seminars to strengthen the organization and management of urban churches. Deets specializes in sponsoring seminars providing help for church leaders to create the kind of efficiency that is necessary if boards and committees are going to accomplish their intended tasks. Resources for music programs, Sunday School, neighborhood outreach, evangelistic meetings, and social service ministries are available. The URC establishes cooperative programs that churches could not provide individually.

The URC develops and facilitates collaborative initiatives for church-based youth ministry programs like Project NEWS (Newspapers, Entrepreneurship, and Winning Students). URC's mission is to be a bridge between urban churches and other resources, so strengths are shared for maximum community impact. Through its programs, URC strengthens the capacity of urban churches to obtain resources for community-building ministries and manages the Inner-City Impact Institute, the Resource Bank, and IKRHM (Institute of Knowledge and Resources for Hispanic Ministries).

The ECIUS also functions as a center for church-based neighborhood job creation. In cooperation with the Philadelphia Development Partnership (PDP), a variety of efforts are being made to encourage churches throughout the city to become incubators for microbusinesses and cottage industries. At its first venture, an interfaith all-day program on economic development, jointly sponsored by Eastern College and EAPE/Kingdomworks, PDP had over 150 church leaders in attendance. Seminars were provided on such subjects as ways to establish small businesses in churches, how to help young people develop productive work habits, and how to work with the government agencies in facilitating welfare-to-work programs. Now plans are being finalized to establish a training center at ECIUS for those who want to be entrepreneurs in faith-based ventures. There will be several microbusinesses established to operate right at the ECIUS site in order to provide demonstrations of how to set up and run neighborhood microenterprises.

Eastern College is making a major commitment to ECIUS by moving some of its undergraduate and graduate courses in urban economic development to this new inner-city campus for the express purpose of attracting into its programs church leaders who want to hone their skills in entrepreneurship. Already, churches such as the Rev. Leon Sullivan's Zion Baptist Church on North Broad Street and the Rev. Benjamin Smith's Deliverance Evangelistic Church on Lehigh Avenue have taken bold steps in faith-based economic development. Both of these churches have started major shopping centers that not only serve African-American communities but also provide employment for neighborhood people. Each of these pastors has established a job-training program of significant size. The Rev. Sullivan's Opportunities Industrialization Corporation includes hundreds of training centers worldwide. The academic courses provided by Eastern College at ECIUS will help other church leaders learn the skills of accounting, management, marketing, legal paperwork, and finance that go into the kind of entrepreneurship demonstrated by the viable church programs of the Rev. Sullivan and the Rev. Smith. With Eastern's help, a major impetus to faith-based economic development will be provided for participating churches.

Among the academic programs that Eastern College will establish at ECIUS is a unique course of graduate studies to train specialists in urban family education and counseling. Ever since the notorious Daniel Patrick Moynihan study on African-American family life, there has been an awareness that no plan for urban renewal would succeed unless the basic societal unit, the family, could be strengthened.[2] Leaders in the African-

American community have increasingly called for new and extensive efforts toward restoring strong biparental family life for those who live in the cities. The old ideology that deemed a male presence in the lives of children as nonessential has been demolished by empirical research. Through the family studies program at Eastern College, every effort will be made to help church leaders learn how to provide the guidance and help that are essential for establishing and strengthening the familial system in the urban African-American community. Eastern now offers a specialized masters degree for those who successfully complete this course of study.

In conjunction with the Hispanic Clergy of Philadelphia, an organization that coordinates community-development corporations for the more than ninety churches in its membership, a first-of-its-kind bilingual junior college will be established. Rev. Luis Cortes, the founder and director of the Hispanic Clergy of Philadelphia, has created a vision for this junior college within the Spanish-speaking churches of the city. Cortes recognizes that many bright and talented young people who have immigrated to Philadelphia from Puerto Rico and the Dominican Republic are having a hard time in the institutions of higher education of the city because adjusting to speaking English instead of Spanish is too much to handle. Cortes views the bilingual junior college as a necessary response to this reality. Furthermore, he wants Hispanic collegians to have the benefits of learning under professors who interpret their subject matter in the context of a Christian worldview. He envisions a new generation of young people who will not only be educated but inspired by a theology of the kingdom of God that will enable them to understand themselves as agents of social change within their own communities.

This junior college will gain instant academic legitimacy because of its connection to Eastern College. In its initial stages, classes will be held at the ECIUS campus, which is located on the edge of the Hispanic section of Philadelphia. In the not-too-distant future, the college will have its own campus but will continue its ongoing relationship with ECIUS, where Eastern will make an array of its unique courses available to the junior college students.

Perhaps one of the most significant contributions of ECIUS to the city of Philadelphia will be in the field of teacher training. Eastern College, through its excellent education department, has long been involved in training teachers for urban schools through its regular bachelor of science program. At ECIUS, the college will be able to provide the opportunity for uncredentialed public and parochial school teachers to secure accreditation and take continuing education courses that will enable them to advance in their fields.

Today, more and more churches are starting day nurseries and their own private Christian schools, and this is creating an increasingly urgent need to train those Christian teachers who are presently *not* credentialed. If the school voucher program advocated by many church leaders becomes a reality, there will be a mushrooming of new church-related elementary and secondary schools across the city. Most of them will be staffed by uncertified teachers in need of further training. There is every expectation that the courses in the field of urban education provided under the auspices of Eastern College will not only help teachers get the academic credits they need, but will also offer them the specialized training they must have to relate the Christian faith to the special needs of inner-city students.

Those directing the Philadelphia Institute for Urban Studies are especially hopeful about the partnership being developed with Eastern Baptist Theological Seminary (EBTS), a leading seminary of the American Baptist Churches. EBTS has a well-established program in the development of public policy. Created by Ron Sider, the founder of Evangelicals for Social Action and one of America's best known Christian apologists on social justice issues, the program is focused on ways to apply the biblical message to the answering of contemporary political problems. One of the things that makes ECIUS an ideal partner for the seminary in this venture is its location—within walking distance of City Hall. Accessibility to the mayor, the city manager, the members of the city council, the judges of the court system, the police commissioner, and various other city officials will facilitate interaction with them by those involved in the seminary's public policy program. Students will have the opportunity for input into the decision making processes of city government, thus developing a model of how a faith-based "think tank" can effect social change.

Perhaps the most significant contribution of ECIUS will be made through its efforts to impact other American cities with its vision for church-based neighborhood development. One of its programs that is already influencing urban ministries across America is the National Urban Youth Workers Convention. This convention, founded and run by Bart and Marty Campolo whose Mission Year program operates out of ECIUS, annually brings together more than 1,000 urban church youth workers for a weekend of training and inspiration through this particular ministry. The vision and programming being developed by the various agencies of ECIUS are gaining wide recognition among those who work with young people in inner-city churches. As efforts in faith-based neighborhood development are turned into success stories, the National Urban Youth Workers convention will provide a means for promoting replications of these programs from coast to coast.

The Mission Year program, discussed earlier, also has its national offices at ECIUS.[3] If this program expands as anticipated, ECIUS will be able to promote its vision for faith-based urban renewal through the hundreds of young people recruited. In various cities, Mission Year workers—who even now are being trained and inspired by the holistic vision of urban salvation outlined in this book—will be at work sharing that vision with other church leaders.

The Eastern College Institute for Urban Studies, like this book, is marked by hope. At stake is not only the role of the church in urban America in the twenty-first century, but the salvation of our cities. Unless the churches of the city respond to the challenges that now confront them, the urban crisis will surely worsen. There is little doubt that the church is being called to an involvement in the social redemption of our decaying inner cities. The government has cut back on its programs for helping urban dwellers, and the corporate community is finding that being involved in urban renewal has diminished the bottom line of its commercial interests. The church is the one institution left amidst the debris of those other social institutions that have been devastated by the onslaught of post-World War II suburbanization and de-industrialization.

The Eastern College Institute for Urban Studies is one attempt to harness the potentialities of urban churches so that they can become the lead institutions for making something of the kingdom of God a reality in our cities. Undoubtedly, there are other ways of doing this. We do not assume that no other models for urban renewal will work. Rather, what has been presented in this book shows the beginning of one particular experimental model for urban social change and offers a challenge to others to give it a try. Only time will tell if this model is viable for Philadelphia, and even if it proves to be, there would still be a question as to whether or not it could be replicated in other cities. Urbanologists are well aware that every city is different. Each has its own unique cultural systems, socioeconomic structures, political machines, and ethnic components. What works in one city will not necessarily work in another. But in spite of all of this, those who are committed to urban ministry can learn much in one city that may be applied to development models in others.

I hope that what has been proposed in this book will have value to those in other cities who are trying to figure out how the Church can be the lead institution for urban renewal.

Chapter 19

What's a Suburban Church to Do at a Time Like This?

Since World War II, America has become increasingly suburbanized. The city of Philadelphia has lost so many people to the suburbs that today it is down to about 1.2 million people from the 2 million that it had in its heyday. Meanwhile, the suburbs have grown so that the greater Philadelphia area has more than 6 million people. Camden, likewise, has been steadily losing people to the suburbs so that it now has less than half the population that it did in 1945.

Gibson Winter, in his popular 1950s book, *The Suburban Captivity of the Churches,* carefully outlined the problems that such population shifts have posed for the church.[1] The most significant problems were those related to the loss of both human and financial resources by inner-city churches to the new congregations that seemed to spring up overnight in the ever-expanding suburban neighborhoods.

Winter strongly advocated that each suburban church link up with a specific inner-city church of its own denomination. He suggested that the two churches have a common board to govern their "linked parish" and that they pool their financial resources and operate on a common fiscal budget. Sunday school teachers could be drawn from a common pool. Certain activities, like the youth program, could bring together persons from both congregations, thus providing crosscultural experiences for all involved. The inner-city church, as a result of such an arrangement, would have not only the money it needed to carry on ministry in the downtown location but also would have a new source from which to recruit the leadership so necessary to sustain and direct the programs that are an essential part of its mission.

When Winter's book was published, it generated far-reaching debate and discussion. Ministers' meetings and denominational gatherings often were organized around examining his proposals. There was a general conclusion that what Winter was suggesting would help urban churches to maintain effective and relevant ministries, but not much resulted in the way of concrete action. Suburban churches, bent on aggrandizing their own programs and expanding their own facilities, were not eager to share either their people or their money with struggling inner-city congregations. It became increasingly clear that inner-city churches were going to be left to die while their suburban sisters flourished with growing congregations and increasing wealth.

But all is not lost! It is encouraging to note that recently there has been a growing sensitivity on the part of suburban churches to the needs of inner-city congregations, as well as an increased willingness to do something to meet those needs. Now, some forty years after Winter made his plea, there is evidence that many suburban churches are taking on the challenge of supporting sister churches that are struggling to survive in the inner-city.

Eastern College, where I teach, is located in a suburb of Philadelphia. Many Eastern students have found a church home at the Wayne Presbyterian Church. This main-line church with its traditional worship service has experienced significant growth of late, in large measure because of its dynamic senior pastor and preacher, Dr. John Galloway. The Sunday morning services are packed, and the upper-middle-class members give generously to the maintainance of the church. But Dr. Galloway's vision was to make his people aware of the needs of those who live in some of the declining neighborhoods in nearby Philadelphia. He brought on to the church staff a young married couple who are working with him to realize his vision.

Gerry and Carey Davis are both graduates of Princeton Theological Seminary. Carey had been an effective and faithful worker in the EAPE/Kingdomworks ministries, which have been so much a part of my own life. I had watched her give herself in service to the children and teenagers who are the focus of what EAPE/Kingdomworks tries to do in the city. Her love for at-risk youth represents some of the best that the church has to offer, and her years of experience in organizing and implementing inner-city programs and in relating to needy city people on a personal level make her an ideal leader for the initiatives of Wayne Presbyterian Church as it seeks to make a difference in the dire conditions that exist in many Philadelphia neighborhoods.

Gerry Davis had served faithfully at two struggling urban churches in one of the poorest ethnic neighborhoods in inner-city Philadelphia. An outstanding preacher and an effective youth leader, Gerry has the kind of commitment and know-how to connect with inner-city youth.

Over the past few years, the Davises and Dr. Galloway have put together a program they call City Lights. They have recruited a significant number of church members who volunteer their time to work in various urban ministries. It is a rare day when Cornerstone Christian Academy, the Christian school developed under the auspices of EAPE/Kingdomworks, does not have volunteers from Wayne Presbyterian Church serving its children. These volunteers serve as tutors, run the library, and are always ready to help out the shorthanded school administrators. Hundreds of thousands of dollars from Wayne Presbyterian Church, both from its budgeted income and from individual members, have been used to undergird Cornerstone Christian Academy and its more than 300 students. It is fair to say that without the generous financial contributions and the countless hours of volunteer service provided by the people of this church, Cornerstone Christian Academy would not exist today. And Cornerstone Christian Academy is only one of the many urban ventures of Wayne Presbyterian Church.

There is an increasing number of men and women who, like John Galloway and the Davises, want to connect suburban churches to those that are struggling in our cites. The resulting partnerships take many different forms. One idea which has great possibilities is that a suburban church commission some of its members to become part of a needy urban church to undergird the ministries there. Utilizing this modified version of Gibson Winter's suggestion, a suburban church would ask some of its best families to transfer their memberships to a struggling inner-city congregation. By singing in the choir, teaching in the Sunday school, and involving their sons and daughters in the youth and children's programs, such families would lend support and encouragement to the ministry of the city church and provide great encouragement to its pastor.

Imagine what a shot in the arm it would be for a discouraged pastor of a dying inner-city congregation to suddenly have ten couples and their children transfer their memberships into his or her church. Obviously, this could stimulate new enthusiasm for that pastor and jump-start a whole new era of effective ministry for the church.

An even more dramatic proposal for assisting inner-city churches comes from Bob Lupton, who heads an urban ministry in Atlanta, Georgia. Lupton increasingly has promoted the idea of *neighboring*. This is an effort to have suburban church members not only commute into the city on Sundays to lend support to a needy church, but to sell their homes in suburbia and move to at-risk urban neighborhoods. This challenge is aimed especially at retired couples who do not have to worry about decent schools because their children are already grown up.

Why is it that people are willing to travel to far-off countries and live among the poor and oppressed of the Third World, but so many do not realize that the Third World is just a few miles away from where they live, in the urban ghettos of the city? Bob Lupton believes that retired couples who are looking for ways to be involved in missionary service ought to consider this option. They should be commissioned and ordained by the sending church, even as they would be if they were going to some overseas mission field. The home church in the suburbs should be ready to undergird such urban missionaries with prayer and with whatever financial support is required for effective ministry. (It should be noted that not much financial support would be needed by most retired couples since they would probably have enough income from their retirement plans and from Social Security to keep them going.) Almost 30 percent of all men between the ages of 55 and 65 are already retired. Add to them the large numbers of vital persons over the age of 65 who are retired, and you can see that there is a virtual army of potential volunteers available to do what needs to be done to make something of the kingdom of God a reality in the city. Not only would these commissioned missionaries from suburban churches lend much-needed support to barely viable urban congregations, but, by moving into the neighborhoods where the churches are located, they would become the kind of transforming "leaven" (Matthew 13:33) that Jesus calls the church to be, challenging those neighborhoods to become like the kingdom of God. A missionary movement like this could have retired persons working on voter registration to create politically effective communities. They could tutor in the schools, helping to provide a caring atmosphere for children, especially those having difficulties. They could join in the "town watch" and work against the spreading of drugs; participate in the Meals on Wheels program, which provides food for shut-ins; work with Habitat for Humanity to rebuild some of the abandoned houses in the neighborhood; provide counseling help for single mothers; and assist those who do not know how to fill out their income tax returns. The list of possibilities goes on and on.

It seems to me that there is a terrible waste of human resources when talented and experienced senior citizens retire to play golf. We need to let them know how very necessary they are for the salvation of our cities.

People who retire to relax are actually mentioned in the bible. Jesus tells this story:

> And he spake a parable unto them, saying, The ground of a certain rich man brought forth plentifully: And he thought within himself, saying, What shall I do, because I have no room where to bestow my fruits? And he said, This will I do: I will pull down my barns, and build greater; and there will I bestow all my fruits and my goods. And I will say to my soul, Soul, thou hast much goods laid up for many years; take thine ease, eat, drink, and be merry. But God said unto him, Thou fool, this night thy soul shall be required of thee: then whose shall those things be, which thou hast provided? So is he that layeth up treasure for himself, and is not rich toward God. (Luke 12:16–21)

These words should be sufficient warning to would-be retirees that having invested in IRAs and retirement plans they had best not take their ease as did the foolish man in the story. Instead, they had best consider how this last part of their lives might be invested in the building of the kingdom of God in the city. Preachers should be preaching sermons that challenge their older members to do this kind of missionary work. After all, why should we challenge only the young and restless to missionary work? Abraham was in his mid-nineties when he responded to God's call to leave the comfort of the Ur of the Chaldeans and create the city of God in another place.

> By faith Abraham, when he was called to go out into a place which he should after receive for an inheritance, obeyed; and he went out, not knowing whither he went. By faith he sojourned in the land of promise, as in a strange country, dwelling in the tabernacles with Isaac and Jacob, the heirs with him of the same promise: For he looked for a city which hath foundations, whose builder and maker is God. (Heb. 11:8–10)

Creative Solutions

I was inspired and challenged by a daring and unique ministry called Urban Dwellers, initiated by some young adults from the Hollywood Presbyterian Church. I first encountered these young people at a college and career conference at Forest Hills Conference Center in California. This is the place where Billy Graham made his decisive commitment to believe that the Bible was an inerrant revelation from God, where Bill Bright developed his vision to start Campus Crusade, and where Dick Halverson began the journey that led him to become the chaplain of the United States Senate. With a history like this, it was not surprising to me that these conference grounds secured and developed for Christian gatherings by Henrietta Mears, the one-time Christian education director at the Hollywood Presbyterian Church, should be the setting in which some young adults committed themselves to a radical version of urban ministry.

The Urban Dwellers are basically people in what some call the yuppie professions, but they are anything but typical yuppies. They live together in a big old house in Hollywood not far from the well-known corner of Hollywood and Vine. Each workday they go to their jobs in the glass towers of the city, but in the evenings they do their missionary work. Out on the streets around Hollywood and Vine they talk with the teenaged runaways who seem omnipresent. They offer friendship to these lost souls, as well as everything else that love requires: a place to sleep, a meal, help to go home, and most important, the opportunity to give their lives over to Jesus. The Urban Dwellers have made their house an oasis in the midst of the desperate thirst for hope of many who know the degradation of living on the streets.

What the Urban Dwellers created in Hollywood inspired me to try something that I thought was a good idea but never quite worked. My wife and I bought a house in West Philadelphia, big enough to house a group of graduate students studying economic development at Eastern College who wanted to live among the poor of the city. The idea was that while taking classes at Eastern College in the suburbs, they would do ministry among the needy people of the city who lived in their neighborhood. Eight fine young people moved into our stately old house and promptly made their presence felt. On the corner of their city block was an apartment building that housed about twenty Cambodian refugee families. The Eastern students reached out to those families, tutoring the children who were having difficulty in school, starting Bible study groups for their neighbors, and even inviting into their own home a teenaged couple who had had a baby out of wedlock. They took legal steps to keep the slum landlord who owned the apartment building in which the Cambodians lived from evicting them in order to make way for more "desirable" tenants.

These young graduate students became known to just about everyone in the neighborhood as caring, ministering servants of Jesus. But as with so many efforts of this kind, over time things changed. The Cambodian people all left the neighborhood, and today, while some very good people who are doing some very good things are living in that house, the original missionary vision is not being fully realized. Nevertheless, the idea is a good one. The church should challenge its young adults to undertake such ventures. Think of the difference it could make if scores of suburban churches bought houses in worn-out urban neighborhoods and filled them with students and/or young professionals from their congregations who viewed their presence in the city as an opportunity to be agents of evangelism and social transformation. By living "in community," they could experience something of the biblical concept of *koinonia* while carrying out a missionary mandate that would enhance their own lives significantly. Besides all of that, they would have the opportunity to live a simple lifestyle by paying low rent and sharing living expenses. Taken together, all of these things would enable them to be a demonstration of the kind of community of faith that ideally lives out the requisite of scripture as set forth in the second chapter of Acts.

Still another way that suburban churches can help renew the city may be found in something called The Pittsburgh Project. Headed up by one of my former students, Saleem Ghubril, this program is organized around getting suburban youth groups to come to the city for a couple of weeks during the summer months to do repairs on dilapidated houses generally inhabited by the elderly poor. The city Offices of Licenses and Inspections readily provides a list of houses that ought to be condemned and torn down—and would be except that there would be nowhere for the displaced people to go and live. With equipment and supervisors provided by The Pittsburgh Project staff, youth groups do the kinds of fixing up that these houses require. Everything from the electrical system to the plumbing is brought up to government specifications. The houses are painted and made as attractive as possible. Scores of ruined houses are restored, and many elderly people have their lives immeasurably brightened by The Pittsburgh Project.

A rather daring program to help the urban homeless was instituted by a small church-related college on the West Coast. When I had the opportunity to speak at that school for a series of lectures sponsored by the Staley Foundation of New York, I used the opportunity to challenge the students to reach out to the poor and oppressed, not only in Third World countries, but in the city nearby.

After I left the campus, some of the students decided to take up that challenge. They worked out an arrangement with the administration of the college to go into the city each night and bring out to the campus those who wanted a meal and a place to sleep. The homeless were invited to eat with the students in the school cafeteria and to spend the night in unused dormitory rooms. The program worked beautifully, and the president of the school told me that it not only enriched the experience of the students who interacted with the street people (most of them for the first time), but also enhanced the image of the college throughout the city. Rotary clubs and charitable foundations got behind the effort, and this hitherto unrecognized little college was suddenly a front page story.

Great things are beginning to happen as suburban Christians are becoming aware that they need not travel overseas to become involved in Third World missions. I have only touched on those examples with which I am directly acquainted, but there are many others. The stories of unique programs connecting suburban Christians with inner-city churches and the urban poor are abundant. I could tell about the LaSalle Street Church in Chicago, which has a host of members who drive in from the suburbs because they want to be involved in inner-city ministries. This church is into everything imaginable from providing legal and medical services for the poor to sponsoring a beautiful low-income housing development as an alternative to the infamous project called Cabrini Green.

There are many more innovative ideas being tried out by suburbanites responding to the call to minister in the inner-city, but the ones that work best are the ones that involve relocation. Even as Jesus moved in to be among us in order to be our salvation, so we who want to bring his salvation to those who live the city must also move into those neighborhoods. The power of the gospel is at its best when the Word becomes flesh and blood in those places where we want to see social transformation. Other attempts for relevancy have made their impact, but when the Word becomes flesh through those who incarnate it by becoming one with those whom they seek to serve, the finest and best work of the kingdom is most likely to be seen.

Chapter 20

A Brief Theology of the City

A city can be a wonderful thing. The kingdom of God that will be ultimately realized in history is a city. The Bible teaches that the New Jerusalem, which symbolizes the kingdom of God in the book of Revelation, is a city that descends out of heaven. It is a compact entity that holds the promise of God's fulfillment and joy.

When the Hebrew prophets fell under the inspiration of the Holy Spirit, they envisioned a city in which the hopes and dreams of all the peoples of the world would be actualized. Their faith was expressed in their vision of a city where the citizenry would enjoy good health and the curses such as those that presently mark urban America would be wiped away and forgotten. These prophets preached that in that city there would be an end to the infant mortality that plagues our present-day ghettos and slums and that there would be no more weeping for teenagers whose lives are cut short by gang violence. They looked toward a city where men and women would live out the full cycles of their lives without fear of an old age that would doom their tortured bodies to isolated charity wards. They believed God would create a city where there would be adequate housing and full employment for all of its people. In such a city, no children would be born only to face a troubled future and eventually be overwhelmed with a sense of nihilistic despair. The city of which the prophets dreamed would be environmentally clean, negating the effects of human abuse. Nature would be renewed and the violence that characterizes the struggle for survival would be no more. All of this was expressed symbolically by the biblical image of the lion and the lamb lying down together in peace. The prophet Isaiah envisioned that city when he wrote:

> For, behold, I create new heavens and a new earth: and the former shall not be remembered, nor come into mind. But be ye glad and rejoice for ever in that which I create: for, behold, I create Jerusalem a rejoicing, and her people a joy. And I will rejoice in Jerusalem, and joy in my people: and the voice of weeping shall be no more heard in her, nor the voice of crying. There shall be no more thence an infant of days nor an old man that not filled his days: for the child shall die a hundred years old; but the sinner being a hundred years old shall be accursed. And they shall build houses, and inhabit them; and they shall plant vineyards, and eat the fruit of them. They shall not build, and another inhabit, they shall not plant, and another eat; for as the days of a tree are the days of my people, and mine elect shall long enjoy the work of their hands. They shall not labor in vain, nor bring forth for trouble; for they are the seed of the blessed of the Lord, and their offspring with them. And it shall come to pass, that before they call, I will answer; and while they are yet speaking, I will hear. The wolf and the lamb shall feed together, and the lion shall eat straw like the bullock: and dust shall be the serpent's meat. They shall not hurt nor destroy in all my holy mountain, saith the Lord. (Isaiah 65:17–25)

But the city, as it was meant to be, has been spoiled by the one who has been called "The Great Destroyer." There is a real, though invisible, demonic presence in urban America that transcends the empirical realities studied by sociologists. When social scientists gather data on such things as crime, homelessness, urban blight, disintegrating families, teenaged prostitutes, growing joblessness, racial conflict, and the alienated elderly, they are at a loss to fully explain why such things are increasingly evident. Theoretical interpretations of the evils they survey do not convince them that they completely understand what is going on. On a subliminal level, these social scientists know that something more is unfolding in the city than that which is objectively available to their scientific instruments of investigation. The word demonic is not part of their politically correct academic jargon and, as practitioners of a discipline that invented the word "positivism," they are at a loss to make sense out of what is unfolding before their eyes.

But things *are* changing. Some social scientists are beginning to talk of the need to go beyond the categories of reason and empirical science to give serious attention to postmodern perspectives on the ugly urban realities that defy their comprehension. Some of these postmodernists go so far as to criticize colleagues who, in their sophistication, will not admit that the full explanation of the evil and chaos of the city does not lie in modern categories of understanding. These postmodernists argue that such explanations can only begin to be found in the context of a worldview that is ready to consider evil as a strategizing intelligence that is systematically destroying the city and creating what appears to be insane behavior among its inhabitants.

The idea of Satan or the Devil does not compute in the minds of most pure empiricists who think that ideas like that are medieval. However, there was room for such "mystical" thinking in one of the most brilliant of them, Emile Durkheim. This seminal thinker in the field of sociology believed that there were, among the "social facts" of the city, certain nonmaterial realities that significantly controlled its people.[1] It was Durkheim who talked about a "collective effervescence" that could emerge *sui generis* from the interaction of the inhabitants of the city and which seemed to have a life of its own. He further argued that this collective effervescence of the city could not simply be traced back to the personal traits of the group of individuals who created it.[2] Consequently, it is not unreasonable to ask if there might be a collective spirit, evident in a city like Calcutta, which is named after and dedicated to the god, Kali, who is, in Hindu theology, "The Great Destroyer." It seems to me quite legitimate to ask if there is not some kind of link between the impoverished and diseased souls who sleep on the streets of that city each night and some kind of collective consciousness that pervades the city. Can some supranatural energy force be at work in Calcutta, leaving hundreds of corpses each morning to be picked up by garbage collectors and burned at the city dump? Is something going on in Calcutta that escapes the observations of those who come with *a priori* commitments to explain in nonmystical terms what they see?

On the other hand, is there something mystically positive about that city on Mt. Zion, given a name that means "The City of Peace"? Should we not take seriously those who visit Jerusalem and readily talk about a "presence" in that place, a presence that all the evil of Israeli and Palestinian terrorists cannot wipe out? Can it be that there is a spiritual reality there that hovers over that city and through the ages has wept over Jerusalem? Might there not be a mystical longing for the realization of that peace that is promised in the name Jerusalem? Is the spirit of The One who once cried out,

> O Jerusalem, Jerusalem, thou that killest the prophets, and stonest them which are sent unto thee, how often would I have gathered thy children together, even as a hen gathereth her chickens under her wings, and ye would not! (Matt. 23:37)

still an overarching presence in that city?

Once, when visiting Liverpool, England, I met some young people who were serving with what is now the largest missionary organization in the world, Youth with a Mission. The YWAM missionaries, as they are called, claimed that they had come to Liverpool to pray against the forces of darkness that dominated that city. They talked about engaging in spiritual warfare, and stated emphatically that no good could come to Liverpool until the demonic forces that held the city in their sway were vanquished. And so they stood in the middle of Liverpool—praying in the name of Jesus, commanding the demonic forces to be gone.

What the YWAM missionaries said seems to belong to another place and another time. To listen to those young people quote scripture and declare, "Resist the devil, and he will flee from you!" (James 4:7b) seems out of sync with the mind-set of those who hold to more sophisticated interpretations of reality. And yet the intellectuals who would scoff at these young people might feel a bit threatened if they could recall the words of the ancient apostle who once referred to his own intellectualism as "dung" (Philippians 3:8) and went on to say:

> For it is written, I will destroy the wisdom of the wise, and will bring to nothing the understanding of the prudent. Where is the wise? where is the scribe? Where is the disputer of this world? Hath not God made foolish the wisdom of this world? For after that in the wisdom of God the world by wisdom knew not God, it pleased God by the foolishness of preaching to save them that believe.
>
> . . . .
>
> But God hath chosen the foolish things of the world to confound the wise; and God hath chosen the weak things of the world to confound the things which are mighty; and base things of the world, and things which are despised, hath God chosen, yea, and things which are not, to bring to nought things that are. (1 Cor. 1:19–21; 27–28)

Religious talk about evil spirits controlling a city and dominating the workings of its institutions was, not so long ago, the kind of thing you might hear only from backwoods Pentecostal preachers, perhaps from those in snake-handling cults. But this is not the case anymore. Today, even respected twentieth-century theologians are talking the same kind of talk. Prominent among these theologians are Hendrick Berkoff, Walter Wink, and Albert van den Heuvel, each of whom is doing exegesis on the biblical references to the "principalities and powers" referred to in Pauline theology (Ephesians 6:12).[3] Wink and Berkoff have started some serious speculation about the possibilities of such evil spirits. The idea that demonic forces might pervade the institutional structures of a societal order and constrain those who live within that social system to behave in ways that bring destruction on themselves and on others is gaining credibility these days.[4] Berkoff and van den Heuvel contend that when Paul wrote about the principalities and powers almost twenty centuries ago, he was referring to the supranatural forces that have gained control of societal institutions and are now wreaking havoc among us. According to Berkoff and van den Heuvel, economic, political, familial, and educational systems are not simply sociological accidents. Rather, these institutions have been willed into existence by God for the good and well-being of God's people. However, Berkoff and Wink contend that certain evil spiritual powers, perhaps akin to fallen angels, have gained control of those organizational systems and are employing them as instruments for destruction. According to Berkoff and van den Heuvel, demonic powers are at work in the various institutions of the urban community, and these structures, once ordained for the good of God's people, are now oppressing them.[5]

Can there be any doubt that *something* has gone haywire in the societal systems of the city? Schools created to enhance the lives of boys and girls are, in many cities, marked by violence and even the teaching of anti-God values. Young people in such systems are given the illusion of receiving an education but left without the skills that they need to earn a living and contribute effectively to the societal good.

Governmental structures purposed by God to hold back evildoers (Romans 13:1–3) are too often corrupted into agencies that serve the selfish designs of special interest groups instead of the welfare of all the people. Politicians called by God to do good (Romans 13:4–5) fall into graft, corruption, and the abuse of power, using their offices to exploit the city for their own benefit.

Economic institutions, created to provide employment and give workers the opportunity to produce things that people need, end up doing neither, caring only that production maximizes profits. The public is manipulated through advertising into spending its hard-earned cash for consumer goods it does not need, leading biblically based prophets to ask again, "Wherefore do ye spend money for that which is not bread?

and your labor for that which satisfieth not?" (Isaiah 55:1–2). And even as such demonically controlled economic systems are enslaving people through credit buying, they further exercise their destructive powers by polluting air, land, and sea with their industrial waste.

Other evil forces at work in the city are well on their way to destroying the fabric of family life. The easy acceptance of divorce, the high rate of premarital pregnancies, the use of abortion as a means of birth control, the rebellion of children against their parents, and the abuse of children by parents all seem to be orchestrated by an evil intelligence bent on familial destruction. The extended family, which once provided economic security, a network of caring relatives, and a deep sense of community, has been replaced in the city by smaller nuclear families that more easily tend toward being isolated and/or pathological. The heightened individualistic selfishness and egocentricity of children raised in such micro units creates a sullenness and anger among the urban youth of this generation that does not bode well for the future of the city.

Berkoff and Wink contend that, in our efforts to save the people in the city, we must engage in spiritual warfare against the demonic forces that control the institutions of the social order. They admonish us to give serious consideration to Paul's words in the Epistle to the Ephesians:

> For we wrestle not against flesh and blood, but against principalities, against powers, against the rulers of the darkness of this world, against spiritual wickedness in high places. (Eph. 6:12)

Paul further reminds us that the principalities and powers usually pose as agents of good, even as they do us evil. We can see this in the faces of those politicians who mask their evil agendas as they smile, glad-hand us, and make empty promises on election day.

Not even the religious establishment is free from the possibility of demonic control. Those churches in Northern Ireland that set Catholics against Protestants and Protestants against Catholics, churches in America that teach a prosperity theology that contradicts everything that Jesus taught us about wealth, the "official religion" of some churches in Third World countries that legitimates the oppression of the weak by supporting regimes of ungodly power, and all of the churches everywhere that foster racism, sexism, homophobia, nationalistic chauvinism, and militarism—all are evidence that even those institutions which God intended to be agents of deliverance can become instruments of the Evil One.

Berkoff and van den Heuvel remind us that the Apostle Paul pointed out that Christ was crucified by principalities and powers that purported to be servants of God, but were, in reality, servants of Satan. If they had been servants of God, said Paul, they never would have conspired to put Jesus to death. Because they did crucify Jesus, their true nature was exposed.

> But we speak the wisdom of God in a mystery, even the hidden wisdom, which God ordained before the world unto our glory; Which none of the princes of this world knew, for had they known it, they would not have crucified the Lord of glory. (1 Cor. 2:7–8)

More recently, Walter Wink has taken up the challenge of examining the nature of evil as it expresses itself through institutional structures. Along with the French sociologist Emile Durkheim, Wink believes that institutions, over time, develop "a life of their own." Societal institutions, he claims, have an emerging collective consciousness that possesses the power to do spiritual, psychological, and social harm to the people of a city. However, Wink does not believe that such principalities and powers have any *a priori* existence to the societies that they permeate with their influence, as do Berkoff and van den Heuval.[6] In short, Wink does not hold that the principalities and powers that wreak havoc in a city are controlled by transcendental demons or fallen angels. Like Durkheim, he believes that they emerge *sui generis* from the people of a given urban collective over time. Nevertheless, Wink contends that any attempt to bring about social change requires that we deal with these suprahuman realities and figure out ways to counteract their evil powers. As the church takes up the challenge of participating with God in transforming the city, it is imperative that it devise a strategy for combating those principalities and powers that, according to scripture, are in rebellion against the will of their Creator.

William Stringfellow, in his book, *An Ethic for Christians and Other Aliens in a Strange and Distant Land,* contends that it was a failure to recognize the presence and influence of the principalities and powers at work in the city that reduced the effectiveness of attempts to create justice and economic well-being in Harlem during the '50s and '60s.[7] During those explosive years, Stringfellow worked with a variety of Harlem-based social action organizations but always felt that they were making little, if any, headway. Looking back on those days, he says that their mistake was in dealing only with the *visible* expressions of social evil and not recognizing that there were *invisible* powers behind the institutional structures of Harlem that provided strength and gave direction to those institutions. They thought that if they could just get rid of an evil school superintendent here and a corrupt politician there, the social system would change. Stringfellow later bemoaned the naïveté of himself and his coworkers in thinking that, simply by endorsing progressive social policies, they could counteract the poverty, prejudices, and crime that wreaked havoc among the Harlem populace. Stringfellow came to believe that they were constantly defeated in their attempts to realize something of the kingdom of God in Harlem because they did not recognize that there were invisible demonic powers in control of the structural evils that were so visibly evident. It was his belief that their modern logical empirical mind-sets did not allow them even to consider whom their ultimate enemies might be.

In the spiritual warfare which requires that we do battle with the principalities and powers that exercise rule over the city, we are told to be properly equipped. Paul writes:

> Wherefore take unto you the whole armor of God, that ye may be able to withstand in the evil day, and having done all, to stand. Stand therefore, having your loins girt about with truth, and having on the breastplate of righteousness; And your feet shod with the preparation of the gospel of peace: Above all, taking the shield of faith, wherewith ye shall be able to quench all the fiery darts of the wicked. And take the helmet of salvation, and the sword of the Spirit, which is the word of God: Praying always with all prayer and supplication in the Spirit, and watching thereunto with all perseverance, and supplication for all saints; (Eph. 6:13–18)

Going forth with your loins girt about with truth means that we have to be a people who know what we are talking about. Sometimes we want to be prophetic in attacking the injustices we find within institutional structures, but we do not have accurate facts and end up making sensationalistic statements that are not true. As a case in point, we evangelicals have recently been protesting the removal of anything having to do with the Judeo-Christian faith, not only from the public school system, but from any place in the public sector. It is true that Stephen Carter, the Yale Law School scholar, has made the case brilliantly that what is going on under the auspices of court rulings and under pressure generated by the American Civil Liberties Union is out of line with what the framers of the U.S. Constitution had in mind when they passed the First Amendment of the Bill of Rights. Religion, contends Carter, *should* be part of the educational experience of every child. All that was intended by our nation's founders was that no one sectarian version of religion be established in a favored position over others. Certainly, there is a need for us to call for openness to God in our educational institutions. However, in our zeal to make our case, we evangelicals have been prone to exaggerations and even downright misrepresentations of what is really going on.

We will not get to any good place if we do battle with the principalities and powers without having our "loins girt about with truth." It has been said, "Beware when you fight a dragon—lest you become a dragon." Indeed, all too often, we Christians, in our struggle for causes that are just, adopt the ways of the Evil One and distort the truth, believing that it is somehow right to fight evil with evil.

Christians should recognize that in challenging the evils that are inherent in the structural systems of social institutions, truth is our greatest ally. Nothing diminishes the hold that evil principalities and powers have over the city as much as having the truth about their evil made public. In Colossians, the Apostle Paul tells us that one of the things Jesus accomplished on the cross was to expose the true nature of the principalities and powers that were at work in the city of Jerusalem.

The religious leaders of that city paraded themselves as good public servants and claimed to be preserving the party of true religion, maintaining public order, and ridding the community of a blasphemer. But if they really had been people of God, they would not have crucified Jesus because they would have recognized him for who he was.

The Roman soldiers who drilled the nails through the hands and feet of Jesus and then lifted his bloodied body up to hang on the cross claimed that, as agents of *Pax Romana,* they were an army of deliverance. But had they really been the agents of good, and not of evil, all of them would have joined with that solitary Roman soldier who cried out at the end, "Truly this man was the Son of God" (Mark 15:39).

As Jesus hung on that Roman cross, the true nature of all those civil and religious leaders and of the institutions they represented were exposed as being under the direction of the Evil One. Paul makes this clear as he writes:

> And having spoiled principalities and power, he made a show of them openly, triumphing over them in it. (Col. 2:15)

In Philadelphia, many real estate agents used to make a practice of not showing homes that were for sale in white neighborhoods to African-American families. They never came right out and said they were doing this because to do so would have been illegal, but the system was well known in the white neighborhoods that they were trying to "protect."

People putting their houses up for sale were discouraged by these agents from displaying For Sale signs. African-American families that came looking to buy homes were not shown listings of the houses that were on the market in "protected" neighborhoods.

Church leaders, who had long been aware of what had been happening, devised a plan to expose these real estate agents as promoters of racist policies. They would send an African-American couple to the office of a suspected agent and ask about available housing, carefully tape-recording what was said in response to their inquiry. Immediately after the African-American couple had been told that no housing was available in a certain neighborhood, a white couple would go to the same office and ask about the availability of housing in the same neighborhood. This second couple, who also tape-recorded their conversation with the real estate agent, usually found that there really were houses for sale in the neighborhood in question.

Making both tapes available to the press not only exposed this covert racial discrimination, but set up such an uproar in the city that agents were forced to end their efforts to maintain segregated neighborhoods. An evil practice was brought to an end, simply by letting the truth be known.

The 1950s Supreme Court decision that permitted busing and ended *de facto* segregation in the public schools was built on careful sociological research. Studies proved that when African-American students left segregated schools and attended schools with white children their learning improved, while the learning of the white children showed no decline from being in integrated schools. Knowing this truth provided the basis for the court ruling that set huge numbers of African-American children free from having to put up with inferior educations.

There are many fronts in the war against principalities and powers. For example, if churches are going to win the battle to keep gambling out of their cities, it will be because they have found ways to expose the devastating truth about the effects of gambling on individuals and families. Conclusive studies show that gambling destroys huge numbers of people who become addicted to it. Studies also show that the revenues from gambling have failed to deliver to the general public promised benefits such as funding for improved education for children and expanded programs for senior citizens. Furthermore, there is empirical evidence that gambling fosters such a host of social pathologies (for example, burglaries, wife beatings, and child neglect) that it ends up costing a community more than the monies it produces for the public coffers.[8] As churches strip bare the phony case for gambling made by politicians too often tied in with the casinos, the evil principalities and powers that bring this curse into urban communities will lose their hold on people and may even collapse when exposed in the light of truth.

"Put on the breastplate of righteousness!" is another directive of the Apostle Paul. This second piece of armor was what the temple priests would put on when they went forth into the community to ferret out social injustices and signs of oppression.

In those ancient days, the Israelite judges were not simply legal experts who waited for culprits to be brought before them so that sentences might be pronounced and punishments meted out. Instead, those judges served as agents of God who had been called to roam among the people for the express purposes of listening to the cries of the victims of injustice and being champions of the poor and oppressed who had no voice. Furthermore, they had the authority to call for the correctives that would make things right. Before discharging their judicial responsibilities, these judges always put on the symbol of their office, which was the Breastplate of Righteousness.

In our own struggles with the principalities and powers of this age, we too are called on by scripture to equip ourselves with the authority that is required to carry out the calling of those long-ago judges we read about in the Bible.

In spite of all the weaknesses, hypocrisies, and shortcomings of which the church is accused, we who are the church must be aware that we still speak with considerable authority in our world. We must learn to use that authority to speak out against the social injustices that are all too evident in the city. We too must put on the Breastplate of Righteousness in our struggle against the principalities and powers of this age.

Some years ago our missionary organization, EAPE/Kingdomworks, supported the Adrian Sisters, a Roman Catholic order based in Michigan, as its members sought to bring some of the kingdom of God into the lives of the poor sugar workers in the Dominican Republic. Like the Adrian Sisters, EAPE/Kingdomworks had been at work evangelizing and providing some basic social services to those who worked in the sugar fields located in the eastern half of the country.

As we ministered among these very poor people, we heard their stories. Many of them expressed a great deal of anger toward their primary employer, Gulf and Western. This corporate conglomerate had gained control over most of the sugar production in the Dominican Republic following the invasion of the country by the U.S. Marines in 1965.[9]

The people who worked in these fields cutting sugar were not being paid a living wage. They lacked basic medical care for their families and had little means for educating their children. Over and over we heard their stories of privation and suffering. We knew that it was not enough to minister to the victims of what this company was doing. We had to do something to change things so that Gulf and Western might become a blessing rather than a curse to the people.

We, like the Adrian Sisters, bought a few shares of stock in Gulf and Western. This entitled us to go to stockholders' meetings where we could demand justice for the poor. We wanted the stockholders to hear what we had heard from the people who were working their lands. We would call them to repentance and ask that Gulf and Western make things right.

The results were astounding. After several confrontations on the floor of the stockholders' meetings, and long discussions in the corporate offices of Gulf and Western, some major changes and innovations were instituted. The company helped to develop a network of village schools and a university, which provided new and better educational opportunities for the people of the Dominican Republic.

An arrangement was made with Mt. Sinai Medical Center in New York City for clinics and medical dispensaries to be established in the eastern part of the country. "Industrial zones" were established where various companies from abroad might find attractive places to develop manufacturing ventures, thus delivering the economy of the area from being dependent on sugar alone. Perhaps most important was a program to shift, insofar as it was possible, agricultural production from sugar to produce, thereby making more food available for the indigenous population. It is fair to say that, over the years, Gulf and Western has moved significantly toward becoming the kind of principality and power that does the will of God when it comes to economic justice.[10]

If the church is to live out its calling in the city, it must learn how to engage the principalities and powers. The church must, as did the judges of the Bible, go out into the community, listen to the people to learn how they are being oppressed by institutional evils, and then become the advocate of the oppressed, demanding justice on their behalf.

Third, according to the Apostle Paul, challenging the principalities and powers requires that we be a people whose feet are "shod with the preparation of the gospel of peace" (Ephesians 6:15). This translates into our learning to understand ourselves as agents of reconciliation (2 Corinthians 5:18). We must be a people that does not let the Evil One destroy the potentialities for good inherent in the principalities and powers by turning them against each other in destructive fashion. For example, in city after city throughout America, corporations and labor unions have done battle with each other in ways that have mortally wounded them both, as well as bringing economic disaster to the people of the city. In my own city of Philadelphia, I watched as one of our major newspapers closed down because of unreasonable demands by a labor union on the one hand, and intransigent selfishness by owners and management on the other. Thousands of families were impacted because of the ensuing loss of jobs, and the city lost a valuable instrument for communication. Something of the spirit of the city of Philadelphia was diminished when *The Evening Bulletin* ceased to be. None of this *had* to happen. The newspaper was economically viable and very much needed. But in the midst of the labor/management dispute that destroyed *The Evening Bulletin,* there was no agent of reconciliation to step in and try to bring the two sides together. The churches of the city failed to recognize that they had a responsibility to shoe their feet with the preparation of the gospel of peace and run between the warring parties to bring about a just settlement of the problem.

One of the ministries to which I have given a good bit of my time over the years is the Value of the Person (VOP) program based in Pittsburgh. Founded by Wayne Alderson, the former CEO of Pitron Steel, this organization has as its mission the bringing of peace to the corporate community and goes so far as to try to foster love between those in labor and those in management. Alderson has put together a team that includes persons with experience as labor union leaders as well as corporate executives. This team negotiates with major corporations to bring together for a few days their key employees from both union and management. The VOP staff helps these people unburden themselves and brings to light repressed hostilities in ways that lead to repentance and forgiveness. Labor and management, which previously may have known each other only in adversarial relationships, tap into each other's emotions and each comes to understand the other in new ways. Complaints are heard and dealt with outside the context of contract negotiations. Having participated in these VOP seminars, I can verify that the unexpected and unbelievable often happens. Labor and management sometimes become friends and even come to love each other. One manager told me that when his wife was in the hospital members of the union regularly visited her and prayed for her. Employees, who once had viewed him as an enemy, had come to know him as a brother. Attitudes at his factory changed; a positive spirit now prevails.

Through the work of VOP, there are many places where labor and management have a new sense of trust that makes for rapid, honest, and open contract settlements. Strikes have been avoided, and the economies of cities have been rescued from collapse. Redemptive forces have been set loose in the marketplace. The VOP program recognizes the interrelationship between what goes on in the home and what goes on in the workplace, and the family lives of all involved are very much impacted. My particular role as a member of the VOP team is to address the concerns of the family and to help both labor and management recognize what must be done to bring love, dignity, and respect to their family relationships.[11]

The VOP seminars are overtly Christian. It is quite usual for us to talk about what the Bible says about the problems being faced in labor/management relationships. A major effort to bring something of God's kingdom to the workplace is behind all that we do. The entire staff understands its calling to be agents of reconciliation whose "feet are shod with the preparation of the gospel of peace."

The shield of faith described by Paul in Ephesians 6 is essential to ward off the fiery darts of the wicked. In the struggle against the principalities and powers, we must be people who wholly rely on God. The true safeguard in the difficult struggle lies not in introspection, but in looking Godward to see the essence of our faith (Psalm 25:15). Those who thought they could overcome the evils that distort social institutions underestimate what they are up against. In the Bible we find that even Michael, the archangel of heaven, backs off in the face of Satan and asks God to do battle on his behalf (Jude 9). It is ignorance or arrogance to think that anyone other than God can ultimately overcome that Evil One who uses the principalities and powers to work in the world.

In South Africa during some of the darkest days in the struggle against apartheid, David Cassidy, a prominent Christian leader and founder of the evangelistic organization African Enterprise, recognized that political strategies would not be enough to bring an end to the racist government that had reduced blacks to second-class citizenship. Cassidy put out a call to all South Africans to set aside a day of prayer to call on God to do what seemed humanly impossible—to bring an end to white domination of the country.

The president of South Africa, Pieter Willem Botha, did not take Cassidy's proposal lightly. He called Cassidy to his office and made a not-too-veiled threat of bodily harm that was aimed at getting Cassidy to call off the day of prayer. But David Cassidy would not back down.

On the day of the prayer vigil, roads leading into the city of Johannesburg were empty. The newspapers carried front-page photographs of carless highways and the story of how just about the entire black population had stayed home from work to support this special day of prayer. Leaning on God alone for help, the overwhelming majority of South Africans set loose through prayer a power that eventually would bring down the oppressive Botha regime and pave the way for the creation of a free nation. In miraculous fashion, circumstances changed and it was not long before Nelson Mandela was released from prison, elections were held, and apartheid ended. Some credit economic sanctions for what happened in South Africa. Others will contend that it was political pressure from outside the country that brought about the change. But those who were there will tell you that something more mysterious and more powerful was at work. There were too many "crucial coincidences" as events in this struggle for freedom unfolded to chalk the victory up to anything other than the intervention of God. As the history of South Africa is written, the faith of the people, expressed in prayer, will have to be given serious consideration.

Sometimes, in strategizing for social change, Christian leaders talk like secular politicians. They speak only of the power that they can muster from voting blocs and the manipulation of public opinion. Frequently, there is a cynicism about them as they assume that all the players involved are governed only by the most base motivations. These leaders have no confidence in appeals to the people to do what is right because they believe that the general public acts only out of self-interest. These Christian leaders function as though God were not in any way involved in what is transpiring. In short, they do not go to do battle with the principalities and powers equipped with the shield of faith.

When the counterattack comes from the Evil One, they are overwhelmed. Not having tapped into the power of God through prayer, they are too weak to gain any victories. I have heard leaders like this complain and attribute their defeats to the fact that, historically, the righteous have always lost out in the struggle for justice. There is no recognition of the reality that their failures might be the result of a lack of faith in God and in people. The Bible tells us:

> These things I have spoken unto you, that in me ye might have
> peace. In the world ye shall have tribulation: but be of good cheer;
> I have overcome the world. (John 16:33)

But not only do these leaders fail to use the Bible as a guidebook for social change, they also treat as irrelevant a biblically based faith that would make them "more than conquerors" (Romans 8:37).

This replacement of prayer with positive strategizing has become especially evident in the civil rights movement. When Martin Luther King was among us, every action of the movement was bathed in prayer. Those who practiced civil disobedience through passive resistance did so only after all-night prayer meetings. Tapping into the power of God through prayer, armies of demonstrators went forth with their shields of faith to do battle, saying to one another, "If God be for us, who can be against us?" (Romans 8:31).

Recently I went to a planning session of African-American ministers in a large city who had come together to deal with concerns about instances of racially motivated harassment by the police. At the meeting there were no prayers, no talk of God, no references to the Bible, and no allusion to faith. Instead, there was talk only of what political threats could be made and which special interest groups could be mobilized to put pressure on City Hall.[12]

These same ministers decried the fact that so many of the gains made during the '60s were eroding in the '90s. It never occurred to them that the difference might be that the movement in the '60s was dependent on faith in God's power while their movement in the '90s was dependent on how much personal power certain African-American leaders could muster for themselves.

The helmet of salvation is the fifth piece of armor that Paul prescribes for those engaging in spiritual warfare against the principalities and powers. As any "knight of faith" knows, the helmet is the most important piece of protective armor. In the face of mortal combat, the head must be protected at all cost.

Christians need constant reminders that, in the context of a spiritual battle, the God who has saved them is a God who will protect them. When the time comes to act, Satan has a way of doing thing to our heads so that we become filled with doubts and fears, and we lose that edge of confidence that would carry us through. There are risks involved when we stop talking and start acting, and at such times we can be sure that the Evil One will bombard us with reasons as to why we might be doing the wrong thing. We need to be constantly reminded that the God who saves us is a God who sends angels to watch over us (Luke 4:10) and who will not allow us to be tested beyond what we are able to handle:

> There hath no temptation taken you but such as is common to man: but God is faithful, who will not suffer you to be tempted above that ye are able; but will with the temptation also make a way to escape, that ye may be able to bear it. (1 Corinthians 10:13)

All too often when I am demonstrating for social justice or speaking out on behalf of the poor and the oppressed, I am accused of being some kind of a "leftover" from the '60s. I am told that the kind of radical ideology that I preach belongs to another place and another time. My critics remind me that now most of the social activists of the '60s have become part of the establishment and are holding down jobs in the very societal system they once challenged so boldly.

These critics give me a great opportunity to witness to the power of the gospel. I explain to them that most of those who paraded for social justice in the '60s were motivated by a value system that was built on secular humanism. They were good values, but they were based on a philosophy of human origin. Most of those people, who took their stand against the principalities and powers that were wreaking havoc on the dignity of blacks and enmeshing us in a horrendous war in Southeast Asia, were not rooted in eternity. They lacked the assurance that belongs to those who are in Christ and have Christ in them. Those who have "the helmet of salvation" are protected against such claims as "The system cannot be changed!" or "We'll never have enough power to challenge the establishment!" Knowing that God has saved them and has called them, they are in for the long haul. Nobody can do things to their heads. They know that they may lose battles—but that they will do so in a cause that will ultimately win. And they can say, under the influence of the Holy Spirit, "Better to lose in a cause that will ultimately win than to win in a cause that will ultimately lose." When other advocates for social justice give up in the face of an evil social system that seems unchangeable, those who wear the helmet of salvation will fight on, knowing that they are on the victory side. Their confidence lies in their weapon which is *the sword of the spirit which is the Word of God.* They have read the Bible and they know the good news—"We win!"

When Jesus is tempted by Satan, he is able to be victorious by quoting the Bible (Matthew 4:1–11). Being grounded in the scriptures is essential to those who struggle for social justice against the diabolical presence who uses the principalities and powers to do evil. Too often there is a divide between those who are versed in scripture and those who are into social justice. The former tend to be evangelicals who are constantly studying and memorizing scripture, while the latter tend to be "liberals," who seem to study just about everything else. I really do believe in that creedal statement that declares the Bible to be "an infallible guide for faith and practice."

I am constantly surprised at how situations in the Bible parallel those situations that are part of the struggle for justice in modern times. In the late '50s, I had an encounter that demonstrated this correlation and exercised an important influence on my whole approach to struggling against the principalities and powers.

I had just finished delivering a great lecture at a small church-related college in Indiana, and I opened myself up to questions from the floor. A disheveled-looking student stood, and then asked me if I believed it was ever right to practice civil disobedience. In a cavalier manner, I flipped through my King James Bible and read:

> Let every soul be subject unto the higher powers. For there is no power but of God: the powers that be are ordained of God. Whosoever therefore resisteth the power, resisteth the ordinance of God: and they that resist shall receive to themselves damnation. For rulers are not a terror to good works, but to the evil. Wilt thou then not be afraid of the power? do that which is good, and thou shalt have praise of the same: (Rom. 13:1–3)

"That should answer your question," I said.

Instead of sitting down, as I had expected him to do after being confronted with what I believed to be the final word of God, this young man stood there silently for several moments. Then, slowly and thoughtfully, he asked, "By the way, preacher—where was Paul when he wrote those verses?"

Where he was going hit me right away. I gulped before I replied, "In jail."

"That's what I thought," answered my young interrogator. "Let me tell you how he got there. It seems they were having a race relations problem down there in Jerusalem. The Jews and Gentiles weren't getting along too well. Some Jewish people thought those other people weren't like them and that they ought to have their own church. They didn't think they should even eat together. Isn't that right?"

I tried to interrupt, but he wouldn't let me.

"Paul decided to go down there to Jerusalem to straighten out those racist Christians and, to make his point, he took along a Gentile to travel on the boat with him. Now I don't know what you call that, but it sounds like the first freedom ride to me. And that wasn't all. When Paul got to Jerusalem, he decided to eat out in public with his Gentile brother. Back in those days Jews didn't eat with people from other races—but Paul showed them that all that segregated eating was over and done with for those who were in Christ Jesus. I don't know what you think was happening down there, preacher, but it sounds like the first sit-in to me.

"After that, Paul decided to take his Gentile friend into the Temple of Jerusalem to do some worshiping. Now it's one thing to have a freedom ride, and it's another to stage a sit-in. And when Paul got into racially integrating the Temple with some kind of "pray-in," well, he'd gone too far—in the opinion of some folks. So they rioted! Now you've got to ask how good a Christian Paul was with him going around stirring up race riots. But that's what he did. He caused so much trouble that the police had to come and take old Paul into protective custody. And when they got him down at the jail, there was a little police brutality. When they finished beating on him, Paul said, 'You've messed with the wrong man! You think I'm just some ordinary Jew. Well, I'm not. I'm a Roman citizen! And I demand my rights. I'm taking this case to the Supreme Court. Just you wait and see!'

"It was on his way to have his case heard in the Supreme Court—which in those days was in Rome—that Paul wrote to the Roman Christians that they should be subject to the higher powers. After violating the laws and customs of the people of Jerusalem, Paul goes on to tell those people that they had better not resist or disobey the authorities. Now, explain all of that to me, preacher. Why would Paul say to always be subject to the law after doing what he did? Or maybe there are some times when civil disobedience is okay!"

I knew I was, as they say, dead meat. He had cut me down with the Sword of the Spirit which is the word of God.

Appendix

As you read through this book, you may have been inspired to want to support the EAPE/Kingdomworks ministries. Thousands of children are being touched daily by God's love through these ministries, and it is our hope and prayer that one day some of them will replicate what our young missionaries are contributing toward urban renewal. These missionaries are certainly deserving of your loving support and prayers and will be grateful for your financial support. Together with them, we believe that this city (and any city) can be turned around. Won't you help us turn dreams into reality and hopes into actuality? Won't you give a gift to:

EAPE/Kingdomworks
P.O. Box 7238
St. Davids, PA 19087

Notes

Chapter 1

1. All the stories in this chapter were written by Bruce Main, the executive director of Urban Promise. This is an urban ministry initiated in 1988 in Camden, New Jersey. Urban Promise has extended its outreach through affiliates now established in Vancouver, Canada; Toronto, Canada; and Wilmington, Del. Its Camden offices are located at 3700 Rudderrow Avenue, Camden, N.J. 08105.

Chapter 2

1. An article describing the plight of Camden appeared in *Time* (January 30, 1992), 21–22.
2. Ibid.
3. The definition of "natural barrier" was developed by Robert Park to describe those physical and social characteristics of a part of the city that divided a city into distinct zones or neighborhoods.
4. Red-lining is now illegal, but it is still practiced *de facto*.
5. See the *Philadelphia Inquirer* (October 31, 1991, and November 1, 1991), 1.
6. Statistics available at the office of the mayor of Philadelphia, the honorable Edward Rendell.
7. Brett Pulley, "While a Dying City Languishes, a State Battles to Take Control," *The New York Times* (May 19, 1996).
8. Ibid.
9. An excellent study of "the principalities and powers" as systemic evil can be found in Walter Wink, *Engaging the Powers* (Minneapolis: Fortress Press, 1992).

Chapter 3

1. Charles Murray, *Losing Ground* (New York: Basic Books, 1984).
2. Herbert Gans, *The War Against the Poor* (New York: Basic Books, 1995).
3. John J. DiIulio, Jr. of the Brookings Institution contends that to date there is only anecdotal information on the subject.
4. Marvin Olasky, *The Tragedy of American Compassion* (Wheaton, Ill.: Crossway Books, 1995).
5. Keith J. Hardmen, *Charles Grandison Finney: Revivalists and Reformer* (Grand Rapids: Baker Book House, 1987).

265

6. Ibid. Arthur and Lewis Tappan were two of the wealthiest men in America. Committed to the antislavery movement they invested their vast fortunes to this cause and died penniless. They were able to get significant numbers of other wealthy philanthropists to make large contributions to support church-based programs to help the poor.
7. Arthur Bonner, *Jerry McAuley and His Mission* (Neptune, N.J.: Loizeaux Brothers, 1967) supports this thesis in his examination of what was happening in New York City in the 1800s.
8. Research on costs to churches for carrying the burden of welfare can be secured from the Polis Center in Indianapolis, Ind.
9. Op cit., Olasky, 99–115.
10. See *Sojourners*, "With Unconditional Love" (September–October 1997), 16–22.
11. See House Bill HR 4255.
12. See *Sojourners*, "The Cry for Renewal" (May 1995).
13. See *The Washington Post* (October 18, 1997), 8.

Chapter 4

1. An overview of Talcott Parsons and his views on social change is outlined in his book, *The System of Modern Societies* (Englewood Cliffs, N.J.: Prentice Hall, 1971).
2. The concept of the "Invisible Hand" comes from the theories of Adam Smith and John Maynard Keynes. See Robert L. Heilbroner, *The Worldly Philosophers* (New York: Simon & Shuster, 1953).
3. Witold Tybczynski, *City Life* (New York: Charles Scribner's Sons, 1995).
4. Max Weber, *The Theory of Social and Economic Organization* (New York: Free Press of Glencoe, 1964), 64 ff.
5. Ibid.

Chapter 5

1. Roberta Hestenes pastors the Solona Beach Presbyterian Church in Solona Beach, Calif.
2. William H. Willimon, *The Intrusive Word* (Grand Rapids: Wm. B. Eerdmans Publishing Co., 1994).
3. D. James Kennedy, *Evangelism Explosion: A Manual for Outreach* (Wheaton, Ill.: Tyndale House Publishers, Inc., 1996).

Chapter 6

1. Robert Linthicum, *Empowering the Poor* (Monrovia, Calif., MARC, 1991), 5–6. Copyright 1991 Robert C. Linthicum. Published by MARC, a division of World Vision.

Chapter 7

1. Alexis de Tocqueville, *Democracy in America*, vol. 1 (New York: Schocken Books, 1967), 53 ff.
2. Saul D. Alinsky, *Reveille for Radicals* (New York: Vintage Books, 1989).
3. *President's Initiative on Race*, ed. John Hope Franklin (Washington, D.C.: U.S. Government Printing Office, 1998).
4. "Ten Point Plan to Mobilize the Churches," *Sojourners* (February–March

1994), 13. Excerpted with permission from *Sojourners.* (800)714–7474, www.sojourners.com.

Chapter 8

1. See Marvin Olasky, *The Tragedy of American Compassion,* (Wheaton, Ill.: Crossway Books, 1995).
2. See Arthur Bonner, *Jerry McAuley and His Mission* (Neptune, N.J.: Loizeaux Brothers, 1967).
3. See Daniel P. Moynihan, "The Negro Family: The Case for National Action" (Washington, D.C.: Office of Policy Planning and Research, U.S. Department of Labor, 1965).
4. See Lewis A. Coser, *Masters of Sociological Thought* (New York: Harcourt Brace Jovanovich, 1977).
5. Alexis de Tocqueville, *Democracy in America* (New York: Schocken Books, 1967).
6. Emile Durkheim, *The Division of Labor* (Chicago: Free Press, 1956).
7. E. Digby Baltzell, *The Protestant Establishment* (New York: Vintage Books, 1965).
8. John Kenneth Galbraith, *The Affluent Society,* 2d ed. (New York: New American Library of World Literature, 1969).
9. Robert A. Taft introduced the Taft-Hartley Act in 1947. This dealt with the legal protection of labor and unions.
10. Bill Bradley, *Value of the Game* (New York: Artisan Press, 1998).

Chapter 9

1. William Julius Wilson, *When Work Disappears* (New York: Alfred A. Knopf, 1996), 29–30.
2. Ibid., 11.
3. Ibid., 29–30.
4. Ibid., 159 ff.
5. Ibid., 87–88.
6. See Elliot Liebow, *Tally's Corner* (New York: Little, Brown & Co., 1967).
7. Ibid.
8. Op. Cit., Wilson, 92.
9. See Kathryn Edin, "The Myths of Dependence and Self-Sufficiency: Women, Welfare, and Low Wage Work" (unpublished manuscript, Center for Urban Policy Research, Rutgers, 1994).
10. Op. Cit., Wilson, 61.
11. See Marie Jahoda, Paul F. Lazarsfeld, and Hans Zeisel, *Marienthal: The Sociology of an Unemployed Community* (Chicago: Aldine-Atherton, 1971).
12. Op. Cit., Wilson, 124 ff.
13. E.F. Schumacher, *Small Is Beautiful* (New York: Harper Perennial, 1975).

Chapter 10

1. Tom Jones serves as a senior advisor for U.S. field operations for World Vision, the largest faith-based development agency in the world.
2. This material was gathered by Shelly Goehring, a graduate research assistant at Eastern College during 1997.

3. Ibid.
4. The Philadelphia Leadership Foundation is presently under the leadership of Linwyrd Crowe. Using the model of the Pittsburgh Leadership Foundation, it was created in October 1983 to be the nonprofit legal and administrative structure to carry out the city-wide kingdom agenda. In response to the call of the Philadelphia Leadership Foundation board, Lin Crowe took on the full-time role of president in 1988 and opened an office in downtown Philadelphia.

   The board has adopted the Values Statement as a set of guiding principles for its philosophy and ministry. The Values Statement emphasizes the following: valuing the city in that they "seek the spiritual renewal of persons and the social renewal of places;" valuing the vulnerable in that the Foundation "commits itself to the leadership of the city, but always in partnership with the vulnerable;" valuing empowerment in that the Foundation "calls the powerful to partnership with the vulnerable, so that the Gospel has equal and full effect on both groups;" valuing reconciliation in that the Foundation "will work to bring together urban and suburban, Protestant and Catholic, mainline and evangelical as well as Anglos and non-Anglos;" valuing risk in that "urbanization will require creative vision and bold initiative from individuals, churches, and other institutions if renewal of persons and cities is to take place;" and valuing leadership which requires "transformational leadership characterized by openness to change, personal growth, and strong faith."

Chapter 11
1. Marvin Olasky, *The Tragedy of American Compassion* (Wheaton, Ill,: Crossway Books, 1995).
2. See the interview of John J. DiIulio, Jr., by Jim Wallis in *Sojourners* (September–October 1997), 16–22. Also see the article by John J. DiIulio, Jr., "The Church and the Civil Society Sector," *Brookings* (Fall 1997).
3. Peter Berger, *Invitation to Sociology* (New York: Doubleday, 1963), Chapter 3.
4. William James, *The Varieties of Religious Experience* (New York: New American Library of World Literature, 1958), 157.
5. Max Weber, *The Protestant Ethic and the Spirit of Capitalism,* trans. Talcott Parsons (London: George Allen, and Unwin Ltd., 1930).
6. Robert Southey, *The Life of Wesley; and the Rise of Progress of Methodism,* vol. 2 (London: Longman, Brown, Green, and Longmans, 1846), 369–70.
7. Edward C. Banfield, *The Unheavenly City, Revisited* (Boston: Little, Brown & Co., 1974).
8. Milton Yinger, *Sociology Looks at Religion* (New York: Macmillan Co., 1961).

Chapter 12
1. Oscar Lewis, *La Vida* (New York: Vintage Books, 1968), xliii ff.
2. A further description of a "natural barrier" can be found in the essay by Robert Park, "The City: Suggestions for the Investigation of Human Behavior in the Urban Environment," *American Journal of Sociology,* vol. xx (Chicago: University of Chicago, 1916).

3. See Lydia Morris, *Dangerous Class: The Underclass and Social Citizenship* (London: Routledge, 1994), 15.
4. Franz Fanon, *The Wretched of the Earth,* trans. Constance Farrington (New York: Grove Press, 1966).
5. Charles H. Cooley, *Human Nature and the Social Order* (New York: Schocken, 1904), 182–85.
6. William James, *The Varieties of Religious Experience* (New York: New American Library of World Literature, 1958), 157
7. A good survey of neo-Pentecostal revivals can be found in Donald E. Miller, *Reinventing American Protestantism* (Berkeley, Calif.: University of California Press, 1997).
8. Herman Schmalenbach, "The Sociological Category of Communion," *Theories of Society,* ed. Talcott Parson (New York: Free Press, 1961), 331 ff.
9. John J. DiIulio, Jr. (unpublished manuscript, Washington, D.C.: Brookings Institution).
10. Congressman Chaka Fattah is a faithful member of Mt. Carmel Baptist Church, which is the church where I serve as an associate pastor. He has been especially effective in developing policies for improving public education.
11. Op. Cit., DiIulio.
12. Op. Cit., Fanon.

Chapter 13
1. Roberta Hestenes, *Using the Bible in Groups* (Philadelphia: Westminster Press, 1984).
2. *Serendipity New Testaments for Groups,* ed. Lyman Coleman, 2d ed. (Grand Rapids: Zondervan Publishing House, 1986).
3. See Tony Campolo, *The Kingdom of God Is a Party* (Waco, Tex.: Word Corp., 1990), 17–21.
4. Tony Campolo, *Wake Up America* (New York: HarpersCollins, 1991). Chapter IV gives a more extensive view of how base communities developed.
5. Kenneth E. Sharpe, *Peasant Politics,* (Baltimore: Johns Hopkins University Press, 1977).

Chapter 14
1. Neil Postman, *Amusing Ourselves to Death* (New York: Penguin Books, 1986). Postman gives a good explanation as to how television impacts the attention students give to teachers at school.
2. Richard J. Herrstein and Charles Murray, *The Bell Curve* (New York: Free Press, 1996).
3. Amitai Etzioni, *The Spirit of Community* (New York: Simon and Schuster, 1993), 147–57.
4. Stephen L. Carter, *The Culture of Disbelief* (New York: Basic Books, 1993).

Chapter 16
1. Edwin H. Southerland, "White Collar Criminality," *American Sociological Review* (February 5, 1940), 1–12.
2. See Fox Butterfield, *New York Times* (October 6, 1995) and John J.

DiIulio, Jr. (unpublished manuscript, Philadelphia: Public/Private Ventures) on young blacks in the criminal justice system.

3. Cornel West, *Race Matters* (New York: Vintage Books, 1993), 17–31.
4. Robert K. Merton, *Social Theory and Social Structure,* chap. VI and VII (New York: Free Press, 1968).
5. Paul C. Vitz, *Psychology as Religion* (Grand Rapids: Wm. B. Eerdmans Publishing Co., 1977), 37–57.
6. See Abraham H. Maslow, *Religion, Values, and Peak Experiences* (New York: Viking Press, 1970).
7. Irving Goffman, *Asylums* (Garden City, N. Y.: Anchor Books, 1961).
8. There is a debate on this issue. An argument against capital punishment as a deterrent is by Harry Elmer Barnes and Negley F. Tecters, *New Horizons in Criminology* (Englewood Cliffs, N.J.: Prentice-Hall, 1959), 319. Contrary studies have been made by Gary Mauser of Simon Frazier University. Also, see Thorsten Sellin, *Capital Punishment* (New York: Harper and Row, 1967).
9. Diana Scielly and Joseph Marolla, "Riding the Bull Gilley's," *Down to Earth Sociology,* ed. James Henslin, 7th ed. (New York: Free Press, 1993).
10. Prison Fellowship, P.O. Box 17500, Washington, D.C., 20041-0500 has provided leadership in starting Christian prisons in Colombia.

Chapter 17
1. A good review of ways in which church congregations can partner with financial institutions in urban American can be found in the July–August 1999 edition of the *Harvard Business Review,* 57–68.
2. A survey of the early development of Cardone Industries is available in the biography of Michael Cardone, Sr., *Never Too Late* (Old Tappan, N.J.: Fleming H. Revell Co., 1988).

Chapter 18
1. ECIUS is located at Tenth and Springarden Streets in Philadelphia. It is ideally located within walking distance of city hall and is situated on the edge of the Hispanic community.
2. Daniel P. Moynihan, "The Negro Family: The Case for National Action" (Washington, D.C.: U.S. Department of Labor, 1965).
3. The Mission Year Program is described in Chapter 6.

Chapter 19
1. Gibson Winter, The Suburban Captivity of the Churches (New York: Doubleday, 1961).

Chapter 20
1. See Emile Durkheim, *The Rules of the Sociological Method,* trans. W. D. Halls (New York: Free Press, 1982), 2 ff.
2. See Emile Durkheim, *The Elementary Forms of the Religious Life,* trans. Joseph W. Swarn (New York: Free Press, 1947), 47.
3. Albert van den Heuvel, *These Republican Powers* (London: SCM Press, 1966). Also H. Berkhof, *Christ and the Powers* (Scottsdale, Pa.: Herald Press, 1962).
4. Walter Wink, *Engaging the Powers* (Minneapolis: Fortress Press, 1992).

5. Op. Cit., van den Heuvel, 39 ff.
6. Op. Cit., Wink.
7. William Stringfellow, *An Ethic for Christians and Other Aliens in a Strange Land* (Waco, Tex.: Word Books, 1976).
8. See Robert D. Herman, *Gambling* (New York: Harper & Row, 1967).
9. See Theodore Draper, *The Dominican Revolt* (New York: Commentary, 1968).
10. Anthony Campolo, "The Greening of Gulf and Western," *Eternity* (January 1981), 30–32.
11. Information can be secured from the Interfaith Center for Corporate Responsibility, Riverside Drive, New York.
12. A good overall description of Ed Rendell's interaction and conflicts with African-American and Hispanic clergy can be found in Buzz Bissinger, *A Prayer for the City* (New York: Random House, 1997).

Subject Index

Scripture Index